DISCARD

Why Do We Fall in Love?

The Psychology of Choosing a Partner

Cathy Troupp

St. Martin's Press
New York

For Chris and for Jane

Library of Congress Cataloging-in-Publication Data

Troupp, Cathy.
Why do we fall in love? : the psychology of choosing a
partner / Cathy Troupp.
p.   cm.
ISBN 0-312-13215-8
1. Mate selection—Psychological aspects.   2. Love.
I. Title.
HQ801.T778   1995
152.4'1—dc20   95-782   CIP

First published in Great Britain by Virago Press

First U.S. Edition: June 1995
10 9 8 7 6 5 4 3 2 1

Contents

Acknowledgements

MY first and profoundest thanks go to all the couples who welcomed me into their homes and their lives during the course of the interviews which make up this book. They gave their time and commitment for free, as well as a great deal of emotional energy and thought. My life has been enriched through learning so much about theirs. I hope that they think the result was worth it.

Naturally thanks are due to Virago and to my editor, Melanie Silgardo, for asking me to write a book and for being enthusiastic about my original idea. I am also grateful to my agent, Sara Menguc at Murray Pollinger, for her support at all stages of the project, and for solicitously looking after my interests as an author, especially while I was abroad.

Judy Cunnington, Assistant Director of London Marriage Guidance and a very experienced marital counsellor, acted as my consultant for the book. She gave me invaluable help and advice in the early stages particularly, with suggestions for questions, advice on formulating open-ended questions, and ideas for structuring the five interviews. She also helped me to think about and clarify the boundaries of my role as interviewer. Further, she gave a lot of time to reading and commenting on the first drafts of many of the couples' stories. Her ideas were always interesting and stimulating, but I want to emphasise that

I bear full responsibility for the case histories and interpretations as they appear in the book. Many thanks also to Christopher Clulow, Director of the Tavistock Institute of Marital Studies, for reading and commenting on the manuscript.

Linda Kelsey, editor of *She Magazine*, really set me off down this road several years ago, in 1989, when she asked me to write a monthly column entitled 'Couples Counsel'. That is where my professional interest in couple dynamics began (as opposed to my private fascination with relationships which I think I must share with most women). I am indebted to Linda for her continued support for my writing. My very warm thanks, too, to the marital counsellor with whom I collaborated on 'Couples Counsel', although I cannot name her because of the need to protect her clients. We had many interesting and exciting discussions, and I learned a lot from her.

Special credit is due to my friend Becky Abrams for all the conversations about relationships, emotions and unconscious motives that we have had over more than ten years, and which have woven their way into the book as they are part of me. I am also grateful for the benefit of her advice and experience as a fellow author. My friend Jane Haynes was a catalyst to many of the insights in this book. And many other friends helped me by showing interest and asking questions which made me think hard and sometimes by finding me interview subjects.

My parents gave support in so many ways, by offering an occasional base with access to a word processor, meals and encouragement, as well as the challenges that sprung from their different way of viewing relationships. In trying to answer them, I was often helped to clarify and think through my own ideas. Thanks especially to my mother who put her wide knowledge of literature at my service and often rang me from Finland with suggestions for quotations (and paid for the phone bill).

I could not have completed the book without Abby-Lee

Knight, my son's nanny. Knowing that Gabriel was happy and contented on the days he was with her allowed me to concentrate at the word processor.

And finally, thanks to Chris, my husband, for everything that matters: moral and emotional support, meals, care and love.

Preface

WHY do we fall in love with the people we do? Why did we choose as our partner the woman or man we did? What is it in one person that responds to another?

We like to think of love as a mystery, especially the beginning, the moment of falling in love. According to the myth, blind Cupid shoots his golden arrows haphazardly, and wherever they land passion takes hold. Our mind becomes prisoner to thoughts of the loved one. Falling in love is supposed to be involuntary and outside our control.

At the same time one of our favourite pastimes is analysing and trying to understand the dynamics of couples' attraction and relationships. What does she see in him? Why does she stay with him? Will it last? Often people are trying to solve problems: why do they quarrel all the time? Why has their sex life dropped off when it was so good? Why does he never show her affection? Why does she criticise him all the time? And occasionally people even puzzle over what makes a relationship good: how come they get on so well when they seem so different? How come they still find each other fascinating to talk to after so many years?

This book is based on in-depth interviews with sixteen couples. I saw each couple five times in a sequence of two joint interviews, one individual interview each, and a final joint interview. The first interview was about how they met and the course of their relationship to date. The second interview focused on their family backgrounds and involved each partner drawing up a kind of family tree, called a geneogram, and marking on it relationships within the family. (For an example of a geneogram, see p. 266.) The third and fourth interviews allowed each partner to talk alone, and in the fifth interview loose ends might be tied up and the most important issues gone over again. (For a fuller account of the interview process, see Chapter 7.)

The couples are presented in detail in the chapters that follow. Drawing on their stories and on psychoanalytic theory, this book proposes and examines the psychological factors that draw two people together. I am especially concerned with the unconscious elements in our choice of partner: the hopes and needs that we seek to have fulfilled without our being aware of it.

The couples in this book had been together between ten months and twenty years. After learning as much as I could about their present relationship, I attempted to trace backwards towards an understanding of their original choice of each other. My premiss was that the outstanding features of a relationship would have been there in seedling form at the beginning, and this applies both to weaknesses and strengths, problems and pleasures. I argue below that the original, unconscious choice is often 'problem based', even in a working and flourishing relationship. This is because falling in love, or choosing a partner, contains the hope of resolving one's inner conflicts and starting afresh. This is part of what lends the experience its power and intensity.

This book is about the beginning of relationships. For many people, falling in love is the most intense and exhilarating experience of their lives. The presence of the other is needed as food and water; being parted feels, in the words of one of those interviewed, 'as if my whole world walked away from me'. Not everyone 'falls in love', of course. In some of the accounts in this book, falling in love was never mentioned. Many couples preferred to emphasise an early feeling of comfort, or security, or recognition. 'I felt there was nothing to worry about.' 'It felt comfortable, and comforting.' 'I felt as if I'd known her for ages.' 'I felt I could relax and be myself with him.' Why did they feel like that? Such feelings at the beginning of a relationship, no less than the passion of falling in love, deserve investigation.

Chapter 1 sets the theoretical framework for the real-life stories that follow. The rest of the book is structured according to a loose chronology. Chapters 2 and 3 cover 'the early days', the time of deciding whether or not to make a commitment, and the time shortly after a commitment has been made, by marriage or in other ways. Chapter 4 looks at established couples who were facing some specific change in their lives; Chapter 5 examines conflicts that may arise and how couples try to solve them, while Chapter 6 describes some patterns that partners may settle into. Throughout, the focus remains the unconscious, original choice.

I could have adopted a structure with each chapter devoted to a 'type' of attraction, but I favoured the chronological, real-life structure for two reasons. First, I wanted to share with the reader the whole impression I gained of each couple, so that she might also share the detective work – the process of working backwards towards an understanding of the original choice. Often, the light in which I saw the choice would inevitably be slanted by the particular stage of the relationship. Secondly, since many of the psychological ideas and concepts are abstract, I wanted to have it borne in mind that the couples in the interviews were people living day-to-day lives and grappling with issues that were current for them.

Love and our choice of a loved one may be a mystery, but in part it is also explicable and understandable. Naturally I hope that readers will use the ideas and insights offered to make sense of their own experiences of relationships.

CHAPTER ONE

The Unconscious Choice

HERE are snapshots of a few of the couples who appear in this book.

Elaine and Greg have been together five years and are wondering whether or not to get married. Elaine wants to start a family. But she has doubts about Greg: is he an assertive enough man to satisfy her? For his part, Greg says he is happy to marry Elaine – so why does he never propose?

Cheryl and Michael married after a six-month courtship when they were only 19. Now in their thirties, they have three children and a warm, secure home life. Yet recently Cheryl suspected Michael of having an affair. He swears he didn't and she says she believes him, but she can't let it drop. Why?

Caroline and Kathleen were each other's first women lovers. Now they have a child and describe themselves as 'an old married couple' – a description which seems to include the absence of a sex life. But does sex matter when they give each other so much else?

Patricia is black and Peter is white; Patricia is the breadwinner while Peter hasn't settled to a career; Patricia is bold and assertive while Peter is shy and withdrawn. Does it work when 'opposites attract'? And does their colour have anything to do with it?

James and Linda met through Dateline, and a year and a half later they were married. Linda longs to create a stable home and to fill it with children. James says he does too. So why do they keep stumbling into ferocious quarrels?

The stories of these and other interview couples are told in depth in the chapters that follow. In each case, the unconscious aspects of their choice of one another is examined both through what they said, and through the issues and dilemmas that were current in their relationship. This chapter sets the theoretical framework. The starting point is the unconscious hopes and longings with which people embark on a relationship. It introduces certain concepts and ideas drawn from psychoanalytic theory, which seem particularly to illuminate the mystery of partner choice.

The first part of this chapter is devoted to four types of dynamic that characterise early relationships in general (hope, projection, disillusionment, attachment). The second part highlights four factors in the specific choice (complementarity, similarity, shared defence, repetition of patterns from the past).

General Themes: Hope, Projection, Disillusionment, Attachment

When people first fall in love they are usually imbued with *hope* – for happiness, for fulfilment, for the future. One relationship dynamic that may be particularly prominent at this early stage is that of *projection*: seeing in the other exaggeratedly wonderful and desirable personality traits. I shall try to show that often these are in fact characteristics one longs for in oneself and hopes to acquire through the loved one. After projection comes a certain *disillusionment*, when one begins to see one's partner with more clarity and reality. This stage, though it may be painful, is crucial for transforming the state of being in love to a loving relationship. Finally, *attachment theory* explains why we seek an intimate relationship with one other special person at all. Let us examine these four concepts in detail.

Hope

When two people fall in love, they experience a great surge of hope. There is the hope of being exclusively loved – of becoming the most important person in someone else's world. There is also the hope of being able to give love without reserve. There is a great sense of possibility – the future lies ahead, open and golden as an untrampled cornfield. No choices, compromises or sacrifices have yet had to be made, no disappointments and disillusionments absorbed. The achievement of eternal love seems quite possible. 'Perhaps, this time, I will really be happy for ever. Perhaps, this time, I can really make a fresh start.'

The nature of people's hopes of love depends on their personal histories, their personalities and their imaginations, what they can conceive of. It depends on their experience, their notion of reality, and what they feel they deserve.

But underlying all the individual variations, it is the contention of this book that all lovers share at least two kinds of hope. Firstly, there is the hope, for some, of reproducing and reexperiencing the comfort and safety of childhood and the warmth of belonging to a family; for others, the hope of making up for bad aspects of the past, for recouping love and security that ought to have been there and were not. For many, this hope may be quite conscious and spoken. This is the hope of finding a lasting attachment, in the sense of the word as it will be defined below.

Secondly, often more unconsciously, there is the hope of achieving some individual psychological growth towards wholeness: the hope of discovering more of one's self, the secret recesses of one's being, both ugly and beautiful. Think about the way people often say, when they first fall in love, 'He brings out the best in me.' Or, once the relationship has progressed and there have begun to be arguments: 'He really knows how to bring out the worst in me!' These well-worn phrases may actually mean, 'Through my relationship I am able to bring to light and get to know parts of myself I didn't know I had.' Then, too, there is the hope of having one's self, the old and the emerging, accepted by one's new partner: 'I feel I can relax and really be myself with him.'

When I use the word 'unconscious' I am referring to those parts of our selves, those feelings and traits, of which we are not aware, and which seem alien to our conscious image of ourselves. Often these hidden parts 'conflict with consciously held ideals' and may therefore be 'denied, suppressed, or disowned'.

An idea may be unconscious because it is actively repressed owing to its unthinkable nature – a memory, fantasy, thought, or feeling which conflicts with our view of ourselves, and of what is acceptable, and which would cause too much anxiety, guilt, or psychic pain if it were acknowledged. Repression may weaken at times so that previously unconscious mental contents become manifest, for example, during sleep in the form of dreams, at times of stress in the form of symptoms, or in the emergence of apparently alien impulses under the influence of drugs or alcohol.[1]

To that I would add: repression may weaken, too, when we fall in love. Or to put it the other way round: we fall in love because we actually hope to bring to light the secret, repressed parts of ourselves. John A. Desteian, a Jungian analyst, believes that falling in love is usually preceded by a period of psychological stagnation: 'The stagnation is necessary because it is symptomatic of no longer being able to find meaning or satisfaction within the confines of our old ways of being and seeing things.' He compares the process to a fairy tale where stagnation 'is symbolized by the old king who is weary and fragile and whose kingdom has become unproductive. His people have become lethargic. Suddenly, a young, handsome hero, a prince, appears and rescues the king's daughter. He wins her hand by overcoming threatening obstacles and assumes the throne when the old king dies. The palace and the kingdom are restored to their former glory and all the subjects are released from their lethargy. This myth is enacted again and again in our society.[2]

Falling in love is the most common way in which people try to become whole, which means 'to become reconciled with those sides of personality which have not been taken into account'.[3] Or in the more lyrical words of the poet John Donne:

> *But as all several souls contain*
> *Mixture of things, they know not what,*
> *Love these mixed souls doth mix again,*
> *And makes both one, each this and that.*[4]

For example, a couple called Tom and Clara met and quickly fell in love. Within only a few months they began to look for a house to live in together, and spoke of getting married. While Clara was a tough and sometimes aggressively independent woman who found it hard to show tender feelings, Tom was a kind, gentle and nurturing type of man, but also very shy. Friends were intrigued: would this relationship work? Would Clara allow Tom to care for her and soften a little? Would he learn to stand up to her?

The strength of their attraction can be explained by the tidal wave of hope that accompanied their meeting. Each had overdeveloped one side of their personality at the expense of others, but now, having found each other, there was every hope of becoming complete. Clara hoped, more or less unconsciously, that she would dare to feel and show all the love and caring inside her that so far she had repressed, without of course relinquishing her strengths. Tom hoped that he might become more assertive and able to stand up for himself, while continuing to be gentle and caring too. Each hoped that their partner would be the one to bring to light in their personality feelings and traits which so far had been buried. Through their relationship with each other, they hoped to become more rounded and complete as individuals.

'The desire and pursuit of the whole'

We fall in love in order to become who and what we could be. This statement is founded on the belief that all humans strive for psychological expansion, for self-expression, and wholeness. I believe that an intimate relationship with one other person is the chief means by which this natural striving can be achieved. Of course, the notion of love as the pursuit of psychological wholeness, the union of two halves, is as old as the ancient Greeks. It was Plato who wrote in *The Symposium*, 'love is simply the name for the desire and pursuit of the whole'.[5] In recent times, this idea has been taken up particularly in Jungian psychology, where the two halves have been defined as masculine and feminine and named 'animus' and 'anima'. The animus of a woman and the anima of a man is said to contain her or his counter-sexual traits. So, for example, a woman's animus, once she has made contact with it in herself, may give her access to her ambitious, competent parts.[6] When a man is able to make himself conscious of his anima, he makes contact with the more emotional parts of himself. Indeed, Jung sometimes equated the anima with man's soul.[7]

Of course, as the case of Tom and Clara shows, the hidden parts of ourselves need not be 'counter-sexual' or gender bound in any way, although in Jung's day this may have been more likely. Jung also called them 'shadow' traits. For all of us, our personal history and experiences in our family, at school, with friends and peers and so on, will have encouraged us to develop in ourselves certain character traits at the expense of others. For example, it could be that Clara changed school several times when she was young, and developed a tough skin to cope with the uncertainties of her shifting situation. Tom might have grown up in a family where pushiness was frowned upon and putting others first rewarded. So when I talk about the missing, hidden or repressed parts of ourselves, I do not mean that we have a fully formed shadow self sitting inside us somewhere and waiting to pop out; rather I mean *potential* aspects of our personality which, by chance or design, have not had the opportunity to grow. When we fall in love and seek union with our loved one, it is at least partly with our unknown, because undeveloped, selves that we long to be united.

The ancient Greeks had no doubt that the finest union was between two male halves, and was less a sexual union than a union of souls and minds. The union between a man and a woman was considered to be of an altogether baser kind, regrettably necessary only for procreation. However, if we can put aside for a moment our reaction to this anachronistic affront to women, a look at Plato's story of wholeness, told in the voice of the comedian Aristophanes, offers us many threads to pursue when thinking about psychological wholeness in modern love relationships.

In the beginning, according to Aristophanes, each human being was a self-contained whole with four hands and four legs and two identical faces on one neck, turned in opposite directions, and with 'two organs of generation and everything else to correspond'. Such super-beings suffered from an overweening pride, however, and the gods decided that something had to be done to put them in their place. Eventually Zeus had an idea: 'I will cut each of them in two; in this way they will be weaker, and at the same time more profitable to us by being more numerous. If there is any sign of wantonness in them after that, and they will not keep quiet, I will bisect them again, and they shall hop on one leg.'

Aristophanes continued: 'Man's original body having been

thus cut in two, each half yearned for the half from which it had been severed. When they met they threw their arms round one another and embraced, in their longing to grow together again.'[8]

A psychologically minded interpretation of this ancient state of wholeness might suggest that it refers to our time in the womb, when we were indeed part of our mother, and she was part of us. Once we are born we are severed from her and can never return to that state of oneness. Alternatively, this early state of blissful union may be seen not so much as the time in the womb as that shortly after when, many psychoanalysts believe, the baby cannot distinguish between its self and its mother, its mouth and her breast, its body and her arms.[9] Thus for a short time the baby can maintain the glorious illusion that it is omnipotent and self-sufficient. It is as though it feeds itself and comforts itself. Perhaps it is this kind of oneness, an illusion of complete, contented self-sufficiency, which Plato's story evokes?

What does wholeness mean? How does it come about? Does it really presuppose two identical halves, as in Aristophanes' account? Or is it more like two opposite halves which fit together and complement each other, like Jack Sprat and his wife?[10]

My contention is that with the passage of time and the course of the relationship, wholeness comes by nurturing in oneself the differences perceived in one's partner.

Taken to its extreme, this idea would mean that at the end of a long life in common each partner would be the proud possessor of all traits, all characteristics and all feelings, and, paradoxically, the partners would be mirror images of each other. Of course this sounds absurd and doesn't happen, although people do say that long-time married couples grow to be more and more alike, even in appearance! Certainly a long-term, intimate relationship changes us: love transforms, but rarely so radically. What is here meant is a movement towards wholeness, a constant flow and exchange between two different people leading to the discovery of wider spaces and greater depths in oneself. A genuine acceptance and appreciation of the other's difference is an important prerequisite for a satisfying union.

For example, it might be as with Louisa and Jason who appear in Chapter 2: she expressed great admiration for his enterprising spirit and get-up-and-go, while she saw herself as a rather cautious type whose fear of the consequences made her hesitate before undertaking any big action. Yet not so long afterwards, as the story will tell, she was the one to really get up and go. Or James and Linda (Chapter 3): James, who had always been a slightly cold fish, was powerfully drawn to Linda's emotional expressiveness. On a conscious level he admired it. On a level as yet unconscious, he also sought some of it for himself by experimentally giving vent to more feelings of his own. This wrought complications in the relationship which are presented and discussed in Chapter 4.

Hope is a fount which starts to flow whenever two people fall in love. The hope of psychological wholeness, or perhaps more accurately, psychological expansion, is a powerful ingredient in the early days of any relationship. The actual, detailed nature of this hope will be different for each individual, depending on his or her own nature – both the part in the light and the part in the shadows.

Projection

Projection[11] is part of falling in love. It is the means by which one sees gold streaks in one's lover's brown hair, senses deep thoughts in his post-prandial digestive silence, or perceives an irresistible mix of tough and tender in the way he handles the gearstick of his car. As George Eliot says in *Middlemarch* about Dorothea's infatuation with Casaubon: 'Her faith supplied all that Mr Casaubon's words seemed to leave unsaid: what believer sees a disturbing omission or infelicity? The text, whether of prophet or of poet, expands for whatever we can put into it, and even his bad grammar is sublime.' Projection is a psychological term for rose-coloured spectacles.

Projection doesn't only happen in love. In psychoanalytic literature, the term 'projection' has several meanings, depending on the context, whether it is child development, individual psychology or marital dynamics. Often the term is used to imply pathology, but this is not how I intend it here, unless one considers being in love a pathological state, an 'extraordinary hallucination'. Projection means attributing to others feelings and traits which really belong to one's self but of which one has remained unconscious because these traits are undeveloped or repressed.

Projection can happen in any relationship, as casual as that between a shop assistant and a customer, or as close as that between a parent and child, or a couple married for thirty years. It can be a brief mechanism, or a deeply entrenched pattern of relating.

An everyday example of projection is a child requesting a night-light because teddy is afraid of the dark. The child itself is not *aware* that he is projecting his own fear of the dark on to teddy.[12] So projection contains a 'double unconscious': we are unconscious of the contents of our projection, as well as of the mechanism itself. How, then, can projection be proven to happen? Usually only afterwards, when the projections are untangled and restored to their rightful owners.

The mechanism of projection starts in infancy. Infants cannot hold inside themselves strong conflicting feelings of good and bad – for example, love for mother cannot coexist with anger with mother for not coming the moment she is needed. An infant cannot acknowledge, 'I have mixed feelings'. Infants split the good and the bad feelings and project the bad into those around them. The result would be that the baby continues to hold on to its loving feelings towards its mother, but when mother fails to satisfy it, the baby 'thinks', not 'I am angry with mother', but '*She* is angry with *me*, and that's why she is not doing what I want'. Projection, as we have seen, is attributing to others feelings or motives that really belong to the self.

In childhood, we begin the task of healing the split between good and bad and learning to tolerate both sides of ourselves. Children's fascination with the good and evil in fairy stories – princesses and witches, monsters and heroes – suggests this. The process continues in adulthood. To hold on to the knowledge that you love your partner at the same time as you are furious with him or her indicates a certain maturity. So does the ability to distinguish between a real cause for being angry with one's partner and taking out one's own bad mood on him or her. Splits in oneself are not just between good and bad, but between dependence and independence, vulnerability and toughness, sadness and cheerfulness; indeed, all the conflicting feelings in the world can shack up inside one heaving breast.

Rare is the adult who is so self-aware as to know exactly what they are feeling all of the time. In adulthood we continue to project some of our own feelings on to others, sometimes permanently so that we always remain unaware of them, sometimes only as a prelude to acknowledging them in ourselves. In daily life, these projections are probably more often negative or ambivalent than positive. In order to understand the process better, let us first look at this kind of projection, and then turn again to the happy projections of falling in love. As I will try to show below, projection plays a prominent part in the early days of a couple's relationship; indeed, the more intense the exchange of projections, the more people feel themselves to be in love.

For an example of everyday projection, take Rose, who worked in a publishing company and was frustrated and angry with her boss, the divisional director, for failing to promote her. However, he was also her mentor and friend, and regularly pushed little perks her way: free books, invitations to publishing events and so on. In this delicate situation, Rose could not afford to admit to herself her negative feelings about her boss. Instead, she periodically projected them on to him. She often convinced herself that he was angry with her, and would interpret a brief 'good morning' or a preoccupied expression as signs of extreme displeasure with her. Sometimes she felt afraid to go into his office; indeed, she began to feel quite 'paranoid'. Only after she was finally promoted and moved divisions, so reducing the intensity of their relationship, was Rose able to understand the pattern of feeling that had developed: that her growing anger with her boss, denied in herself and projected on to him, had made her feel more and more persecuted by him.

Temporary projections can become especially evident during quarrels. Who hasn't come home cross and bothered after a hard day at work and a rush-hour traffic jam, and quickly found themselves embroiled in a series of accusations and counter-accusations:

'What's the matter with you?'

'With me? I could say the same to you. You barely said hello when you came in the door.'

'Rubbish. Something's obviously bugging you and you're taking it out on me.'

'How can you say that? I was feeling fine until you came home and started having a go at me for nothing.'

And so on. Charging each other with identical offences is typical of an exchange of projections. More than likely neither partner was feeling fine, each in need of some end-of-day care and cosseting. It then becomes easier to project and blame, than to search one's own self to discover, and own, how one is really feeling.

Whereas in the case of Rose and her boss she was the one sending out projections and he the screen, the example above illustrates an *exchange* of projections, as is more common in close relationships. In established couple relationships, exchanging projections can become a way of life. Then you get Jack Sprat and his wife. Jack Sprat will eat no fat – instead, he projects the greedy, fat-loving part of himself on to his wife. She *receives* his projection and expresses his greed for him, as well as her own. She in turn projects the more controlled aspects of her personality on to her husband, so at mealtimes Jack eats with restraint 'for both of them'. They have a deal going, and according to the nursery rhyme it worked well, because 'betwixt them both, you see, they licked the platter clean'.

When projections get stuck

But projection as a way of life has its dangers and in the long run stops being satisfying. If one partner is always required to 'carry' and express a certain emotion for the other one, in addition to his or her own, this double burden eventually becomes too heavy. Always having to be 'the angry one' or 'the calm one' comes to feel restrictive for the partner at the receiving end of the projection. For the projecting partner, too, it becomes frustrating. After all, the hope was to discover in oneself that which one began by projecting on to one's partner. If this does not happen, if the projection gets stuck, the hope of wholeness is not being fulfilled.

An extreme example encountered in the literature of marital therapy is the case of the upright, hard-working, clean-living wife and mother who keeps her house and children spotless, while her feckless husband drinks, farts, snores, and never changes his underwear. She complains about him continuously, but she doesn't leave him. One might interpret that the couple have evolved a division of emotional labour that suits them both and fits with their personal histories: she projects all her 'dirtiness' on to her husband, while he projects all his 'cleanliness' on to his wife. The 'dirtiness' and 'cleanliness', although quite literal on one level, also refer to how the two feel inside themselves.[13] Perhaps, for example, she cannot bear to know about her own inner 'dirtiness', that is, her bad and angry feelings, having grown up with a mother who would not permit them. He, by contrast, might be profoundly uncomfortable with his own gentler, more considerate side, perhaps because he models himself on a father who taught him that all such feelings were weak and unmasculine. So their mutual projections allow them to live in the way with which they are most familiar.

This kind of extreme division of emotional labour, 'although a precarious balance may be established, remains inherently conflictful,' writes Lily Pincus. This is because people often feel compelled to attack their projection as it appears in their partner. As we saw, the 'clean' wife complains constantly about her 'dirty' husband. No doubt Jack Sprat berates his wife for being so greedy. It is often not enough to project one's unwanted qualities on to the other; they also have to be punished. As long as projection is a way of life, 'a more mature integration may be very difficult for the partners to achieve'.[14]

Another type of projection that may become established in couple relationships is for the two partners to unite in the joint projection of everything unpleasant on to people and things in the outside world. This is also a way of defending oneself against one's bad and uncomfortable sides – with the added advantage that one's own relationship is allowed to remain pure and free of conflict. '*We* are good nice people who never harbour mean thoughts, but everyone else is conspiring against us,' is the theme of such a couple, who may embroil themselves in a series of battles with relatives and in-laws, or employers, or even institutions such as a company or the council. Marital therapists call couples who use this kind of projection 'babes in the wood'; they cling to each other for protection against what they see as the hostile world beyond. The hostility they see in it comes in part from inside themselves.[15]

A splendid example of a couple jointly projecting outwards appears in the story, as told by Phyllis Rose,[16] of the marriage of Thomas Carlyle, the nineteenth-century historian, and Jane Welsh, his erudite wife, whose letters and diary he published after her death. For a long period in their marriage, they joined forces to fight an obsessive, relentless battle against the cocks in their neighbour's yard. Thomas was extremely sensitive to noise: 'A dog barking kept him from work; a cock crowing kept him from sleep. Beyond that, the noises aroused in him a fury which in itself upset his work.' Jane took it upon herself to fight the cocks on his behalf, paying regular visits to the owners to plead for the needs of her husband's genius, one time giving private tuition to the neighbours' son in return for the silencing of the cocks, another time actually considering buying the neighbour's house. In the end, they built a sound-proof room at the top of the house for Thomas to work in, but even this measure failed, as the room became unbearably hot. Jane dreamed about cocks, left parties early to go on cock business, and was constantly on the alert for the dreaded sound of crowing. As her husband said: 'We must extinguish those demon fowls or they will extinguish us.'[17]

Cock-crowing can be an irritating noise. But the passion and energy Jane put into the crusade, the feeling of being threatened expressed by Thomas, and above all the way in which they were united by the fight, suggest that a 'babes in the wood' type of projection was in operation. This becomes especially plausible in the context of the rest of Rose's account of their marriage, in which there were plenty of unexpressed resentments and dissatisfactions. The purpose of projecting negative feelings out on to the world is precisely to prevent those feelings from erupting between the two partners. Rose writes: 'Against the world's hostility, whatever form it took – tiresome visitors, hapless servants, a recalcitrant, hard-to-run house, bedbugs, ugly interiors, maddening noises – they stood united, with Mrs Carlyle firmly and joyously playing the role of her husband's protector.'[18] (Further examples of this kind of interaction of the couple with the world appear in some of the stories in Chapters 4 and 5.)

The potential of projection

The concept of projection was introduced in the context of falling in love: a psychological term for rose-coloured spectacles. The illustrations above show how projection can make a relationship go awry. The implication is that projection is a mechanism that most of us use to some extent in daily life, but that if it is allowed to become an entrenched way of relating, it spells blame and dissatisfaction. Projection as a way of life leads to the partners getting stuck in polarised roles and their stagnation both as individuals and as a couple. When roles become set – she is the cheerful one while he is always depressed, she is the one who remembers to pay the bills while he is wildly creative – then the partners are no longer helping each other to grow more whole. One might say that people who routinely project do not know themselves very well. They can't distinguish between their own feelings and those of others.

And yet the projections that happen between the two partners of a newly in-love couple can be the first step to the grand end of psychological wholeness. Our attraction to a partner has much to do with the unconscious parts of ourselves, which yearn for release and expression. By projecting these on to our newly beloved, we come face to face with them, can experience them vicariously, and familiarise ourselves with them. Our beloved is like a mirror reflecting our hidden parts.

At first the projections tend to be purely positive, desirable, admirable, touching – though it *is* possible for a love affair to start with negative projections: 'When I first met Sebastian I took an instant dislike to him – I thought he was really arrogant and full of himself.' The speaker then goes on to describe how she was nevertheless intrigued by Sebastian and perhaps how, gradually, she was won over by him. A personality clash also contains a projection, though its content is perceived as negative: something in ourselves that we don't want to know about and of which we disapprove. But a 'bad' projection may feel just as exciting as a good one. In a personality clash we invest something of ourselves in the disliked other person, just as we do when we fall in love. Both are passionate experiences, and sometimes the initial revulsion turns into attraction.

Mostly, though, the good projections come first, like a hail of golden arrows from Cupid's quiver. But whereas Cupid was said to be blind and his arrows randomly distributed, projections are not quite so haphazard. The content of our projections is determined by our own longings, certainly, but also by the character of our love target, what little we know of it. Projection arrows must be accurate enough to come to rest in the flesh of their target: a projection that is sent must also be received; it must 'fit' well enough for the recipient to accept it, to go along with it. The projection must correspond closely enough with the recipient's self-image.

As an example, let us return to Tom and Clara. Clara projected on to Tom the loving, nurturing qualities that were embryonic in herself. This projection was accepted by Tom, as it fitted his dominant personality and his self-image. He felt he had a lot of love to give; he liked to think of himself as a caring sort of person. He in turn projected on to Clara an assertiveness that was underdeveloped in himself, which projection was well received by Clara as it fitted her self-image: she saw herself as tough and competent in the world. No wonder that at the start of their relationship they felt completed by each other: the perfect fit.

Often, then, a projection exaggerates a partner's actual characteristics, or singles out one character trait without paying attention to the others. As long as our relationship is based on projection, we see only a bit of our partner, the bit we want to see, magnified. Projections cloak the real, complex person behind.

For the early projections to lead to fulfilment of the hope of greater wholeness, they must be *reclaimed*. We must absorb the projections back into ourselves, this time more consciously, rather than continuing to see the projected qualities only in our partner. We must adapt and change ourselves sufficiently to take account of these new, inner discoveries. In this way we may grow into fuller personalities, with a greater range and experience of human emotions. Clara must find in herself the capacity for being loving and Tom must become assertive too. This idea seemed to be understood by the lyrically minded advertiser in the personal columns of the *New York Review of Books*, who was looking for:

> *A woman, to share, to laugh, to hold,*
> *Allowing the best of life to unfold.*
> *Expanding of soul, body, and mind,*
> *Traits I possess and seek to find.*[19]

Is love selfish?

When we view partner choice as being motivated by an individual's hope for achieving greater psychological wholeness, the question poses itself: is love selfish? Is it a therapist we really want in a lover? Is it only ourselves that we are concerned for when we fall in love?

What about genuine care and concern for the other's wellbeing? What about sharing one another's joys and sorrows, the small daily ones and the great life-events? And what about a sustained curiosity and real interest in the other person? One early reader of this book commented, 'You have not said much about the delight in exploring and always finding new aspects to the other person, which can go on for ever.'

The time of attraction, of falling in love, is here separated from the time when a relationship, and mutual love, has become established. I do not cynically believe that love is selfish: on the contrary. But if readers interpret my analysis of *falling* in love as selfish, with its emphasis on hopes for psychological wholeness, then it must be so. If hope and projection are 'selfish' then so is falling in love. And yet their aim is a noble one. If the relationship goes on and goes well, and the projections are withdrawn and reclaimed, then the scene is all set for the transformation of in-love to love.

How then can we go about reclaiming projections? How can the hope of wholeness be fulfilled? How is the early attraction transformed into a lasting relationship?

Disillusionment

At the beginning we cast over our lover a beautiful silk cloak of our own design, and at first it is mainly this that we love. Only gradually will our lover emerge from behind the cloak dressed in his own everyday clothes, giving us the chance to really examine the cut and the colours. His or her own clothes will not all be made of silk – indeed, we might find that some of them are really quite frayed and tattered and made of everyday cloth. We will inevitably feel some measure of disappointment and disillusion. This is a necessary prelude to reclaiming one's projections.

Lovers often think that simply by meeting each other, the hope of becoming whole has already been fulfilled, because the other one 'makes' them feel so good. People plead with each other and with fate, 'Let's always keep it like this. Let's never let it change.'

Inevitably, though, it has to change. At first, the two lovers feel very close and 'at one'; they may almost feel as if their two separate beings are merging into one. But if the passionate encounter is to turn into a real relationship between two separate individuals, if the hopes of individual psychological growth are to be fulfilled, the lovers must take a few steps back in order to see each other more clearly. The commotion dislodges the rose-coloured specs, and this is experienced as disillusionment and disappointment: 'he wasn't as he seemed'. This phase must be survived and accepted, not denied, nor the partner punished, in order for the couple to be able to set off on a new, more realistic phase of the relationship.

In *Marriage Inside Out*, marital therapists Clulow and Mattinson write: 'The active lover is distinguished from the spellbound lover by a measure of dispassion and a commitment to another "warts and all". To be an active lover is to have survived disappointment and disillusion.'[20] Surviving disillusionment requires one to reclaim one's projections. This means that each partner must come to feel that he or she also to some extent possesses those qualities which at first he or she only saw in her partner. Let us see how this process might take place.

When the good turns to bad

People usually remember the moment of that first disappointment, even though they may try to forget it or make light of it. For a woman we can call Jessame, it was when she and her new lover Eugene broke down in his car on the way back from a weekend in the country. She realised, when she saw him standing by the open bonnet scratching his head, that he knew nothing about fixing engines. She felt a jolt of revulsion. 'He's pathetic,' she thought, and walked away from him, ostensibly to try to flag down another car. What an unkind reaction, one may think – but her reaction was understandable in the context of her early love projections. One of the things that she had seen in him and to which she was powerfully attracted was the sense of calm and competence that he seemed to exude. It was as if she had heard him say, when they first met, 'Don't worry, I can deal with things, I'll look after you as well as everything else.' Now he'd shown that he wasn't always competent. He could also be helpless; as helpless as she in this situation. Well, that was human enough, but she could not rid herself of her disappointment, and her contempt. As she stood there in the road, she wondered whether she could continue the relationship after this.

Jessame was disturbed by the vehemence of her reaction. She recognised that it was extreme. So the car had broken down; so he didn't know what to do any more than she did. How could such a commonplace episode make her think about ending the relationship when she had been so happy only minutes before? She was silent most of the way back in the AA car, and for a couple of days afterwards she didn't return Eugene's calls, while she tried to sort out her feelings and understand what had happened. Eventually she began to see that the contempt she had felt was actually for herself – her own helplessness, her own weakness. Why should it be OK for her not to know what to do when the car broke down, and not for him? The competence that she projected on to her lover and then admired in him was a quality that, if she was honest with herself, she feared that she herself lacked. She feared she was weak and pathetic. To see her own least-liked side suddenly reflected in her lover there on the road had been more than she could stand. In turning away from the 'weakness' of her lover, she was turning away from similar weakness in herself.

One cannot tolerate in a partner a quality for which one punishes oneself. To be able to forgive Eugene for his weaknesses, Jessame would also need to forgive herself. She would need to confront her own failures – a recent example was failing to get a job that she wanted. This was not accomplished overnight, but was a slow process of self-discovery: identifying the occasions on which she was too hard on herself, living through her feelings of self-contempt, and finally forgiving herself. When she knew more about her own weaknesses, she could afford to show Eugene more compassion for his.

This is what is meant by reclaiming projections. The moment of disillusionment cannot be survived without some measure of reclamation, which in turn cannot be accomplished without becoming at least partly conscious of the existence and content of one's projections. Jessame was surprised into searching her soul by the violence of her own feelings, and also by the knowledge that she did not want to lose her relationship with Eugene.

This illustration of the chronology of the early stages of a relationship is particularly stark and of course not everyone experiences such searing moments of disappointment or such clear reclamations of their projections. Nevertheless some version of this process is necessary for the transition from the in-love stage to a permanent, loving relationship. The moment of disillusionment has an important function. It spells the first psychological separation, the taking of a step back from the closeness and seeing the other's separateness. Only when one's partner can be seen with a little more clarity and reality can the process of reclaiming one's projections be begun. That the step back has to be prompted by a negative feeling does not have to spell the end for the relationship. Of course, many love affairs don't make it. They break at the disillusionment stage, not surprisingly, as the feeling of separation, and the disappointment that has to precede it, can be intensely painful. People think, 'it's all going wrong'; they don't recognise the value of what is happening but try to scrabble back to that early feeling of oneness. When it fails they give up and say that they must have picked the wrong person, that they were not what they seemed, and so on.

It is at the stage of disillusionment that the early good projections may turn 'bad'. Jessame's positive projection of competence on to Eugene was followed by the negative projection of weakness, as symbolised for her by his lack of skill as a car mechanic. This projection, too, derived from inside her, although it was a part of her that she had hitherto preferred not to think much about. But in seeing her own weakness projected on to Eugene, she was confronted with it. After the first feelings of shock and contempt, she began to try to synthesise the two – the competence and the weakness. They must be allowed to coexist, both in Eugene and in herself. In this way Jessame began to 'allow' Eugene to emerge from behind the screen of her projections, and to accept him as a more complex person with both strengths and weaknesses. He *was* competent in many areas of life – our early projections may fit one part of our loved one. In other areas of life he was less competent.

The 'bad' projections that succeed the good ones are often just their underside: 'lively' becomes frivolous and superficial; 'kind' can become cloying; 'reliable and dependable' come to be euphemisms for staid and boring, and so on. In a successful long-term relationship, couples usually appreciate both the positive and negative of their partners' characters, and readily acknowledge that that which they love also sometimes annoys and angers them. The acceptance of both good and bad is crucial to the transformation of an attraction into a 'real' relationship. If Jessame and Eugene looked as if they would make it, the prognosis seemed less hopeful for Katharine and Sally, a lesbian couple who were interviewed.

Katharine grew up in a turbulent household with a father who drank heavily, and the family regularly moved across the country with his changing jobs. Sally, by contrast, grew up in circumstances of great stability, in the bosom of her extended family: mother and father, grandmother and grandfather, aunts and uncles, all living round the corner from each other. Sally exuded calm, stability and capability which Katharine, with her unsettled background, found enormously attractive and reassuring. Katharine radiated a restlessness and probing energy which Sally, somewhat sedated by her life so far, found enlivening and exciting. They seemed to complement each other well, and their original getting together was passionate and intense.

At the time of the interviews they had been going out for two and a half years, and the original attraction was no longer holding water. Katharine now complained that Sally was cursed by 'an extreme caution and an extraordinary lack of curiosity about the world outside. I find it incredible that someone who has lived all their life in the same street in the same town should actually choose to go to college in that town as well!' She felt that Sally was clingy, and holding her back in her attempts to go out into the outside world. She wanted to start new projects and meet new people, but Sally just wanted to have cosy nights in.

Sally, for her part, was upset that Katharine didn't seem to need her any more and wanted to put all her energy into outside enterprises. She complained that she had nurtured and cared for Katharine through several crises, but now that Katharine felt better again, she was being cast aside. The early good projections turned bad: to Katharine, Sally's caring became invasive and her calm sluggish. For her part Sally came to experience Katharine's energy and excitingness as unloving.

Disillusionment is a bridge between romance and a realistic relationship that has to be crossed. If the relationship survives it, we come to see our partner more clearly, we are free to learn to love them as they really are. Disillusionment will give way to the joy of mature love. Even the magic will return, for, as C. S. Lewis writes, 'This is one of the miracles of love; it gives – to both, but perhaps especially to the woman – a power of seeing through its own enchantments and yet not being disenchanted.'[21]

Attachment

Why do most of us want to unite our selves and our lives with one other, specific individual? Is it just a socially and culturally motivated arrangement for the perpetuation of the species and the raising of children? Is it a way of warding off loneliness? Is it the endowment of sexual desire with a social face? Why is being single not enough?

Some people argue that if society were not predicated upon the couple and singles not discriminated against – if double hotel rooms were not cheaper than singles, if women did not cancel dates with their girlfriends in favour of their boyfriends, if couples who spent all their time together were socially ostracised instead of admired – then coupledom would not be nearly so popular. Certainly one cannot deny the existence of powerful social pressures towards coupling up, marriage and procreation, in the assumptions and images shown daily in the media, as well as in the attitudes of friends and family. But although social mores are in part responsible for the popularity of couples, they also act to reinforce nature, although to what extent is impossible to disentangle. For example, Louisa and Jason (see Chapter 2), said: 'We hadn't really thought of marriage until last summer when we went to four weddings in a row – and they were all great! So we thought, why don't we have one of those?' They may get married to imitate their friends, but to claim that they are a couple because all their friends are would be too simplistic.

So why are they a couple?

Are twosomes natural?

Most psychological writers on couple relationships liken them to the very first relationship of life, that between mother and baby.

> A lot of basic patterns of parent–child behaviour are carried over into the courting situation. Many forms of intimacy indulged in – baby-talk, hand-holding, embracing, kissing, sucking, and biting – are reminiscent of parent–child contact. In fact, a great deal of the behaviour of lovers can be viewed and understood as a return to a parent–infant style of tenderness and caring, with the two lovers taking turns in playing the roles of parent and infant.[22]

Attachment theory, the psychoanalyst John Bowlby's great contribution to human psychology, offers an explanation for why we seek to form a lasting bond in life with one other, special person. The mother–baby bond was the focus of his pioneering research in the 1950s and 1960s. He wrote:

> In so far as psychologists and psychoanalysts have attempted to account for the existence of affectional bonds, the motives of food and sex have almost always been invoked. Thus in attempting to explain why a child becomes attached to his mother, both learning theorists and psychoanalysts have independently assumed that it is because mother *feeds* child. In attempting to understand why adults become attached to one another, sex has commonly been seen as the obvious and sufficient explanation. Yet, once the evidence is scrutinized, these explanations are found wanting. There is now abundant evidence that, not only in birds but in mammals also,

young become attached to mother-objects despite not being fed from that source, and that by no means all affectional bonding between adults is accompanied by sexual relations; whereas, conversely, sexual relations often occur independently of any persisting affectional bonds.[23]

One of the best-known experiments to support the claim that it was not mother's milk that was the chief bond between mother and baby was that conducted by Harlow with rhesus monkeys.[24] Baby monkeys were removed from their mothers at birth and raised with 'mother' models, one made of wire netting only, and the other of wire covered with soft cloth. Some were fed by bottle from one model, and some from the other. But irrespective of which model they were fed from, all baby monkeys soon came to spend most of their time clinging to the cloth-covered model. Some even managed to lean over to feed from the wire model while maintaining their hold on the cloth one.

The explanation that Bowlby developed for attachment behaviour centred on our need for protection from potential danger, and for a 'secure base', in childhood especially, but throughout life also. Attachment behaviour is characterised by, first, the *specificity* of the attachment figure – only one chosen person will do. Secondly, attachment endures for a long time; childhood attachments are attenuated in adulthood but rarely completely broken, while a new adult attachment is sought. And thirdly, attachment involves strong feelings:

The formation of a bond is described as falling in love, maintaining a bond as loving someone, and losing a partner as grieving over someone. Similarly, threat of loss arouses anxiety and actual loss gives rise to sorrow; whilst each of these situations is likely to arouse anger. The unchallenged maintenance of a bond is experienced as a source of security and the renewal of a bond as a source of joy.[25]

In so far as attachment behaviour has to do with protection from potential dangers, Bowlby conceived of it mainly in evolutionary terms. That is, although in society today there are still plenty of situations in which it is safer to be two than one, the origin lies in the shared desire, or instinct, of mother and infant to ensure the infant's survival.

The notion of the 'secure base' also derives from childhood behaviour. As long as mother is around, and within sight, small children feel able to make forays away from her to explore the world around them. But if she goes away, they try to follow her, and if the separation lasts long they may cry or cling, once reunited. (The effect on the child of long separations, in the context of young children going into hospital, was particularly studied by Bowlby. The less secure the attachment, the more disturbed the child's behaviour becomes. Children reunited with their mothers after weeks of separation exhibited both extreme clinging and anxiety and aloof detachment, and sometimes seemed hardly to recognise their mothers.)

All our lives we need a secure base, with an 'attachment figure', someone we can trust, who will be there for us, who will care for us in a consistent way. It is our focal point, a safe haven where we go for comfort and to gather strength for repeated excursions into the world, such as work and social life. People without a secure base are 'rootless and lonely', says Bowlby, however defiantly independent they may appear.

Attachment sits alongside the biological imperative for procreation as a motive for becoming a couple, and probably often outweighs it. The nature of our childhood attachments – whether they were secure or interrupted, whether they aroused feelings of trust or anxiety – plays an important part in our choice of partner. Some people choose someone with whom they can repeat important aspects of their past, while others look for someone with whom to live out the very opposite of their past (for more on this theme, see the section on '*Repetition*', p.44ff). for example, a person who suffered breaches of attachment in childhood may not recognise a reliable 'attachment figure' in adulthood, says Bowlby. He or she may choose a partner with whom sad patterns from the past end up repeating themselves, albeit in adult forms such as divorce or unfaithfulness. It is not surprising that 'divorce is transmitted through generations; children whose parents have divorced are themselves more likely to divorce'.[26] A secure childhood attachment may similarly make one's antennae go out to potential partners with whom the pattern can be repeated.

Another famous psychoanalyst who wrote about the mother–baby bond was Donald Winnicott. His observations of the interactions of a mother and her baby often convey their intense, absorbed quality, and the idea of the mother and baby as a unit. 'There is no such thing as a baby,'[27] he wrote, rather a 'nursing couple', a mother-and-baby. He subscribed to the idea that in infancy babies conceive of mother as an extension of themselves. 'What does the baby see when he or she looks at the mother's face?' asked Winnicott, and answered, 'I am suggesting that, ordinarily, what the baby sees is himself or herself.'[28] Through this kind of *mirroring*, through seeing itself as it were reflected in its mother's expression, in her smile, the baby gains its first rudimentary notions of its self.

The search for 'lost happiness'

We come into the world not alone, but in immediate relation to another person. At first it is not so much a relation to a perceived other as a sense of oneness. Many writers talk about the infant's 'belief' in its own omnipotence, by which they mean, perhaps, that the infant believes it has the power to conjure forth its own feeds and changes and caresses, since it cannot distinguish between its own skin and its mother's, its self and hers.

The perfect fusion of two adults when they fall in love may feel something like the good part of being a very young baby – a seamless union with the loved one, being at peace with oneself and the world. All frustrations and bad feelings are temporarily at bay. For a brief moment, everything becomes good. During or after making love, when we lie entwined with our lover, touching skin, breathing each other's scent, hearing each other's breath, the peace and contentment we feel can echo that of our earliest days.

One of Plato's definitions of love is that it is a search for lost happiness. In a psychological interpretation, this lost happiness might be the infant moments of oneness with its mother/its world – the omnipotent, content moments.

'What is it, mortals, that you hope to gain from one another? . . . Is the object of your desire to be always together as much as possible, and never to be separated from one another day or night? If that is what you want, I am ready to melt and weld you together, so that, instead of two, you shall be one flesh; as long as you live you shall live a common life, and when you die, you shall suffer a common death, and be still one, not two, even in the next world. Would such a fate as this content you, and satisfy your longings?' We know what their answer would be; no one would refuse the offer; it would be plain that this is what everybody wants, and everybody would regard it as the precise expression of the desire which he had long felt but had been unable to formulate, that he should melt into his beloved, and that henceforth they should be one being instead of two. The reason is that this was our primitive condition when we were wholes, and love is simply the name for the desire and pursuit of the whole.[29]

Plato says, in the voice of Aristophanes: 'It is from this distant epoch, then, that we may date the innate love which human beings feel for one another, the love which restores us to our ancient state by attempting to weld two beings into one and to heal the wounds which humanity suffered.[30] The wounds can, perhaps, be conceived as disillusioning recognition by the baby, as it grows older, that mother is not part of it after all, but an other, different, with her own wishes, and that the world is not at the baby's command at all, but full of frustrations and difficulties.

Similarly, no adult in-love state can last for ever. It either ends, or it is transformed into a relationship between two individuals, who may sometimes feel very united, but who more often will interact with the recognition of the other's difference and separateness. When the spell of falling in love is broken and the complex good-and-bad reality bursts in, the real work of forging a relationship starts. As we saw in the previous section, disillusionment is inevitable in this process. It has its antecedent in the experiences of infancy, just as does the longing for union that is fulfilled in falling in love.

It should be noted, though, that while the usual image of being newly in love is of the two lovers welded into one, miserable when apart and blissful together, just as Plato says, by no means everyone feels like this, or even wants to feel like this. On the contrary, the possibility of great intimacy and closeness can be frightening to people, because it spells vulnerability. 'Indeed, the positive emotions are frequently more threatening than the negative ones because they open us up to others, and they allow us to become lost in causes greater than ourselves. Fusion, like separation, brings the fear of losing oneself.'[31] So while many new lovers are almost as inseparable as mother and newborn baby, others play it casually for fear of returning to that early state of helplessness. Plato's scenario would make many recoil with a strong fear that such merging would lead to the suffocation of their individuality. Where some new couples repair to the bedroom and only emerge for a take-away pizza after dark, others take care to spend a good part of their courtship in the company of friends and relatives. For example, one interview couple who were at separate universities, and only saw each other during the holidays, spent most of their vacations with one or other of their families – even, one summer, sharing a caravan with his parents. And some couples arrange early on to dilute the intensity of the twosome by having a baby and becoming a threesome.

The importance of attachment

The discussion above should go some way towards explaining why a twosome is a natural state of being to seek (and sometimes to fear as well). Of course, an adult couple is not the same as a mother-and-baby couple. An adult couple is not (at least, should not be) a union of one dependent partner and one to be depended on, but of two equals. Therefore, writes Lily Pincus,

> marriage makes possible an interaction of two
> personalities at greater depth and intimacy than is
> possible in any other relationships except those in early
> childhood . . . It recapitulates much from past
> experience, perpetuating the security and goodness of
> childhood relationships while providing opportunity for
> their intimate enjoyment to be transformed from
> immature and dependent modes of gratification into the
> give-and-take of an interdependent relationship. For
> these reasons marriage has great potentialities for
> psychological and biological growth and for creative
> attainment.[32]

Finally, I want to add that although 'attachment' has been presented as having to do with our need for security, and does not sound as exciting as falling in love, the two cannot be so easily disentangled. There is no chronology whereby first we fall in love and then become attached. For many people a certain degree of attachment develops very early on, or may even precede falling in love, for example if the two partners were friends before they became lovers. For a love affair to survive the end of 'oneness' and to make it through the stage of disillusionment and beyond, there needs to be attachment.

Attachment and the persistence of the original hopes of wholeness can together counter the disappointment of finding that one must withdraw one's early, one-sidedly rosy projections. In order to have the courage to undertake the psychological work of reclaiming one's projections, one needs to feel a level of trust in one's partner and safety in the relationship. Change is painful; it involves confronting and coming to terms with the unknown bad as well as the good in oneself. It involves self-questioning and strong feelings. For most people, a secure attachment is a prerequisite for daring to let go and really showing who they are, to themselves and to their partner.

In a mature love relationship, the feelings of intimacy and separateness alternate. The partners can move back and forth between them – from making love to spending a week or two apart, from being very close on holiday to being very busy back at work. This flexibility grows along with the growth of trust in the attachment.

Specific Factors in the Choice: Complementarity, Similarity, Defence, Repetition

'Most strong attachments are based on a mixture of these three processes – identification of feeling, complementarity of feeling and mutual defensive avoidance of other feelings. All these three processes can be conscious or unconscious.'[33] To these three factors in the specific choice of partner I would add the perceived opportunity for repetition of patterns from the past, or conversely, for avoiding or breaking patterns from the past. Under the headings of *complementarity*, *similarity*, *shared defences*, and *repetition*, I want to give real-life examples of each 'type' of attraction.

Complementarity

We saw that falling in love involves projecting one's 'shadow' traits on to the beloved. To recapitulate: the point of this, the unconscious hope, is to develop greater psychological wholeness in oneself. This can be done by reclaiming those projections after having viewed them in full daylight, so to speak, in the other one. Further, although the earliest projections are usually purely positive, their negative underside also comes to light somewhat later on, at the stage of disillusionment. Both the desirable and less desirable of our projections must be absorbed back into ourselves. And finally, we rarely project qualities that are wholly inappropriate to the other person. So one could also describe projection as a partial and exaggerated vision of the actual characteristics of the newly beloved. The choice of what to see and what not to see is determined by the longings of our own unconscious.

Since our shadow traits play such an important part in projection, does this mean that we always fall in love with someone complementary to ourselves? Do opposites always attract? Do we always look for someone who will reflect our shadow traits, our hidden self, our own, *inner* 'other half'?

The search for completion through another is always a factor in an attraction, but it may not always be the most powerful factor. It may be outweighed by an emphasis on similarity, or a shared defence, as we will see below. A complementary attraction implies that there will have to be change. Some people fear change very much, in which case they may choose their partner because they hope he or she will let them stay as they are. In such a choice, projection may not play a very prominent part. Then people may talk more about a feeling of comfort than about excitement and falling in love.

An attraction with a good dose of complementarity may be the 'healthiest' type of attraction, the one offering most hope and scope for the psychological growth. This may sound paradoxical. After all, the projections of falling in love represent an attempt to liberate the repressed parts of ourselves, to breathe life into the shrivelled parts of our being. Does not this in turn imply that the nexus of our choice of partner is always some problem inside ourselves? It does – but this may be no bad thing. Clulow and Mattinson consider it a 'wise unconscious that falls in love with and marries its own unrecognised problem and then in marriage recreates the problematic situation'. They continue: 'We could say we can divide the world into two: those who marry to avoid their problems and those who marry to tangle with them. The former, not having fallen in love, or with few of their emotions engaged, often continue to feel cheated. The latter, whose emotions are firmly engaged are, we believe, the majority.'[34] In other words, they go so far as to suggest that those whose choice of partner is *not* based on the search for resolutions to their problems, never fully fall in love. Projecting one's shadow traits is the start of an attempt to confront one's problems. For this reason complementarity as the dominant factor seems to be the most hopeful starting point for an attraction.

Susannah and Charles

Susannah, 25, and Charles, 27, had only been together a year when they were interviewed, and they had just started living together. They had known each other since school, but their lives had gone in quite different directions.

After leaving school, Charles had stayed in their home town, and stayed with his first girlfriend, too, for eight years, in a relationship that became less and less rewarding. He did odd jobs but failed to settle to a career, and he carried on living at home. Meanwhile, Susannah went to university where she became passionately involved in politics. After graduating she went travelling, and then worked for the European Community in Brussels. There she had several love affairs with men who, like her, were achieving, intellectual and politically committed, but they were usually married or otherwise unavailable, and none of her relationships lasted more than a few months. After the most recent break-up, which coincided with the non-renewal of her contract, she felt she needed time to lick her wounds. She came back to England and went home to her parents. Back in her home town, she bumped into Charles in the local pub.

Their relationship started gently, with drinks in the pub, and going round to each other's houses, as in their schooldays, sitting round the kitchen table and chatting. Susannah, in her own words, 'was very pleased that I could get on with one of my old friends'. Charles felt, 'it was a breath of fresh air when I met Susannah again'.

When they finally got together, Susannah said, 'He hugged me in such a way as if to say, there was nothing to worry about – and I felt there was nothing to worry about, which in my experience is quite rare. It felt totally risk-free.'

She continued: 'Charles certainly provided the things that were missing for me: stability, and being cared for. His life has lacked change, while mine has had too much. He is an extremely stable person. He immediately made me satisfied with the idea of leading a normal life – living in a town which wasn't even a capital city, and doing an ordinary job. When I first got interested in politics it was all about national and international politics, campaigning and fighting and this, that and the other. But when I met Charles I could imagine being a local councillor in a town and being concerned with local issues and local people, and living happily ever after. That never occurred to me before.'

Charles said: 'I was looking for a change in my life. Susannah represented a lot of things that were missing – being interested in world affairs, committed, ambitious, political, educated, having a slightly more sophisticated outlook on things, greater aspirations. All these things were bothering me a lot. I didn't have any friends who could understand what I was talking about. I don't know why I didn't go to university. I now realise I should have, because my life wasn't stimulating me the way I wanted.' Indeed, since meeting Susannah he had started a degree course as a mature student.

For Susannah, then, her relationship with Charles was a homecoming. For Charles, it was the start of doing something new with his life.

Charles's background

Charles's apparent stability, indeed his lack of adventurousness, had developed in reaction to his turbulent family. He said, 'Both my parents are very loud and talk incessantly, which is why it is very difficult to talk to them. My older brothers are very fiery. Tempers flew fast and furious. There was no violence but plenty of shouting and smashing of plates. They're all nutcases!'

Charles remembered his father as being always preoccupied. 'I never felt I could expect time. If I asked a question he would point to a book for me to read.' His mother, meanwhile, was preoccupied with his oldest brother Walter, whom Charles described as 'emotionally unstable, erratic and unpredictable, spiteful and malicious'. He seemed to take special pleasure in taunting and bullying Charles.

Further, Charles felt, 'He kept my parents away from me by creating so much hell. He is always depressed; they are much more sure that I will always be fine and will always cope, so they don't really think about me.' Even just the other day he had been round at his mother's house, 'and every time I tried to talk about something important to me, or something that was worrying me, she just turned the conversation to something Walter was up to'.

Charles thought that the wild tempers and tantrums in his house caused him 'to make the decision in life to try to be calmer, reasonable, not smash plates, not abuse people unnecessarily'. He envisaged himself as a bubble of calm, or imperturbability, in the midst of a tempest. But the price he paid seemed to have been a certain withdrawal from the very currents of life. He himself wondered 'if I am very unperceptive about other people's emotions and relationships, and tension in relationships. I never seem to pick up on things.' He added, 'Susannah is much more astute than I am.'

This determined solidity was one of the qualities which Susannah found attractive in Charles. It made her feel safe. Its reverse was his fear of change and of initiating change in his life. His delay in leaving home and creating his own life appeared a kind of waiting for his turn; 'if I hang around long enough perhaps they'll notice me in the end'.

Susannah's background

Susannah always experienced a conflict of identification between her father's side of the family, which was academic, intellectual and achieving, and her mother's side, which was suburban and 'proper' and conventional. As she grew older, Susannah began to despise her mother's side of the family and resolutely embraced the values of her father's side. She pursued career success, a politicised attitude to life, and a notion of 'being special'. The men she was interested in were similar, but always unavailable for a long-term relationship. Her mother's way didn't seem to be bringing her happiness in relationships.

For Susannah, then, her relationship with Charles opened a way for her to settle down and allow herself to be a little less harshly demanding of herself. Meeting Charles was part of her return to her home town and reconnecting with her childhood. She wanted a steady relationship, to set down roots and start living an 'ordinary' life – but at the same time she still wanted to be 'special'. It was as if she hoped through her relationship with Charles, to heal the split inside herself between her mother's side and her father's side. She consciously likened Charles to her mother.

The couple, the choice

For Charles, meeting Susannah was a way to get out of the rut of dead-end jobs, the grip of his ex-girlfriend, and over-involvement with his family. To Charles, Susannah's go-ahead approach to life and firm opinions must have seemed the kind of strength he so needed to inspire him to take control of his life, for example by going to university, and to lever himself away from home, both physically and mentally.

Susannah thought Charles was 'an extraordinarily stable person'. She needed stability in her life. Charles thought Susannah interesting and exciting, just what he needed in his life. According to their descriptions of each other, they complemented one another perfectly.

But paradoxically, the hope, held by both Charles and Susannah, was for the chance to break out of their respective personality moulds. How could they satisfy each other in the long term, when their satisfaction seemed to depend on keeping their partner in the very mould from which he – and she – was trying to escape?

Susannah was looking for stability through Charles; Charles was looking for change through Susannah. To cope with growing up in his tempestuous family Charles had been forced to develop an imperturbability that probably felt imprisoning. Would Susannah be able to accept it if Charles revealed aspects of himself that were far from placid and calm? Would Charles ultimately be disappointed with Susannah's longing to 'lead a normal life, living in a town which wasn't even a capital city, and doing an ordinary job'?

Their original, complementary exchange of projections would be hard pushed to sustain them through a long relationship. The challenge for their relationship would be to mix and match and swap roles, until there were no longer any fixed roles, but 'each this and that'.

Similarity

What about 'like seeks like'? Don't people often explain the success of their relationship by saying, 'We have so much in common'?

Certainly, studies by social psychologists often show like seeking like, at least in the areas that can be quantified. More often than not husbands and wives are very alike in religion, ethnic background, race, socioeconomic status, age and political views (a 'coefficient correlation' of 0.9 where 1.0 would mean perfect correspondence). There is some correlation on 'personality' measures such as IQ (0.4), and they have even been shown to resemble each other physically – slightly, but still with statistical significance (0.2).[35] Social psychologists also emphasise similarity of social attitudes and values as a factor in people's choice of partner, 'because human beings need to feel that their view of reality is correct'.[36] In other words, couples can validate each other's world views and moral and social opinions: '*we* think that hitting children is wrong'; '*we* believe in the value of education'; '*we* think it's important to save money for a rainy day'. Agreement in such areas certainly helps the smooth running of a relationship. And further, shared interests and hobbies, such as rock climbing, gourmet cooking or playing Trivial Pursuit, can provide a channel for pleasant companionship and a way of feeling close without too great intensity.

But does similarity in external, observable areas tell us anything about the nature of the psychological choice? Of all the white, middle-class, college-educated men that a white, middle-class, college-educated woman meets during the course of school, university and working life, why does she marry the particular one that she does? We cannot assume that because two partners' social backgrounds are alike, their psyches are too. The findings of social psychology tell us little about the unconscious choice.

But what about psychological similarity? What if, in our newly chosen partner, we perceive not our shadow traits but our conscious traits? What is the nature of the attraction when two people who perceive each other as similar get together: two equally easygoing people, or two emotionally volatile people, or two shy people?

For one thing, it can feel comforting to be with someone who seems to feel the same as oneself: it makes one feel understood, whereas the falling in love sequence of projection, disillusionment and reclaiming projections can be both challenging and discomfiting. It arouses strong emotions, and many people have limited stamina for emotional turbulence.

Difference is always challenging. If the emphasis in a relationship is very much on similarity, it may be that both partners have grown up to regard difference as dangerous: it spells disagreement, perhaps arguments and anger. It may be that the two chose each other because they sensed that here was a person who tacitly agreed not to bring such troublesome emotions into the relationship. In this way similarity can be a defensive type of attraction, a way of avoiding confronting one's hidden self. At the same time, there is nothing wrong with enjoying the comfort that comes from feeling 'we understand each other because we feel the same'. It is a question of to what degree identification played its part in the attraction, and how far it acts as a defence against difference.

Janet and Robin

An example of a couple whose attraction was founded on similarity were Janet and Robin. (For a fuller account, see Chapter 5.) They themselves agreed that what they had in common was a lack of confidence and self-esteem – or at least, had had when they met. In the interviews, Robin recalled how amazed he had been to find someone who actually seemed to want him. They soon moved in together and became inseparable. They explained that through their relationship they had helped one another to grow stronger and more confident. They encouraged each other, for example, to apply for jobs, and to believe that they could do it. 'Individually we are not up to much, but together we are strong,' they said, and this became their refrain.

From what they told about their respective backgrounds, it appeared that both Janet and Robin had grown up without any certainty that they were loved. Janet's parents divorced when she was 10. They were preoccupied with her father's infidelities and their own frequent tempestuous quarrels, and seemed to have little time left over for her. In addition, she was overshadowed by her older sister Sarah, who was considered pretty and clever while Janet was not.

Robin was the youngest in his family and there was a big gap between him and his older siblings. His father took no interest in him, and when he was grown up he learned that his father had not wanted any more children. But his mother had her own way and Robin was born, 'her' child only. She was a forceful woman who could not tolerate him showing much independence or difference of opinion. He now believed that his mother wanted him only 'as a pawn in their marriage', never for himself. This was his background of feeling unwanted.

Despite surface differences in Janet and Robin's backgrounds and indeed also in their personalities, Janet being quite sharp while Robin was more gentle, the fundamental similarity between them was that each felt as badly about himself or herself as the other. By choosing a partner so like themselves, they expressed a double hope: of finding someone who understood what it felt like to feel unloved, and of having the past made up for, of being loved at last.

In many ways their hopes had been fulfilled. And yet this achievement was not without certain costs and sacrifices in other areas of their lives. These will be looked at more closely in Chapter 5.

Shared defences

All couples share defences to some extent, in so far as there are emotional no-go areas or taboos in their relationship. 'Most couples will tangle with some mutual problems and leave others firmly alone, retaining some well-defended areas in their personalities and in their partnership.'[37]

Such areas are usually determined by a shared fear of certain emotions. Typical shared fears include a fear of dependency, or intimacy, or anger or depression. These are powerful states of being, and it is not surprising that people should often try to avoid them. But if this avoidance has become a central feature of the way two partners relate to each other – as if they were joining hands to dance around a fire burning right in the middle of the living-room floor without ever acknowledging that it's there – then we may speak of a shared defence.

If this happens then obviously the partners are no longer helping each other to become more whole. Instead, they are co-operating (or put pejoratively, colluding), to avoid the challenge of bringing the emotional skeletons out of their shared closet and incorporating them into their lives. They are joining together to protect each other from the pain of change.

Whether a shared defence is actually part of the attraction right at the beginning, or whether it is an attraction 'gone wrong' is hard to say. Perhaps, for some people, past experience weighs so heavily that what they most desire is a partner who will leave them be and let them continue to arm themselves against their fears without challenge. The antennae go out and report the message, 'Here is someone who, for reasons of their own, is not going to try to get too close; or someone who also loathes conflict and therefore is not going to provoke it', and so on.

But others may be drawn to each other with ambivalent hopes: on the one hand, the hope of being allowed to maintain their defences, and on the other the hope of having them bull-dozed and finding a new courage. Indeed, Clulow and Mattinson suggest that for the majority, 'the unconscious choice of partner is governed by a mix of hopes and fears, the prospect of repairing and making whole, and the fear of doing so'.[38]

Harriet and Bernard

A striking example of a couple whose attraction was based on a shared defence were Harriet and Bernard.[39] They were both painfully shy. They were at the same college, both studying science, both far more comfortable alone in the lab than in the company of other people. Harriet always looked visibly startled when spoken to: her eyes would widen and she would start stammering. Bernard was monosyllabic and couldn't look people in the eye. No doubt their backgrounds bore much of the responsibility for their deficit in social skills: Harriet grew up on a remote farm, the only child of elderly parents who were unworldly and self-reliant. They were possessive of their only daughter and discouraged her from making friends. Bernard was the youngest of three children, two girls and a boy. His mother was a powerful, voluble woman while his father was singularly withdrawn and content to leave to his wife all dealings with the outside world. The family seemed to divide along sex lines with the girls taking after their mother and Bernard identifying strongly with his father.

Somewhat incongruously, Bernard and Harriet met at a student party. They were introduced by their hostess, who had it in mind that they might suit each other. They spent the evening sitting next to each other on a windowseat, exchanging a few sparing words, until the end of the party, when Bernard plucked up the courage to suggest another meeting. They became each other's first girlfriend and boyfriend, and married after graduating. Both continued to work in university settings and settled into a quiet life together. They were as unsociable as ever, except now there were two of them. Thus they could carry on avoiding the world and at the same time have insulation against loneliness.

The fuel for their attraction was a shared defence against the vagaries of the emotions – both those from inside themselves and those provoked by other people. Their backgrounds, different as they were, had in each of them contributed to a fear of emotional expression and a failure to develop more than a limited range of emotional responses to the world.

However, when after some years they had children, dramatic changes ensued. Their two children, a girl and a boy, were quite 'wild'. They were big and bouncy and full of energy, curious and fearless about the world – quite the opposite of their stunned parents, who nevertheless began to adapt. Bernard became a tireless player of romping games, emitting whoops and shouts in a way he had never done when he was a child.

Harriet gradually met other mothers, took some part in community activities and made at least one good new friend. So while Harriet and Bernard's relationship as a couple seemed mainly 'defensive', one might well argue that it also contained the hope of some psychological growth, of finding other parts of themselves, which was at least partly fulfilled when they became a family. Their children were the ones to bring some movement towards 'wholeness'.

Repetition

While I was writing this book, a friend commented: 'Surely your choice of partner is determined by your parents! I mean, either you choose someone who is just like your opposite-sex parent, or someone who is as unlike them as possible.' He went on to describe the ways in which his wife was the very antithesis of his mother: his mother was orderly and organised while his wife was a messy scatterbrain; his mother was She Who Must Be Obeyed while his wife would never frighten a fly. At this point his wife joined in the conversation. She began to point out the ways in which she was very *like* her mother-in-law: both of them had a strong sense of family and placed great value on family occasions and regular contact between family members. Neither of them was prone to emotional outbursts and losing their temper; usually they maintained a cheerful, 'let's get on with it' ethos in the house. And so on: while he emphasised the differences between the specific characters of his wife and his mother, she emphasised the way in which the atmosphere in their family was similar to the one in which he had grown up.

The opportunity for repetition, as a factor in partner choice, is surely almost always a mixture of things similar and things different from the past. The man in the example above, who was happily married with three children, had managed to recreate in his own family the feeling of security and family orientation which he valued from his childhood. At the same time, he had escaped the more overwhelming aspects of his mother.

Rationally, one would always choose to repeat what felt good and leave behind that which felt bad. However, the choice of partner is not rational and the pull of what feels familiar, whether good or bad, can often override a conscious wish to find a relationship that will be quite different from those of one's childhood.

All relationships in one's family of origin play their part. Some were observed, such as the relationship between mother and father, or between father and an older brother. Others were experienced and have become part of one's psychological make-up, that is, one's own relationships with mother and father and siblings. As we have seen, it is 'a wise unconscious' which chooses to tangle with its problems through the choice of partner. The unresolved issues from the past will certainly be part of the repetition factor. Perhaps surprisingly, people often elect unconsciously to repeat the bad, difficult aspects of past relationships. Sibling jealousy, or a feeling of being loved not for oneself but for one's achievements, or a lack of trust in the reliability of the other, may all flare up again in our adult couple relationship.

For example, a person who suffered from powerful sibling rivalry may find it hard to offer their partner encouragement and praise, because of a misplaced feeling that if they do, 'he or she will be better than me'. A person who felt as a child that love was conditional on achievement may feel afraid to reveal the vulnerable parts of themselves to their partner, and may place more emphasis on *appearing* a successful couple than really finding intimacy. And so on: the permutations are, of course, endless.

The point of bringing such legacies into one's couple relationship is the hope of having them resolved. How can this be done? It is rather like acting out the same play a hundred times, but each time with a slightly different ending. At first the ending seems tragic and inevitable, as in a Greek drama, but gradually it is modified. This modification can come about if one's partner does not take on exactly the same roles as the people in one's childhood, and if you, as the main actor, gradually come to perceive this. Changing patterns requires a certain level of consciousness about the existence of the patterns in the first place. For example, Elaine and Greg (see Chapter 2) worked over several years to create better ways of solving conflicts than they had inherited from their families. Elaine had to become aware of her tendency to prod and needle Greg when she was annoyed about something, and had to learn to say it openly. Greg had to resist his impulse to walk away from conflict, and instead to stay and confront it with Elaine.

This kind of reworking of early patterns is certainly difficult to achieve. One partner can be provoked into re-enacting the other's scenario. Indeed, often the partner seems to be chosen for their very suitability for the old role(s).

Lorraine and Howard

An example of a couple who got stuck appears in Marion Solomon's book *Narcissism and Intimacy*.[40] 'Lorraine and Howard' did not make each other happy, yet were unable to part. For example, Howard wanted to move to the country while Lorraine did not, because she feared that she would lose her friends and have nothing to do. When Lorraine did not do what Howard wanted, he got angry and started shouting and fuming. Lorraine's response was to back down temporarily, to say that maybe it would be all right after all, and to plead with him not to get angry. Once equilibrium was restored, Lorraine would again assert her own wishes, Howard would get angry, and the cycle would be repeated. This pattern seemed to erupt over just about everything – even such petty things as Lorraine stacking new packets of mince in front of the old packets in the freezer.

After a few sessions of marital therapy it began to appear that the cycle of Howard's anger and Lorraine's withdrawal had direct roots in their childhoods. Howard was the somewhat neglected child of busy parents, and he remembered that even as a child the best way to get attention was to become angry and start shouting. Then his parents would come running (if they were there). Lorraine, meanwhile, had grown up in a family where her father was prone to erupt into rages and her mother fell into long depressions. It fell to her and her siblings to try to keep things calm in the house.

Lorraine and Howard brought their early child selves and environments into their marriage more or less unchanged. Howard erupted into rages when he felt neglected, which was especially when Lorraine didn't go along with his wishes. Lorraine was quite used to having a raging man in the house, and instinctively reacted by trying to calm things down. For both of them, the scene was a familiar one.

Although on one level it was unpleasant to have so much anger around, on another level it was quite comfortable because it was familiar. What could stop such a fruitless interaction continuing for ever? Howard and Lorraine came to therapy because the rages were no longer working for Howard. He got angry, as he had always done, he got his way, as he was used to – but then, after he had calmed down, Lorraine 'betrayed' him by asserting her own wishes again. They were not getting anywhere with making a decision about moving to the country. One can see how a sense of familiarity was a strong factor in Lorraine and Howard's choice of each other: here was someone with whom old patterns could be repeated. At the same time this attraction must have been coupled with the hope of breaking out of the old ways: endlessly repeating what they had learned in childhood was making neither of them happy.

Naturally, not all couples seek marital therapy. Some spend a lifetime in thrall to their psychological blueprints from the past. Others succeed in making changes with the help of each other. Just as a projection can contain great hope, so can the opportunity for repetition. And just as the projections must be reclaimed to fulfil the hope, so must the troublesome patterns from the past be reworked.

In the chapters that follow, the influence of the past in the choice of partner will be shown in the stories of almost all the interviewed couples, to a greater or lesser extent. So will the mix of other factors drawing the two partners together, especially psychological complementarity, similarity and defensiveness. The themes that have been explored in this chapter are woven into the narratives.

CHAPTER TWO

To Commit or Not to Commit?

COMMITMENT envelops some couples gradually like a mist without markers, while other couples arrive at a point of declaration, moved, perhaps, by some special event. Remember Doctor Lydgate in *Middlemarch* who was tumbled into a proposal by Rosamond's crying:

> As he raised his eyes now he saw a certain helpless quivering which touched him quite newly, and made him look at Rosamond with a questioning flash. At this moment she was as natural as she had ever been when she was five years old: she felt that her tears had risen, and it was no use to try to do anything else than let them stay like water on a blue flower or let them fall over her cheeks, even as they would.
>
> That moment of naturalness was the crystallizing feathertouch: it shook flirtation into love . . . He left the house an engaged man.[1]

However it happens, all couples sooner or later face decisions about steps that would tie them closer together: whether or not to live together, marry, have a baby, merge their finances, buy a property, and so on. The three couples whose stories are told in this chapter were all, in different ways, grappling with the question of whether, and how, to make a commitment. We look at their choice of each other as partners from this vantage-point: their hopes, the doubts they were experiencing, and the assurances they were looking for.

Two of the couples had been together five years and the third couple nine years. Both the five-year couples were living together, while the nine-year couple was not. In five years, let alone nine, young people go through enormous changes, in the circumstances of their lives, as individuals and as a couple. Through these changes the couples in this chapter had stayed together – but without yet making an overt commitment to do so.

The older couple, Elaine and Greg, were very deliberately trying to make up their minds about whether to get married and start a family, or perhaps start a family without getting married? One of the younger couples, Jason and Louisa, were not considering a particular step or stage such as marriage or having babies, but were circling around a more general issue about whether or not to think of their relationship as being 'for ever'. The third couple, Mary and Ian, lived in different towns and seemed to have no need to express commitment in any conventional manner. Yet they had been together nine years, since the time they were both in the sixth form. What was it that kept them together?

Statistically speaking, it is apparently unusual for couples to be together as long as five years without marrying, let alone nine. (Though not surprisingly, research shows that if you meet your future spouse when you are young, the 'courtship' is likely to be longer.)[2] Hence a certain bias, in these case histories, towards trying to discover what factors were holding them back from commitment. What did they have to resolve before they could entrust themselves to each other?

'Till death us do part?'

Commitment means different things to different people. To many, commitment equals marriage, at least in external form: 85–90 per cent of us still marry at some point in our lives, so in Britain marriage must still count as the most powerful symbol of commitment.

Some people consider themselves committed once they have an exclusive sexual relationship. To others, living together is a sign of commitment. Yet others feel that the greatest commitment is to have a baby together.

The external forms of commitment entwine with the inner, personal meanings. The psychologist R.J. Sternberg defines commitment as having two components: 'in the short term, the decision that one loves the other person, and in the long term a commitment to maintain that love'.[3]

Commitment usually includes the idea of permanence. This is most eloquently spelled out in the marriage vows with the promise to share a future, 'till death us do part'; the promise to be faithful, 'forsaking all other', and perhaps most difficult to fulfil, the promise to work at keeping alive one's love, 'to have and to hold . . . for better for worse, for richer for poorer, in sickness and in health, to love and to cherish'.

Many couples hovering around commitment are understandably uncomfortable with the idea of permanence. For example, Jason and Louisa thought they would stay together for the rest of their lives, but also thought that one could not make such promises. And although Mary said she and Ian were committed, she also said that she would never assume that they would be together next Christmas. To talk about 'for ever' feels like hubris to some, too much to ask for – while to others the idea feels frightening and constraining.

Cohabitation and marriage

Let us look for a moment at the question of marriage versus cohabitation. In all West European countries in the last thirty years, there have been enormous shifts in patterns of relationships. In England, pre-marital sex has become almost completely accepted, pre-marital cohabitation increasingly so, and now that couples have babies together without being married, it seems that living together may become accepted as an alternative to marriage. In addition, the one-in-three divorce rate means that many people will be married twice or more, or married once and cohabit afterwards, which has given rise to the term 'serial monogamy' as a description of the possible dominant relationship pattern of the future.

By comparison with other European countries, England is still quite conservative. In Sweden, the most radical of the West European countries in this context, 90 per cent of couples marrying for the first time have lived together first; in England the equivalent figure is about 50 per cent. In Sweden, where 51 per cent of babies are born out of wedlock, having a baby is no particular incentive for cohabiting couples to marry,[4] whereas in England 'starting a family' is still often the reason why cohabitees turn to marriage – as with Greg and Elaine, below. Of course, this may in part have to do with the different legal situations in England and Sweden. In Sweden, in the 1980s, cohabitation was given many of the same rights in law as marriage, whereas in England a 'common-law marriage' has no legal status (although the DSS chooses to recognise it for benefit purposes). If a cohabiting couple with children break up, the father has no automatic rights to the child and the mother no rights to maintenance for herself. If a cohabiting couple with shared property break up, there is no set framework for dividing it up. Jacqui Jackson, a solicitor specialising in cohabitation disputes, says: 'I think people drift into living together, thinking that it's easier to get out of than marriage, but if they mix up their property or finances in any way, then it isn't.'[5]

'One major difference between cohabitation and marriage is that the former doesn't assume a commitment to permanence at the beginning of the relationship.'[6] Not surprisingly then, cohabitation is far less stable than marriage. Even in Sweden, where it is so much the norm, cohabiting couples are six times as likely to break up as married ones.[7] When cohabiting couples say they are committed, they may mean 'committed for now' rather than 'committed for ever'. However, some people think 'now' is a greater undertaking than 'for ever'. One long-term cohabiting couple I know believe that their commitment to each other can only be true as long as it is voluntary, and that to marry would remove it from their own will and transfer it to a piece of paper. As they are now, whenever there is a hitch or a bad patch, their commitment has to be renegotiated and reaffirmed, and this they consider much more demanding than the once-and-for-all contract of marriage.

Several pieces of research, from Sweden, Norway, Canada and the USA have suggested that once cohabiting couples do marry, they are more likely than average to divorce.[8] A 1981 British study found that 25 per cent of women who were divorced or separated had lived with their partners before marriage, compared with 12 per cent of those still married or widowed.[9] It is an intriguing finding: after all, living together is often supposed to be a 'trial marriage', a way of finding out whether one's relationship is strong and good enough *before* shackling oneself together for ever. As yet there are no conclusive explanations for this statistic. Some researchers have simply suggested that those who cohabit are also those with more 'liberal' values who more easily contemplate divorce. A Dutch study showed that those who cohabited were more likely to be urban-dwellers and non-churchgoers, two characteristics also associated with higher divorce rates.[10] Others have suggested that perhaps cohabiting couples often turn to marriage when their relationship seems to be coming apart, in the mistaken hope that this will glue them together (much as some people have a baby in the hope of patching up their marriage). And yet others have suggested that 'the act of taking on the role of "husband" or "wife", for some people, changes their behaviour and/or expectations of the partner in ways that didn't occur while the couple were just living together'.[11]

This last idea is one to be borne in mind in the next chapter, in the context of the experiences of two newly married couples. In this chapter, for Mary and Ian, it seemed that one factor holding them back from overt commitment was their fear of what they might turn into if they followed in their parents' footsteps and married. As long as a couple is not married, they have not fully conformed – they are different from society's norm, different from the majority of couples, different from their parents. As long as one cannot be assigned a role, 'husband' or 'wife', 'father' or 'mother', one may feel more free as an individual and, just as importantly, more free to see one's partner as an individual. Some people are unconsciously very afraid of what would happen to them and their partner if they began to see each other in traditional roles.

The timing of commitment

In England, cohabitation is still usually a prelude to marriage. Apart from the legal disadvantages of cohabitation, peer pressure also plays its part in making it so. If nearly 90 per cent of us still marry, sooner or later young cohabiting couples are going to find that, one by one, their friends are setting off for the church or the registry office with the inevitability of skittles before a ball. As Louisa and Jason remarked: 'We hadn't really thought of marriage until last summer when we went to four weddings in a row – and they were all great! So we thought, why don't we have one of those?'

Timing becomes a factor the closer one gets to 30. Is the person I'm with now the one I'll stay with? Have I got that much time left to look around? If we split up, will there be any singles left to choose from!? Although we have more control over our lives than Jane Austen heroines, people do still worry about being left on the shelf, and not only women, although the fact that the period of fertility is limited makes it more urgent for them. There was a moment of particular terror in the 1980s when a US study, widely reported in women's magazines, claimed that unmarried women in their thirties had a greater chance of being shot by a terrorist than finding a marriage partner (the study was subsequently shown to be quite falsely constructed and the figures on which it was based did not indicate any such conclusion).

Naturally, there are different degrees of commitment that people want to show at different stages of their relationship. No one would suggest that at the age of 25 people should be in any great hurry to get married. For many people, the twenties are devoted to finding out which field of work they want to be in and establishing themselves in it; earning money, perhaps buying a flat or a car; travelling; going out, socialising and meeting people – in other words, building the structure of an independent adult life. It is also the time of finding out what it means to be independent and adult in one's inner world – recasting relationships with parents, looking back on one's childhood and adolescence and making sense of them, so as to find a base for an adult identity.

A good enough choice?

Apart from timing, the great question underlying people's uncertainty about commitment is, of course, 'Is this person the right one for me?'

The child psychoanalyst D.W. Winnicott is famous, among other things, for coining the concept of the 'good enough mother': a mother who is not perfect, but 'good enough' for her baby; who, although she may fail to respond to its every need or want, offers her child enough love and care and holding to enable it to thrive. We could also talk about a 'good enough relationship', one which offers a soil rich enough to work, although it may be by no means suitable to grow every one of the plants one had in mind. As one man said to his bride-to-be, as if in explanation after proposing to her (and being accepted): 'I feel that you are someone I can do emotional business with.' This reminds one of Clulow and Mattinson's contention that the wisest choice of partner is someone who can help us to tangle with our problems. People hovering around commitment are tacitly looking for an affirmative answer to the question, 'Is this a "good enough" relationship?'

If the question can be answered with a confident yes, then a commitment can be made. If not, then even long-term cohabiting couples may break up. Who hasn't heard of couples who lived together for ten years, averring that they were committed as they were and that marriage was unnecessary and wouldn't change anything – who then split up and married new partners within just a year or two? (An example of this is James in the following chapter.) Afterwards, one or other partner may say that they had known for some time that their ex-partner 'wasn't right'. But it is difficult and frightening to break up a long and established relationship, and easier to do nothing until something forces a move – falling in love with someone else, for example.

The amplification of the ticking of the woman's biological clock is often what precipitates a split (or marriage) for long-term cohabitees. This was the case for Molly and Brian,[12] a drifting sort of couple who fell into things rather than making decisions about them. But when Molly, at the age of 29, began to want a firm commitment from Brian which would allow her to feel secure enough to get pregnant, Brian felt cornered. His response to her unspoken pressure was to go off sex for a prolonged period (as if to make sure no 'accidental' pregnancy could happen). This eventually brought them to marital counselling, where they were able to unravel what was going on.

'Marry in haste, repent at leisure?'

One woman who married her partner within a year of meeting him gave it as her opinion that marriage was a safeguard against splitting up once you started on the real emotional work of forging a relationship. In other words, marry first, then go through the pain – and joy – of 'working it out'. Although she put it more bluntly than most people might, many couples who don't spend years hovering around commitment but who marry within the average two years are doing exactly that.

In one way this chronology makes great sense. As we saw in the previous chapter, we need an 'attachment figure' in adulthood just as much as in childhood. We need someone whom we can trust to be there for us and not abandon us. In infancy and childhood the presence of the attachment figure is vital in bestowing the courage and security for the child to dare to have conflicting feelings, to live out fears and joys without feeling that he or she is going to fragment. Similarly, in adulthood, a couple needs to feel secure in their attachment before they can really let go their love (and its undersides). There is a limit to how deep a couple can go with each other, how far they can explore and how much they can grow, if their attachment is not secure. Attachment is not secure when there is uncertainty about whether the partner will be there in the future.

In the seventeenth century Jeremy Taylor wrote in a sermon about marriage as compared with the single life: 'It hath in it less of Beauty, but more of Safety than the Single Life; it hath more Care, but less Danger; it is more Merry, and more Sad; is fuller of Sorrows, and fuller of Joys: it lies under more Burdens, but is supported by all the Strengths of Love and Charity, and those Burdens are delightful.'[13]

These days, we are unused to the idea that something which is more safe and less dangerous could, at the same time, be fuller of sorrows and fuller of joys. We conceive of safety as bland. But in his lyrical language this theologian was making the same point as above: that until we have the safety of a secure attachment, we will have neither the opportunity nor the courage to experience the emotional life to its fullest. Making a commitment is part of consolidating an attachment.

Elaine and Greg:

'We are not each other's ideal sexual type'

Elaine was 30 and Greg 27, and the question of commitment had become especially acute now because Elaine wanted to 'start a family'. Whether or not to marry was their current big dilemma. They had been going out for five years and had lived together for most of that time in a rented house in east London.

Elaine was dark and petite and moved in a neat, defined sort of way, while Greg was large and blond and a little clumsy. Elaine tended to dominate the joint interviews, not so much by volume of talk, since Greg usually talked more, but he had a tendency to go round and round while Elaine said things more directly, and sometimes cuttingly.

They certainly seemed to contrast each other. As the interviews progressed, it became apparent that a major part of their uncertainty about whether or not to get married and start a family centred around their conflicting feelings about these contrasts. Were they attracted or repelled by them? Was their partner's difference a good thing, a challenge, an inspiration to change? Or was it annoying, irritating, something to try to get rid of, or even give up on?

How they met

They met in London's clubland when Greg had just left college and was working in the foothills of the advertising industry; Elaine was an account executive in public relations. Both had grown up in the Midlands, both had come to London in search of bright lights and adventure, and both were a little lost and lonely. Neither had had a serious boyfriend or girlfriend before. Instead, each tended to fall for 'types'.

Elaine had been through a series of infatuations and short affairs with men whom she described as 'charming Jack-the-lad types who had the gift of the gab'. She said, 'I find that type of person very attractive – socially acceptable, the type lots of girls want to go out with.' The Jack-the-lads tended not to treat her very well. She said she never felt she could be herself with them, but always had to 'make a greater effort than my normal self, be more charming, more amusing, more witty'. She felt herself languish and become dull in the shadow of these men whom she perceived as sparkling and interesting.

Greg said, 'I did and do find blonde girls attractive', but the ones he went out with, he said, didn't have much personality or brains and left him to make all the running and talking and entertaining.

So it was interesting that when they met, they were drawn to each other for quite different character traits. Elaine, far from seeing in Greg a man who did all the talking, liked him because he seemed 'quieter, ironic, quite mature in his outlook – a separate entity, very different from other people I'd met in that environment'. Greg thought that Elaine had more 'personality' than other women he'd met in the clubs. He said, 'She was more than capable of contributing to conversations, even dominating them, telling jokes, and so on.' They both agreed the other one had 'stuck out in a crowd'.

They got together slowly. Over a period of six months they bumped into each other now and again at clubs and parties and chatted, but even after Elaine had given Greg her phone number twice, he didn't ring. Eventually she rang him. They went out that same evening, and then 'everything slotted into place and quickly became a fixture', as Elaine put it. Soon they found that the attractions of the London club scene paled and that they preferred to spend time together, just the two of them. Elaine said that, after her previous glamour boyfriends, it was a great relief to be able to be herself with Greg and 'not always have to wear make-up'.

'The ideal sexual type'

Greg's initial reluctance to follow up Elaine's tendering of her phone number had something to do with his idea of his ideal type. He said, 'I think I still had an ideal girl in mind for a "proper" relationship – Elaine isn't what I'd thought I'd start with.'

Elaine chipped in. 'I can describe his ideal type,' she said. 'Voluptuous, blonde, big baby blue eyes, with a good figure and no brain.'

'Not no brain,' replied Greg, 'but yes, a lot that would fit that description.'

Perhaps it was not surprising, then, that Elaine often returned to the theme of the 'ideal sexual type' and how neither of them fitted it. She conceived of Greg's ideal type as someone very sexual and sexy, which she did not consider herself to be. For her part, she said, 'I always go out with guys who are my own build and colouring, darker and slighter than Greg. He was not someone I thought of as a prospective partner.' So although Greg and Elaine were drawn to each other for being quite different from their previous partners, their supposed ideal sexual types were still the type of people with whom they had had such short, unsatisfactory relationships.

Their own getting together was 'no passionate sexual meeting', in Elaine's words. It was very 'conversation based', according to Greg. Their relationship now, they emphasised, was based on friendship and talking things through. They seemed to imply that sexual passion and a secure long-term relationship were incompatible. They could not have a long-term relationship with their 'ideal sexual type'. Yet by forgoing this type, they were also forgoing passion. This notion of the 'ideal sexual type' seemed to hover over them like a myth, or a regret, impervious to logic, and casting shadows. And yet, for all the 'passion' of her previous encounters, it was only in her relationship with Greg that Elaine had been able to relax and enjoy sex enough to have orgasms.

When the interviews began, Elaine had been made redundant from her company, and was temping while taking a course in business administration, with the plan of setting up as a freelance PR consultant. Greg by now had a demanding job as advertising accounts manager, often working long, late hours. Was this the right time to marry and 'start a family'?

Elaine's background

Elaine was the only child of parents she described as 'strange' and 'unsuited as a couple'. She longed for a sibling, but it seemed that her parents were not able to have more children. Elaine suspected that this was because her father was sub-fertile; her mother had herself 'checked out' but her father always refused to be examined. Indeed, he was terrified of doctors, and although he knew something was wrong a long time before he died, he allowed Elaine's mother to call the doctor only at the very last moment, when his illness was too far advanced to be amenable to treatment.

If he was timid with doctors, he was nevertheless a 'terrifically dominant person,' said Elaine, instilling fear into both her and her mother with his thunderous sulks which lasted for days. He could make her cry just by the way he looked at her. He was secretive both about his doings and his earnings and never told Elaine's mother anything about their financial situation: 'He wanted to avoid criticism – he was very proud,' Elaine said. After his death tens of thousands were discovered to be missing and unaccounted for, which made Elaine bitter as her mother was left with large debts.

On the other hand, Elaine stressed that when her father wasn't sulking he could display a great sense of humour, he was clever and self-educated and, Elaine said she really preferred him 'as a person'. 'He was humorous and intelligent, and we got on well as long as he wasn't moody and I wasn't putting forward dangerous views. In Greg's family differences of opinion can be aired; in my family they were shunned. That restricted us so much. Yet he was obsessed with me, they both were, it was very difficult to have such parental obsession focused on me. I hated being an only child, I would have loved to have had brothers and sisters.'

Elaine's mother had been 'lively and bubbly' as a young woman, and loved dancing. However, she lacked confidence and became increasingly dependent on her husband. 'It got completely out of control, she gave up everything and he did everything for her – and then they began to resent each other: he resented her for having no interests and she him for keeping her away from her friends and never wanting to go out socially.'

So Elaine grew up a somewhat lonely, isolated child in a rather gloomy, fearful household. But when she went to sixth-form college, 'my outlook changed completely. I met loads of people and was subjected to loads of new views. It was the happiest time of my life.' Her parents could not accept her new views, and at 20 she left home, one day when her father was out, so as to avoid 'setting him off on a mood'. From that time on, her relations with her parents grew increasingly distant.

Greg's background

Greg was the third child of four. His parents had married young; they were lively, busy people interested in politics, education and self-improvement, *Guardian* readers, who even went to pop concerts. Their marital relationship was by Greg's account a stormy one, with wild arguments, slammings of the front door and regular declarations that 'this is it, this is the end'. But, he added, his parents never harboured resentments and 'a day later they'd both be obviously completely in love with each other and very happy'. He admitted that as a boy he found the arguments disturbing, but quickly added: 'Looking back, it must have been incredibly stressful for them; my father in a job he didn't like, with four children and not much money.' He felt guilty about having been a burden to his parents. 'Since we left home and got out of their hair officially,' he said, 'they have become discernibly closer.'

In his early teens Greg developed what he called 'psychological problems with hypochondria, a whole load of problems . . . an off-beat heart . . . it still happens when I'm stressed'. For a year and a half he was in 'a grim state', 'panicky', and unhappy at school. Elaine later added that he was bullied at school, although he never told his parents, and he didn't mention it in the interviews either.

Eventually his parents took him to a doctor and then, he said, 'I got better overnight when it seemed that the doctor was blaming my parents for my problems'. If a desire to protect his parents was characteristic of him in his adolescence, it could be seen clearly in the interviews too. Greg very much wanted to give the impression of having grown up in a happy family, and became uncomfortable whenever he found himself saying something that contradicted this. Elaine, in her individual interview, offered her own interpretation of Greg's background. 'To be honest,' she said, 'I don't think his parents paid enough attention to their children. It's always he who phones them, never vice versa. He feels very guilty, but I've told him it's not his fault they had four young children and no money. They were always so busy and I think he was a bit lost in that frantic atmosphere.'

It was quite easy to imagine Greg as a boy: the same air of bewilderment, the slight vagueness, the same pliability and desire to please which perhaps contributed to making him a target for bullies.

The couple, the choice
For the first three and a half years Elaine and Greg's relationship was punctuated by enormous rows, mostly initiated by Elaine. She said, 'I was very uptight. I used to read things into Greg's behaviour and take offence at the slightest thing. I felt he wasn't being considerate or sensitive enough to me, maybe. We have talked about it a lot. He says I am a very demanding person, not easy to keep happy. I probably am.'

Bully and bullied
Elaine admitted that she was a 'goader', who pushed and prodded Greg into a reaction. For his part Greg admitted that he

preferred to avoid confrontation, and attributed this to the negative example of his parents' rows: 'They might have caused a mental block in me about confronting people,' he said speculatively. 'Maybe I had a deep-down fear that they would split up.' Thus Elaine assumed the role of the aggressive partner while Greg became the passive, evasive one. The greatest 'work' of their relationship centred on this dynamic between them.

Elaine thought Greg was hopelessly 'unassertive'. He came home at night exhausted and poured out to her his frustrations with his unreasonable boss – but he never stood up to him, to his face. Elaine said she resented being used as an 'emotional sponge'. She implied that although she goaded and dug holes in Greg, it was good for him; she was helping him to become tougher.

Greg described Elaine's philosophy as 'attack is the best form of defence'. Not surprisingly, he felt somewhat ambivalent about her proddings. He said: 'It's like she is with the cat: she strokes her and prods her, and strokes and prods, until she lashes out. And she definitely gets satisfaction from it!'

He admitted that his lack of assertiveness was a problem, and that he did tend to come home from work and pour out all his frustrations to Elaine as a substitute for doing anything about them, which he agreed was not fair on her. But he said: 'Elaine can be very insensitive to my moods – though at other times she can be endlessly giving. But she is good at getting off her chest what she wants, whether or not the time is right, whereas I wait – though often I end up saying nothing at all. She can be selfish with her emotions at times. She'll be in a mood, wanting to get something said, she will see that I am not in a great mood and not able to take it on board, but she will still go ahead. That's a fairly major criticism I have of her.'

Greg had been bullied as a child. Why, as an adult, would he choose a woman who would continue to bully him – even if, ironically, she bullied him to become less bulliable? Part of the fit between partners is how well they can repeat aspects of their pasts with each other, both happy and troublesome. Of course, living the bad again and again is nobody's choice; the hope is usually that the bad bits of the past can be first relived, then reworked and a new and more positive outcome achieved.

Greg may have hoped that with Elaine's help he might indeed learn to stand up for himself rather than always avoid confrontation. Early on in their relationship there was already a glimmer of suggestion that his hopes might be fulfilled. About three months into it, there was a big row which they both still remembered as a turning point.

'Elaine wanted to go out and I didn't,' Greg explained. 'We had a blazing row at the tube and stalked off in our different directions. But because I had the keys to her flat I had to go back there to wait for her. She came home the next day and we had another blazing row, and I was all prepared to walk out the door. But when it came to it . . . I just didn't. I realised we could have an argument and it not be the end of the relationship.'

They continued to have rows. Although he didn't walk out, for a long time Greg's nature and instinct told him that the more Elaine goaded, the more he should retreat and become passive (and the more she then pursued him).

At times it had seemed a wonder they did not split up. But they explained that they were sustained by their holidays together. 'On holiday, our relationship becomes what we'd like it to be all the time,' said Greg. 'Very relaxed, very close, very carefree.' Elaine added, 'We both like doing the same things on holiday: exploring and avoiding the tourist traps. We become as one on holiday, we rarely have any conflicts then.' Perhaps the pleasure and intimacy of their holidays together gave them hope that if they could survive the confrontations and conflicts of their everyday life, something really good and worth keeping would emerge.

Changes: taking back the projections

Recently there had been a change in their relationship: they had begun to row less and talk more. They were pleased at this achievement, but also subdued. Talking was more depressing. As Elaine said, 'When you are forced to be honest about yourself, what you see is not always that great. It's easier to blow up and have a row where you both shout and resolve nothing. Now we talk at great length in the middle of the night and it's more depressing.' She said this was the first time she had been with someone who made her face parts of her character she didn't like.

In particular, she had to face her *own* timidity which, at the beginning of the relationship, she projected on to Greg. Now she could sometimes see that the character traits for which she bullied him – his passivity, avoidance of confrontation and inability to stand up for himself – were ones she also had, and didn't like in herself. Their flipside was aggression, which was her more dominant characteristic.

She said, 'At the beginning I thought this relationship wouldn't be long term because I found Greg so unassertive that I thought I wouldn't be able to accept it. I am not a particularly assertive person myself, more aggressive, but Greg was always trailing behind.' She turned to him. 'You are slowly getting somewhere. I hate being a nag all the time, but I feel you do push me into that position. You don't do anything without me nagging you – it's a vicious circle.'

But in Greg's opinion, Elaine by no means practised what she preached. 'She does an enormous amount without taking credit. I always saw her as very confident, but now, in the privacy of a close relationship, things can seem very different. On an intimate, personal level, she is not so expressive of self-esteem,' he said.

When Elaine was pushing Greg to stand up for himself, at least half of it was really directed at herself. She, and her mother, had not been able to stand up for themselves to her father: 'We spent most of my childhood creeping around him so as not to set him off for another three days. He was a man one couldn't argue with.'

So she must have been afraid to think that in Greg she had teamed up with yet another man with whom it was impossible to argue. At the beginning of their relationship, she needed to argue and to rub against someone to assert herself, as she had not been able to do in her family. She said, 'I used to be very explosive all the time, even a bit hysterical. I was very black and white and to some extent still am. My parents too are very black and white – if you are unemployed you are a dirty shirker, that kind of thing. But in Greg I found someone who allowed other views. Greg has influenced me. To him, the world is full of shades of grey. He doesn't make decisions about people until he knows them a little. He is a very kind person, a great humanitarian.' The question was only whether he was too permissive, too bendy to provide the other side of what she needed – someone who would stand up to her, and someone who would help *her* to overcome her childhood timidity and be more assertive, without being aggressive.

Meanwhile, Greg had started by projecting on to Elaine the confidence that he felt he lacked and perhaps hoped to discover in himself by being with her. In fact, he had found that she wasn't so confident after all and that her aggression was a smokescreen. What Elaine and Greg were discovering, five years into their relationship, was that their individual, inner make-up was actually quite similar although they expressed it in different, almost opposite, ways. Was this a good thing or a bad thing? Would they be able to help each other or not? This was the implicit question at the moment; hence their indecision about marriage and starting a family.

At the start of their relationship they had got a little stuck in a circular interaction, it seemed, where their roles were simplified through projection. Greg was the retiring one who needed a kick up the backside, and Elaine was the aggressive one who would provide him with that kick. Unfortunately, she often kicked too hard. He would then withdraw into his shell, and Elaine would come after, hammering and yelling to provoke him to come out again.

But they had not given up on each other. They had something to resolve, and they hung on. In the last year or so, their work together had become more constructive, thoughtful and fruitful. They made themselves aware of the patterns they fell into, and tried to break them. They talked and listened to each other more. As we have seen, they felt that their relationship had changed for the better. They agreed that Greg was more assertive – he had even signed up for an assertiveness course off his own bat – and Elaine less aggressive.

Sexual passion – or just great friends?

Another issue which loomed large, and which needed to be resolved before they could reach a decision about commitment, was the one about sexual passion and their ideal sexual type.

In their joint interviews, Greg and Elaine repeatedly emphasised that their relationship was based on being great friends. Greg recalled a moment, a year into their relationship, when he 'realised that as well as being very happy and comfortable with Elaine, she was also a very, very good friend, like my best friend in London, replacing a lot of the transient people from before'.

Elaine said, 'Our friendship has been a stabilising factor. All my relationships before Greg were passionate affairs, but short term. I was besotted with a lot of guys, charming, outgoing guys, but they treated me quite badly and I didn't get a lot out of the relationships. I wasn't besotted with Greg. I was craving stability and that is what I got from my relationship with Greg. Perhaps it was a calculation. But I still feel it's the right calculation, because my feelings in previous relationships were not reciprocated.'

It had taken work and talk and time – three years – to

make their sex life satisfactory. Elaine said, 'I believed that storybook stuff that you should achieve orgasm through penetration and together. Then, because I didn't have orgasm through penetration I began to feel, "God, it's all such an effort, why can't it be easy?? And all that pressure to relax too!" It got better and better, but I still felt that we weren't a normal couple, going through all this palaver for me to have an orgasm. Though I was satisfied that he cared enough, I wished it could be simpler. Recently, though, I feel calmer and happier and can achieve orgasm through penetration.'

She thought that 'sometimes when you are very good friends with your partner you can become too close, do too many things together, and sometimes that diminishes the sexual side of the relationship. It becomes more of a brother/sister relationship. Sometimes that has happened with us. But our sex life has improved in the last couple of years – we are still very close and do a lot together, but it has improved, because I am more confident now.'

To Elaine, all this work, successful as it had been, was not romantic. It was not passion – she said that there had never been any passion between her and Greg. She was beset by 'a niggling doubt that perhaps he doesn't want to get married because I'm not his ideal woman physically'. This doubt had grown from the seed sown right at the beginning, when their friendship had progressed without any show of sexual interest from Greg's side.

Greg, in his individual interview, acknowledged that at first he had not been especially sexually drawn to Elaine. In some ways his attraction to Elaine was less strong than to others with whom he had gone out only briefly. 'In a funny way that thing about the ideal physical type did affect me at the beginning. But it was a sign of immaturity.

'At university I used to see myself as an emotional, romantic sort of person going in and out of relationships and getting my heart broken! A girl once asked me whether I thought I would marry, and I said I would either marry the most beautiful woman in the world, or someone who made her irrelevant. I think Elaine is both. I have never before been out with someone who was a friend, and that has made a substantial difference.'

So although their relationship had started without passion, Greg said, 'I think Elaine and I are developing our spark now. Over the last couple of years I find Elaine growing more attractive to me.'

He added, 'I think Elaine still represses her sexuality at times. Like if I wanted sex in the morning and Elaine had indicated, for example by body language, that she did too – she would then impose daily life on it: "I have to be at work at 9.30." But I think that if there's a mutual urge it's more important to satisfy it.'

Thus while Greg had begun to feel increasingly positive about his and Elaine's sexual relationship, Elaine still entertained doubts. As we have seen, her doubts about Greg's character and suitability as a lifelong partner, as a husband, were also more strongly expressed than any he might have about her. So why was she the one keenest to get married and start a family?

To marry or not to marry?

On one level, the answer lay with Elaine's biological clock. She was 30; she didn't know how long it might take her to conceive, and she wanted to have time for more than one child. They were going through a process of exploration and change in their relationship which could lead them to stay together or move apart – either outcome was possible. Their future was still uncertain, but Elaine didn't have much more time for uncertainty.

Meanwhile Greg was only 27 and did not have the same feeling of urgency. What was Elaine to do? Should she risk sticking with the unfolding of their relationship and see what happened? But what if she and Greg decided to part? She might then be well into her thirties, with not much time left for building another relationship and having babies. By insisting on a decision about whether or not to get married, she wanted to pre-empt the natural outcome of their relationship work.

Interestingly, Elaine always used the phrase 'starting a family'. She never spoke of a longing for a baby or a desire to become a mother. 'Getting married' and 'starting a family' were presented as a conjoint stage of life that she now wanted to set out on. Greg seemed more aware that 'starting a family' meant having a child, becoming a father, and he spoke about his anticipation of both great joy and heavy responsibilities.

It may have been that Elaine always linked 'marriage' and 'starting a family' because she felt that marriage, on its own, was not a worthy goal. In the very first interview she explained that she did not 'rate marriage very highly'. Her mother had always spoken disparagingly about marriage: 'it was something she pooh-poohed – women trying to catch a man, as she called it'. At the same time, as Elaine described it, her mother had less and less to call her own in life, and became utterly dependent on her husband. This contradictory message about marriage must have been confusing to Elaine. Perhaps she felt she had to use the notion of 'starting a family' as a justification for her own wish to get married.

In her individual interview, Elaine made it clear that she very much wanted marriage for its own sake. 'Perhaps,' she said, 'I think that marriage might cement our relationship. I don't think it would change anything, because we have been living together so long. But maybe – I'm not sure – it might make me feel more secure. Maybe it would confirm that Greg loves me and wants to give up a part of his freedom . . . well, not freedom, but that he wants to commit himself to me. I'm always suspicious he may not want to, because he is younger, and because we have spoken about marriage so many times but never get round to doing anything about it.'

In their joint interviews, however, Elaine did not say this. There she kept firmly to the notion of marriage in order to start a family. She did not risk showing herself as vulnerable to Greg by admitting, 'I want you to want to marry me'. Perhaps she feared being seen as 'a woman trying to catch a man'. Greg was left with the impression that Elaine's main concern was to have a baby. And he had several reasons for being wary of introducing a baby into his life right now.

Who's to be the baby?

Greg and Elaine held very different positions within their families. Elaine was the only, and lonely, child, while Greg grew up in a large household where there was perhaps not much room for the individual, but plenty of life. Elaine may have sensed in Greg someone through whom she could experience something of the family life she had lacked. Greg, by contrast, may have sensed in Elaine the only child's knowledge of being special which was so absent from his own childhood. He may have hoped to find some of it for himself by identifying with her, and also by basking in the beam of her attention in their relationship. In this latter sense, we may all enjoy the experience of being the 'only child' in an exclusive adult couple before actual children come along – a sort of honeymoon time which, for some, is a repetition of the earliest days; for others, the first experience of being the only baby.

Greg, as a child, was in danger of being sidelined, if only because his parents were so busy coping. He was not sure he and his siblings were quite wanted; they seemed to cause their parents so much trouble, especially financially. In Elaine he had someone who paid attention to him alone – so much so that he sometimes felt that she focused too much on him and nagged him, though he said that she could also be 'endlessly giving'.

However, now Elaine was proposing to 'start a family'. As she said, 'Because I'm an only child a large family appeals to me – I would like four children. When I told Greg he said, what!!!?' Greg's reluctance may have had to do with his fear that he would once again be squeezed out. No longer would there be room for him to enjoy being 'the only child' and for them to take turns at parenting each other. Now the only child would be a real child – with the prospect of a whole brood to follow. Greg might have good grounds for fearing that the child in him would no longer be attended to.

Certainly he implied that he didn't feel ready to multiply the numbers involved in their relationship when he said: 'We have had a very uncluttered relationship. We have had things just as we want, holidays and so on. I've enjoyed these five years and I would like them to continue. But I can see that at 30 Elaine wants to make a start on a family.'

Greg's anxieties were compounded by their financial situation. Elaine was in the process of changing her career and would have little time to establish herself as a freelancer if she got pregnant soon. The responsibility of bringing home the bread for all three of them would fall to Greg. This was particularly troublesome as, he said, 'I'm not very happy in my job at the moment. I don't want to be in this for the rest of my life. The advertising industry does less for me now than at any other time; on a moral and social level I think it's pretty worthless. I find it difficult to care about how our clients' weekly sales figures are doing. But if it was "300 people have been massacred by this general" or "a company has polluted millions of fish" – then I could get emotional about confronting someone.'

So it seemed that Greg was due for a change of career sooner or later. But if he and Elaine had a baby, he would be stuck in his present job for the foreseeable future at least. His hope, he said, was 'to move very quickly, be very successful, so that in maybe a year and a half I could work less hours, just keep an eye and an overview'. He would then still be under 30. But if his ideal scenario failed to come true? Then he might end up like his father, burdened with family responsibilities and stuck in a job he didn't like.

By the time the interviews ended, Greg and Elaine had 'sort of' agreed on a date to get married, though they were unsure what kind of ceremony to choose. Neither seemed to regard the date as fixed and neither showed much excitement. Conversely, they said that the interviews had prompted them to have many intense conversations. So while the question of whether or not to bind themselves legally still appeared unresolved, their relationship work continued active and alive.

Louisa and Jason:

'Is the future going to be like this?'

Louisa and Jason were a strikingly good-looking couple, who met at university. Their relationship was quick to take root, and they had been together ever since, with no breaks, or even thoughts of breaks: 'There's never been a time when I've thought we should split up,' Louisa said in the first interview. Now both in their mid-twenties, they lived together in Brighton in a rented flat, which was compact and cosy, painted in dark reds and blues, and cluttered with their belongings. Louisa worked in a fashion company – not entirely content, but not quite sure what else to pursue; while Jason had had various jobs in the media and was currently trying his hand at independent documentary film-making.

They seemed a very close, involved couple. Louisa talked about 'a deep connection' between them. Jason repeatedly described himself and Louisa as 'best friends'. He said, 'Our closeness, the degree to which we want to be together – I mean, neither of us is short of friends, but we could probably live without them all tomorrow, we're so close – we're best friends.'

This was not to say that they were an unsociable couple; on the contrary. At the time of the interviews they were both busy at work too – Jason especially was working long irregular hours on a film project. They agreed that too much work and too much social life did not benefit their relationship. 'Our relationship has always thrived on us being together, long holidays just the two of us,' said Louisa. Friction sometimes arose at weekends when Louisa's mother or father wanted to see them and Jason wanted her to himself. Indeed, he admitted to 'a slight jealousy in me of Louisa's mother because they are so close, the warmth between them'. He added, 'Considering my family, it does annoy me that they demand our time quite so frequently.'

Jason's background

Jason's parents divorced when he was two, and his mother was awarded custody. But she was barely out of her teens, and Jason was basically brought up by his grandparents. His mother concentrated on growing up – studying for a degree, building a career, and when she remarried, when Jason was 10, he did not go to live with her. He remembered how he had longed for his mother to come home before his bedtime when he was little, and later to visit him, but how he was always somehow disappointed when she finally came. He treated his grandmother and grandfather as mother and father and said that his first loyalty was to them.

Today, his feelings towards his real mother were cool. He was more fond of his real father, with whom he had established a relationship as a teenager, and liked to point out their similarities in temperament and ways of thinking, as if to emphasise nature over nurture. He drew two lines to him on his geneogram, as he did to his grandmother and grandfather. And yet he was also detached – he didn't really belong anywhere. He saw no reason, he said, to treat relatives as special people just because they were relatives, or to be nice to them if you didn't like them. He hadn't seen his grandparents for months, but that didn't bother him: 'It may sound a cold, rational outlook on the world, but I see no point in seeing someone every fortnight if you have nothing particular to say.'

At the same time, he seemed to trace some of this 'coldness' directly to the atmosphere in which he grew up. 'My parents – by which I mean my grandparents – didn't cuddle or kiss, my mother and my aunt and uncle were not warmly brought up, and nor was I. So I suppose I looked elsewhere: I started my first long-term relationship very young, I was 14.' That relationship lasted until he met Louisa.

He saw his detachment from his family as independence. At the same time, he said, 'I realise I'm not independent because I rely on Louisa. I ask her to be family to me. I'd also like her to rely on me more than on her family. I think she's beginning to do that now although she may not know it – she doesn't feel she has to see her father, and he annoys her, which is a victory for me in a silly way. It's falling into line with how I see the world.'

Louisa's background

Louisa introduced her geneogram saying, 'There is a long history of infidelity in my family.' Her parents separated when she was 13 as a result of her father's affair with another woman. He subsequently married her and had another child, but was now having an affair with someone else, which Louisa knew about even though his wife did not. Meanwhile, Louisa's mother had recently started a new relationship with a man for the first time.

Her mother and father and his new wife were on amicable terms, which Louisa attributed to her mother's efforts. 'My mother is a woman of integrity and courage,' she said. 'My father I feel sorry for; he is an emotional coward who lies because he doesn't want to confront the truth. When they separated he told me he was leaving because he needed to have some quiet and time to himself to work. And when he remarried he didn't tell us for over a year! And the same thing when their child was born: he didn't tell us, until eventually his wife rang us.'

She further compared her parents by saying that

although each was as lacking in confidence as the other, 'my mother is more responsible and reliable, she tries harder'. She called her father a 'general wastrel', talented, but incapable of sustaining a career. He was now supported financially by his second wife.

Louisa felt that she had inherited her mother's sense of responsibility. 'At work it's particularly obvious,' she said. 'People know they can rely on me, which sometimes leads me to feel slightly exploited. It did feel burdensome during a bad patch at work when I wanted to leave and do something else. My mother kept saying, "Oh no, you can't leave, you're the only one in a proper job." Not that she ever asks me for anything but it's the peace of mind factor, she's got me in my slot. If I turned round and said I was going to go round the world, everyone I know would be shocked and horrified.

'I don't know if the responsibility thing extends to our relationship particularly. I don't know if maybe Jason exploits it sometimes . . . but it's certainly a pressure. On the other hand, Jason is much more enterprising and risk-taking than I am. My responsibility is to other people, but it's also a defence against failure, misadventure . . . something going wrong.'

The couple, the choice

Neither Louisa nor Jason was interested in marriage, coming as they did from backgrounds shot through with divorce, infidelity and deception. But both said that they could see themselves staying together for the rest of their lives.

Jason and Louisa had not offered themselves for interview with an overt dilemma about commitment, like Elaine and Greg. And yet there was a touch of uncertainty, a whiff of restlessness, which seemed to be coming from Louisa's direction. It seemed to spring from their different ideas about what was the right balance of togetherness and separate space.

Taker and giver – but who's who?

Jason seemed content to be so heavily dependent on Louisa and implied that although he recognised an imbalance, he did not think it was a problem. He said he was 'amazed at her ability to put up with me', and at her lack of selfishness. He said, I demand an incredible amount of attention from Louisa, much more than I probably . . . should.' However, he thought, 'What Louisa needs to exist is very small. She gives out the rest to me, and would to other people if she had the opportunity, which she doesn't because I demand it all – time, effort, thought. All she needs for herself is a book or a film. That's not to demean her, but she's – I was going to say more secure . . . But I suspect there is a more autonomous individual in Louisa than in me; I turn to her more often than she does to me.'

Paradoxically, Jason ended up doing more of the emotional work in their relationship. He talked more, he was more likely to open up emotional subjects for discussion, he was the one who suggested they should spend Sunday together, and so on. Louisa was the one who liked to curl up with a book or slump in front of a film. They hardly ever had arguments – 'slightly raised voices and retiring to separate rooms for an hour is the worst it gets' – because Louisa was so adept at 'deflating' Jason when he became 'provocative'.

But in her individual interview, Louisa said, 'Sometimes I start to feel got at. Demanded too much of. I feel pressurised because I have a responsibility to him and to work, and I feel got at when he says things like "I thought we'd spend this evening alone", or "Why do you have to stay at work till 9.30?"'

'Now we are both very busy. His film is bringing late nights and travel around the country. I don't know if this will become a problem area – we flourish when we have more time together, that's when we function best. I do feel the pressure of being out four times a week. Either I snap or don't make an effort in front of the TV. Jason is good at not doing that; on the other hand, because I like reading or watching films I can function better on my own. Jason will want to be close, sit with me, and comment on the film and want my reply. Then I feel crowded. There's a scene in the film *Truly, Madly, Deeply* where Juliet Stevenson is in the bath with a facepack and music on when her lover bounds in, chatting, full of stories – and she says leave me alone. It's the beginning of her realisation that she has her own space. It's not as extreme as that in our relationship but it reminded me . . . it's a bit like having a dog, he'll come and push my book away.

'I probably wouldn't like it any different, though. I like it when he's doing his own thing so I can do mine, but I don't like being on my own, I hate being on my own for a long period of time. Recently when he was filming away from home I missed him a lot. On the other hand I liked going to bed at eight and reading my book for two hours. And I also went out and saw people a lot, to prove I could function as a single unit.'

Louisa ended her interview with the thought that 'Jason must be quite exceptional in his capacity for closeness, which seems to be what most women complain about in their boyfriends.'

So Louisa was ambivalent: she wished she had more space, but at the same time was not sure whether more space would be a good thing for their relationship, which flourished on plenty of time together. She was worried that Jason's increasing 'busy-ness', as opposed to her own, would put a strain on the relationship – perhaps because she knew that she relied on him to make the effort for them to be together. Although she could feel 'got at' by him, she wouldn't like him to be different, because then she might have to forgo their closeness. And yet, she didn't seem to be making much of that closeness for herself. When Jason said that he turned to Louisa far more than she turned to him, he might have been stating a *fait accompli*, or he might have been expressing a longing for her to show her need for him a little more, as he showed his for her.

Although Louisa and Jason were both committed to their

relationship and both said how much they valued it, in everyday practice they seemed to be taking up polarised stances. Jason pursued closeness while Louisa sought little oases of separate space. Louisa was becoming emotionally lazy while Jason was over-demanding. How was this imbalance to resolve itself?

Renegotiation

The first four interviews took place over a period of a month. Then holidays and Jason's filming intervened, so that the final interview was not until two months later. It began with the dramatic announcement that Louisa had decided to move out for a month's trial separation, beginning in two days' time.

Her decision had come about in a manner quite characteristic of their relationship. Louisa had seemed down for a few days. 'It was on Monday,' said Jason. 'I turned the television off and said, "Are you all right, Louisa, is there anything you want to talk about?" And she said, "Well yes actually, I'm not very happy about my life" – and that was it.'

'Jason actually suggested the idea,' said Louisa. 'It didn't seem good at first, but then I went to talk to my mother, as one does, and she suggested the same thing independently. So it seemed not a good idea but the best solution. We've been together a long time and never been separated for any length of time and we're not a rowing couple, so there's never been a situation where one or other of us has stomped out for a weekend. It's all been very perfect. So I would find it hard to assess everything honestly while I had the continued security of coming home to this flat and Jason and everything.

'Every now and then for the last couple of months I've thought, "I'm quite young, it's all been very easy and straightforward, is the future going to be like this?" But I thought it would go away. I would probably never have raised it if Jason hadn't asked.'

'If it's what Louisa wants,' said Jason, 'I think she should go. But it's not what I want. I look at the future and think, "That's exactly what I want, as it was."'

Louisa commented that the period of her thinking 'Is this what I want with my life?' coincided with a time when they didn't see each other much, because Jason was so unusually busy with, and absorbed in, his filming. Did this mean that having had more time to herself, she found she wanted even more? Or was it a reaction to a feeling of being somewhat neglected by Jason? Now that he was so busy, did she find herself in the unfamiliar position of being the one to wish they could have more time together? And did she find it uncomfortable to be the needy one for a change?

They talked about their impending trial separation in terms of Louisa taking 'time out' to discover her own needs. These were conceived of as having to do with Louisa needing time to be young, free and single; 'for example,' said Louisa, 'ringing you from work and saying I'd rather like to stay for a drink and you saying oh all right, I'll go to the pub with so-and-so, see you later. We've always done everything together, we are a couple that everyone considers a couple, we are always invited together, we go everywhere together.' So on the one hand it sounded as if Louisa wanted to test her own wings to see if they were still strong enough to hold her up on her own after so long nesting with Jason. On the other hand, her leaving was 'time out' – as if a long overdue holiday from her job caring for Jason.

Jason, for his part, seemed split between his feeling that he didn't want Louisa to go, and a certain excitement at the upheaval. He said, 'At first I looked at the books and the records and thought, that's hers, that's mine, we'll have to put red stickers on them. But afterwards I thought firstly, that she should do it and secondly, that our relationship is good enough to stand it and I think she'll come back. And thirdly, much as I haven't chosen to do it, I will probably benefit too. I think it'll do me good, I'm not very good at existing on my own.' Jason even began to question whether one month would be long enough, 'if we are to get back together having learned something about ourselves'.

Jason had asked Louisa if their sex life played any part in her decision to move out. Louisa explained, 'It's been the case for a while that we haven't been having sex as often as certainly Jason would like – that makes you sound like a fiend! – not just these couple of months recently that I've been feeling this restlessness.'

'You said sex didn't have to do with it,' said Jason.

LOUISA: No . . . at the moment I can't think that it does – I suppose I feel slightly guilty, that something isn't good for you.

JASON: I'm surprised it doesn't worry you more since you're not someone who doesn't enjoy sex.

LOUISA: Yes . . . maybe . . . if I thought about it.

JASON: Therefore for you not to want it I would have thought would worry you.

LOUISA: I haven't thought about it because I've avoided thinking about it.

JASON: In this context or generally?

LOUISA: Generally.

She continued, 'Jason has said I should think about why, but I find it very easy to start thinking and then to drift off and not conclude the thought process. That's why it's important to do this, to have this break, because it's easy not to think hard here. I know what to expect, it's all here, whereas if I were sitting in a room in someone's flat and they've gone out and Jason isn't there . . . I'm apt to be mentally complacent. I've got to get my thoughts sorted out. Because of the person I am I dodge things, I'm an optimist, I think it'll all be all right in the end. Instead I should think: what is it that's happening? We should sort it out.'

By her own admission, Louisa tended to 'dodge' uncomfortable or difficult issues – perhaps somewhat like her father. Having got together with a man who was in many ways emotionally upfront and challenging, she left it all to him, and often found him too much, a hyperactive puppy who wanted her constant attention. Perhaps if Jason had felt he could trust Louisa to do her share of 'relationship work', he might not have demanded so much of her, and might have felt more relaxed about 'giving her space'. At the same time he valued her 'selflessness', as he called it: he needed to be able to take, to feed off Louisa, sometimes voraciously, to make up for all the missed nurturing of his childhood.

But by the time of the interviews they were obviously ready for a renegotiation in their relationship. It was a tribute to the emotional courage of both of them that when they felt things starting to slip slightly, they decided to do something about it. Even though the idea for a trial separation was not Louisa's, she was prepared to lever herself out of her armchair and face the discomfort of the unknown. Jason was gamely prepared to learn from it – to make an effort to be more independent himself, and to put up with the uncertainty: would they or would they not get back together?

'As good as marriage'

There were no further interviews after this, but about five months later I had a note through the post saying 'Back together!' I wrote to Jason and Louisa asking them to write and tell me what had happened.

Louisa wrote back. They had been apart not for one month but three and a half, although they kept in touch throughout.

About her own experience of the trial separation, she wrote: 'I had a very lively time in the sense that when you're on your own you suddenly find a strength within yourself to go to parties on your own and you do 'get out more' and see friends, etc. Also I felt flexible and free to make last-minute arrangements without consulting anyone. I suppose I got what I wanted in the sense that I re-established myself in my own mind as an individual – something which was my particular problem to resolve.'

About Jason, she wrote: 'He says that he was convinced that we would get back together (although he admitted to some very depressed times, and when I actually went with a bag, it really was awful), and that consequently he could do nothing but wait until I sorted things out, trying to put as little pressure on me as possible – which he did. Ironically, I think it gave Jason more self-confidence than me – beyond his unhappiness, he proved to himself that he could function well on his own. He threw himself into his filming and indeed, when I was making moves towards a reconciliation I really felt that I might have lost him to that.

'Funnily enough, it was me who made the first moves towards getting back together. I realised I was absolutely mad to throw away such a fantastic relationship . . . Things are different now in the sense that I have absolutely no doubt that I want to be with Jason. But our relationship was always amazing and nothing, thank God, has been diminished in any way by what happened.

'We both agreed that having got back together we should instigate some fairly major change in order to mark this and act as a confirmation of our renewed commitment. We have therefore bought a house together here in Brighton – which, while not marriage, is to us as good as. We've never seen marriage as the only way to be totally committed, so this is really seen as the equivalent to us. We're immensely happy.'

Louisa and Jason's relationship renegotiation, symbolised by Louisa's leaving, had the effect of making their commitment firmer. Or it could have been the other way round: underlying questions of whether to commit or not to commit prompted them to take a close look at their relationship and to do something to right the imbalances between them. The very idea of having a break was the first step in so far as it was an idea negotiated between them rather than a unilateral walk-out.

While Louisa and Jason's three-month break was something that took place *between* them and which had to do with their interaction as a couple, it also had to do with their individual needs. For Louisa, it was the need to feel freer, to toss off some of the 'responsibility' with which she felt burdened, to 'establish herself as an individual', as she said herself. It allowed her to be a bit less like her responsible mother, without swinging over into inconsiderate and irresponsible behaviour in the manner of her father. For Jason, the break served to show him that he could also cope on his own, that his emotional dependency on Louisa was not total and that he could look after himself when he needed to.

Louisa said in her letter that for her, the break achieved its aims. What about Jason? After all, although he thought he too might benefit from the break, as Louisa's letter suggested he had, he had also been happy with the status quo. Did he feel hurt or abandoned, and if so, how did he handle it? It was Louisa who wrote the follow-up letter; whether Jason emerged from their experiment as satisfied as her, the story does not tell.

Mary and Ian:

'Never take anything for granted'

Mary was 25 and Ian 26. They had been together nine years, since the sixth form, with no significant splits, although their relationship was characterised by continual separations and reunions – in the year after school, in their three years at different universities, and now pursuing careers in different towns. Such a record would suggest a great deal of commitment. Yet in their first interview they came across as a rather casual couple. No – they had never consciously decided to stay together. No – they had never spelled out that they must be faithful to each other (although they were). At each separation they agreed they did not want to finish, but acknowledged that although they would not actively look for others, it was possible that they might meet someone else. But they never did.

As teenagers, Mary and Ian had got together because they liked the look of each other. Mary thought Ian the handsomest boy in his class at the next-door boys' school, and he thought she was pretty and lively and decided that at the next party he would try his luck with her. By the end of the interviews it had become clear that they had a great deal more than good looks to keep them together, even from the beginning. They both came from working-class Irish backgrounds, with large extended families harbouring quite a lot of drunkenness and marital unhappiness. In a sense, they were rescuing each other from home. They replaced for each other families who would hold them back, and instead encouraged each other to re-sit A levels, to go to university, and to find interesting and fulfilling careers. Mary was now a graphic designer for a television company in Manchester, while Ian was making his way in London as a photographer in the competitive magazine world. They were both ambitious and determined to do well, and encouraged each other to reach beyond the close horizons they had grown up with.

Mary's background

Ian's rescue operation for Mary was the more overt one.

By Mary's own description, her father was a 'horrible man', a 'real pig'. He was a builder who only worked for one-third of the time he was employed, spending the rest of the time on sick pay as a chronic alcoholic. He was violent, wrecking the house and breaking the children's toys, though he only actually hit a person once. He was mentally abusive: for example, on family outings he would behave like the 'perfect dad', buying them treats which would immediately be withdrawn when they got back home. He was manipulative; after breaking something in the house he would blame the others and say, 'Now look what you made me do!' On a grander scale, he blamed his family for all his failures. During the time that Mary went abroad for a few months during her year off, her father was finally sacked from his building job. He blamed her: 'It was your fault for going away.' Mary had been his favourite. Paradoxically – or perhaps because of this – she had been the one of all the members of her family to turn the clearest gaze on him, exposing him as an abusive alcoholic and, when she was old enough to leave home, rejecting him. She never visited her parents' house now if she could help it.

Her mother she described as a virtual prisoner in her own home, cut off from friends by embarrassment, fear and illness. Her mother's particular pleasure had been sewing, until her husband broke the sewing machine. Yet her mother had stayed in this marriage for thirty years, always making excuses for why she couldn't leave. Mary was exasperated but tried to understand her too. She saw her now and then when she came back to London to stay with Ian, but felt powerless to help her. She had not been close to her as a child; her older sister had been her mother's favourite, as she had been her father's. The difference was that Mary had not felt close to her father; indeed, she said that as a child she had felt close to no one.

Perhaps her non-aligned position in this family was what enabled her to get up and go and be different from them. Doing her own thing was very important to Mary. 'The people in my family always think, "Wouldn't it be wonderful if I could do this and this" – they envy other people and see their lives as exciting, but for themselves they always have excuses. When I was a child my dad encouraged me. He told me to travel: "Do everything I didn't do." He wanted me to have a good education: "My daughter's going to be PM." But as soon as I actually started to make any tracks it was, "Hang on, why should you be any better?" And my mother is the same, I suppose. She doesn't understand me wanting job satisfaction, that I want more than just to take home money at the end of the week. For her it's just a job, and home, and you're not entitled to anything else.'

Mary said that Ian had helped her to be different from her family and to get away. 'Ian is probably everything people in my family aren't: ambitious, outgoing, confident.' Right from the start she admired his get-up-and-go. She felt that with his example and his support, she had been enabled to lead her own life and pursue her own goals. In the early days especially, she said, 'I could tell Ian what Dad was really like. Everyone else always took the attitude "he can't be all that bad" but Ian if anything over-reacted the other way. I could say anything to him. He completely accepted how I was feeling. He was never judgmental about my saying such horrible things about someone so close. And he voiced his own anger.' Later on, Ian had encouraged her to re-sit her A levels and to go to art school when she was inclined to end her education and get a job. He had helped her to become more outgoing. 'At home we didn't dare open our mouths, there were furtive conversations because we were afraid of it leading to arguments. Everyone would sit quietly and watch whatever Dad wanted to watch on TV.'

Ian's background

Yet Ian's path was in no sense gilded. He was the youngest in a large family, and he speculated that perhaps he had been the baby who was supposed to save his parents' marriage. If so, he failed, for his mother left his father when Ian was not yet two, by which time she had been married to him for over twenty years. His father, too, was an alcoholic, violent and abusive towards both his wife and children. Ian had no conscious memory of him and never met him when he was older, but he said, 'I met scores of "Mary's dads" anyway. Perhaps if I'd been from an "ideal happy family" I wouldn't have gone out with Mary. But because I'm Irish too, I knew straight away. I think that bonded us very early.'

Nevertheless, Ian's father was a great believer in education, and for this Ian would like to have met him. 'I'd like to have seen him after I'd finished my degree. Maybe he would have been proud of me, he was always keen for us to do well. But – I never felt there was a great desire to see me on his part.' He died shortly after Ian graduated, but Ian was not told until after the funeral.

So Ian's older brothers were 'surrogate fathers'. One was a solid family man; the other was 'a wastrel and a drinker', who nevertheless inspired Ian with a desire to be a photographer. 'There is no tradition of get-up-and-go in my family either,' he said. 'Tom, the one who drinks, was an artist, he was the only one with a natural talent but he drowned it all in drink. My sisters got married young; one worked in a factory, one is a clerk, and one is a school dinner lady. They're all very homely, they plod along, talking about their houses. Perhaps that's why I feel slightly detached. I do think at times that they think I am the one who will do something different.'

The couple, the choice
Thus Ian's ambitions for himself were at least as strong as the encouragement he offered Mary. These included not only doing well in his career, but also avoiding the trappings of domesticity, house-buying and colour-of-wallpaper conversations – conventionality, routine, stagnation.

'I never think "next christmas"'
Both Mary and Ian feared a conventional life. Their current commuting pattern – spending weekends and holidays together and the working week apart in different cities – they seemed to experience as simultaneously invigorating and enervating, a way of keeping their relationship fresh and a trial to be endured. Ian spoke of their situation with palpable ambivalence. On the one hand he valued the fact of being able to throw himself into his work 'without worrying that someone is expecting me home at six'. Furthermore, a long-distance relationship was far more conducive to romantic gestures – writing love letters, sending

flowers, or turning up on the doorstep unexpectedly – than living together. Their three years at university had been notable for
this, and Ian remembered them with nostalgia: 'I think I was at
my most thoughtful during that time.' On the other hand, he felt
that now his life was divided into two parts, which hardly over-
lapped. 'In the week I'm almost on autopilot, there is no reality.
I'm never really at ease during the week. Being with Mary completely relaxes me. In her company I'm completely happy. We
can't carry on like this indefinitely, it gets on my nerves . . .
Sunday afternoons, when she's got to go back to Manchester
and I don't want her to, it's the worst day.'

He was similarly ambivalent about how he envisaged their
future. He certainly hoped Mary might find a job in London
soon, and then they would live together, in fact, 'we'd get married pretty soon, why not? We both think it's a romantic idea.'
But he was horrified by the idea of buying a house or a flat. 'I've
always hated the idea, seen it as a barrier to freedom. If you are
renting you can take off – although in reality I don't want to,
I'm not a great traveller, I fancy being in one place. But people
become obsessive about their houses, it's almost a disease. And
it's such a big financial burden. That's the nice thing about
here.' He gestured around the room, which was the communal
sitting-room of the rented house he shared with several others,
student style. It was December and the house was unheated.
The furniture in the sitting-room was institutional and badly
run down, the walls were bare and stained. The plaster was
peeling in the stairwell and the bathroom was icy. But where
one person might have seen a powerful argument in favour of
buying one's own place, Ian clearly saw the opposite. 'And Mary
likes it too,' he added.

If anything, Mary showed even stronger ambivalence
about the external trappings of commitment, such as cohabiting, buying a place, marrying. She too preferred to rent: 'If you
rent you are less fussy and more easygoing.' She was clear that
she did want to live with Ian and also hoped it would only be a

matter of months before she found a job that brought her to London, since the constant meetings and partings were beginning to take their toll. But she was vehemently against marriage. Contrary to what Ian said, she gave no indication at all that she found it a romantic notion.

'I used to despair of anyone who got married, which was a fairly infantile view, rather hardline. But why sign a piece of paper when you are happy and committed as you are? Ian would argue that we would be voicing before family and friends that we want to be a couple. But my Mum and Dad did that . . . Why does it have to be a wedding? Why a ring?

'I know I want to stay with Ian, not because of our youth together but because I think a great deal of him and enjoy his company. I don't know how I could possibly feel more strongly about anyone than Ian. But I'm not sure what that means . . . I still don't think beyond the next weekend or the next holiday. I never think "next Christmas" because I wouldn't take it for granted that we will be together. I mean, I trust him, but I'm still not sure how to gauge it. I never quite believe he's been faithful, that he will always be loyal, that he is really as kind and non-judgmental as he is. I fight inside myself to do so, but something also tells me, "don't trust someone that much because you will end up being hurt".'

At other times, Mary spoke freely about wanting to grow old with Ian, and remarked, 'I find it hard to imagine a future without him. I sometimes say "I'm going to tell our grandchildren this", and it doesn't feel strange.'

For Ian, and even more for Mary, there was something about a formal commitment, signed and sealed, such as a marriage certificate or a mortgage document, which aroused their resistance. Certainly they both wanted and needed security, as their nine-year relationship bore witness. But wherever 'security' became synonymous with ordinariness and tradition, they consciously rejected it.

There was nothing strange or unusual in Mary and Ian's

ambivalent feelings about commitment. Many people want to be different from their elders. Many 25-year-olds quite naturally and sensibly wonder whether they are ready for a commitment, whether it will impede their individual ambitions, whether they will regret it.

The danger of repeating history

Yet Mary and Ian's uncertainty was spiced by an added ingredient. They had both grown up with disastrous parental models of marriage. For Mary's parents, 'commitment' had come to mean 'imprisonment', all choice long since drained away. Ian had grown up without a father, though he learned from his mother and his older siblings that his father, like Mary's, had been a violent, abusive drunkard, who had failed to make anything of himself, and whose defeat marked all the other members of the family too, in one way or another. Together, Mary and Ian had a lot to fight against, to overturn, and to prove to themselves and others. If your parents make a hash of it, one seemingly obvious way to avoid repeating their mistakes is to do the opposite of what they did. In fact, this approach has its own perils: rebelling against one's parents' way can mean that one is just as dominated by their example as when slavishly repeating it.

Mary and Ian's investment in each other was rich with hope: to raise each other out of their depressing origins, to help each other to grow as individuals and to fulfil their potential in work and career terms. For this, some people might have chosen a partner from quite different social circumstances, but they had chosen each other: someone whom they could recognise, who knew where the other one came from, someone with whom they could be themselves.

Yet it seemed they could not trust each other completely. Mary expressed it as not being able to believe that Ian really was as loyal and kind and non-judgmental as he was, and consequently never taking the future 'for granted'. For his part, Ian said 'I'm always thinking that she'll be whisked away by someone else'. After nine years in which they had weathered several patches of turbulence, survived separations and proved themselves faithful and constant, what was it that was impeding their trust?

For Mary and Ian, the thought of making a formal commitment contained the threat of undoing everything they had built up together. If they got married, like their parents before them, and indeed like their many uncles and aunts, most of whom seemed to be trapped in marriages with plenty of alcoholism and misery, what was to stop them from going the same way? How could Mary be sure that she would be exempt – that she would never give up the fight, as her mother had done? How could Ian be sure that he would not end up a drinker and a wastrel like his brother, or the father he never knew? Their very difference from their families was erected as a buffer against the danger of history repeating itself. If they dismantled it, might not the floodgates open and all the horrors of the past come rushing in?

A secure attachment is a prerequisite for daring to experience one's deepest and most secluded self. In Mary and Ian's case, this may have included feelings and behaviour they would rather not know about. Despite their years together, in one sense they were still on 'best behaviour' with one another. They rarely argued or quarrelled, because their short weekends were too precious to be given over to bad moods. They had never lived together long enough to get into habits, rhythms, routines, and become over-familiar with one another. Parts of their lives were kept separate. But if they settled down to live together and even married – what was to stop them from becoming like the parental models which they carried inside themselves, buried deep somewhere?

The possibility of repeating patterns from the past with a partner can be a powerful factor in attracting two people to each other. For Mary and Ian, it might be that the sense of the possibility of repetition was what gave them the feeling of 'knowing' each other and where they came from. At the same time, repetition of the past would be a disaster and a tragedy.

Until Mary and Ian both felt really sure that their difference from their families was truly internal – that they were not the losers and defeatists of life, but its winners – it felt safest not to risk it by taking on the external forms of the lives that they were both trying to escape.

CHAPTER THREE

Setting Out

W HAT happens next, after the commitment has been made? Usually the realisation that one is committed brings changes, both in the way one perceives oneself and one's partner, and in how one is perceived by others.

This chapter presents the stories of two newly married couples, and one cohabiting couple with a new baby. For the newly-weds, Pippa and Timothy, and Linda and James, the stories focus on their efforts to adjust to their altered state. Their expectations of marriage were an important underlying issue. What did it mean to be a 'husband' and a 'wife'? How did the public images fit with their private experience? They were creating their own personal meanings of their marriages; simultaneously revelling in the fairy tale and coping with the discovery of unexpected little goblins.

For Simon and Frances, the third couple in this chapter, the challenge was to balance their needs as a couple with their responsibilities both as new parents and as workers. Their thoughts were turned very much to the future. They were ambitious for themselves and their son; as second-generation black Britons, they were strongly motivated to build on their parents' hard work and were striving for education, career success and material comfort – but also for happiness as a family. Supporting each other in their aspirations was an important theme for them as a couple.

Meanings: husband and wife

When people marry, they are transformed overnight from 'boyfriend and girlfriend' into 'husband and wife'. The ceremony of the wedding, the solemn promises, the excitement of family and friends, not to mention their changed status in the eyes of society and the state, all underline that marriage is a big step. But in what way are you supposed to feel different inside?

Although a wedding is a romantic event, 'husband' and 'wife' are not usually considered very romantic words, but solid, down to earth and timeless: the means of the perpetuation of the species, the cornerstones of hearth and home and everything beyond. According to a Finnish saying, a good husband is one who doesn't drink, doesn't fight, and brings home his pay packet on a Friday night. A good husband provides for his family, helps with the washing up, and speaks kindly to his wife. A good wife keeps the house clean, puts meals on the table, and looks after husband and children. Traditional images of the 'good husband' and 'good wife' hardly allow much excitement or latitude.

Of course, it is even less desirable to have a 'bad husband' – a man who is unfaithful, perhaps, or violent, or 'feckless', a man who can't hold down a job, can't stay off the drink, and can't shoulder the responsibilities of having a family.

And who would want a 'bad wife?' She fails to keep herself attractive or her house in order. She may smoke and drink and lose her temper and smack her children and use foul language, like a 'fishwife'. A bad wife is someone who lets things fall apart, who can't cope.

Then there is a 'modern wife', about whom the media displays deep ambivalence. On the one hand she is superwoman, holding down a career, giving her children quality time in the evenings and maintaining a relationship with her husband on Sunday afternoons. On the other hand, she is a selfish or foolish woman trying to have it all and depriving everyone – her children miss their mum, her husband misses his wife, and she misses her self.

Finally, one strand of wife stereotype emphasises her as a victim: the battered wife, the deserted wife, the bored housewife.

'My husband' and 'my wife'

These are crude types, caricatures compiled in part, certainly, from our own childhoods, but also from children's stories, TV soaps, and shocking and sensationalist newspaper articles. One of the great challenges of marriage these days is to create one's own definitions of 'wife' and 'husband'. A generic wife may well be a broad-hipped woman in an apron blocking a doorway – but 'my wife' and 'my husband' can be terms of great tenderness and even sexual spark. They *can* mean: 'We have given ourselves to each other; we have shown each other the greatest trust a human being can show another; by calling you "my wife", or "my husband", I am repeating and renewing my love for you.'

Becoming a husband or a wife also means that one is taking one's place in the chain of generations. We are repeating history: like our parents, we too are now husband and wife, and soon we may be mother and father also. We are keeping the cycle of life turning. Some people relish this aspect of marriage. It makes them feel anchored and adds to their sense of doing the right thing. Others strongly object to it, feeling that it robs them of their free will. If the scheme of things is thus preordained, how can anyone be an individual?

Being known to the world as 'married', or as an established couple, can feel extremely constraining to some people, a threat to their individuality. I was hissed at by one friend after I introduced her at a party as 'So-and-So, So-and-So's wife'. 'Don't ever call me that again!' she said. She explained that other people lost interest in you once they knew you were married. This is a common complaint, or fear, of couples: that once people know you are hitched, they neither flirt with you nor even want to find out more about you as a person. One interview couple said, 'We must give off "I'm taken" vibes or something, because nobody ever tries to chat us up at parties, even when we're out on our own.'

Thus while 'husband' and 'wife' can come to mean delightful and private things to some newly married couples, others certainly stagger under the weight of history no less than unattractive stereotypes. Everyone who marries needs to find a way of synthesising their own subjective experience of being married with their public personae as husband and wife. For many, this may prove an uncomfortable alliance, especially at the beginning.

Marriage: expectations and fantasies

Definitions are shaped by expectations. When people get married, they bring along a whole trousseau full of expectations – spoken and unspoken, conscious and unconscious. Some have to do with how the externals of married life should look – the house, the lifestyle, the number and upbringing of children, whether they are the type who sit down to meals or grab a sandwich from the fridge. Many of these are inherited from childhood, either in emulation of or opposition to home, or inspired by memories of a friend's family who seemed much more like a 'proper' family than one's own.

Many people disclaim high expectations of marriage. Perhaps they feel they should show that they have absorbed the divorce statistics and are realistic. As Pippa says in the interview below: 'This is wonderful now, and I can see it going on for a long time, but forever is a completely different thing. I don't see how anyone can think like that.'

Couples who have lived together before getting married often say they don't expect anything to change. This may of course mean that they don't expect things to take a turn for the worse, but it also suggests that they are not going to expect fireworks.

And yet, on another level, people have higher expectations of intimate relationships such as marriage than ever before. The psychotherapist Anthony Storr, in his study of solitude, writes: 'Current wisdom assumes that man is a social being who needs the companionship and affection of other human beings from cradle to grave. It is widely believed that interpersonal relationships of an intimate kind are the chief, if not the only, source of human happiness.[1]

The apparently hard-headed realism of those who claim to have only limited expectations of marriage can coexist with soaring hopes of marriage and the relationship; indeed, the former may be used as a defence against the latter. Buried somewhere deep in their hearts people still hold the expectation of being each other's fairy prince and princess. People do still expect to be loved and cherished and held. Why would almost 90 per cent of us marry if we did not expect marriage to bring us happiness?

This is not to say that all the high hopes can be fulfilled. Part of marriage is accepting the 'good enough' instead of the perfect. One of the tasks, of early marriage especially, is coming to terms with disappointment.

Let us take the example of one woman whose unconscious longing was that after being married, her husband would take care of her more fully than she had ever been cared for before. Soon after her return from honeymoon she became unaccountably depressed. She woke in the mornings feeling miserable and anxious, and stayed in bed until her husband had left for work. In the evenings when he returned home, more often than not she greeted him with sulks or tears, which led to arguments. What was the matter? Neither of them could understand it, and her husband began to feel demoralised and helpless. He thought that by marrying her he was making her happy – and look at them now!

After a while this woman sought psychotherapy and eventually identified her depression as a consequence of the disappointment of her unconscious expectation that her husband would be some kind of mother substitute. He was supposed to stay by her side. So why did he leave her to go to work every day? This simple routine of life made her feel neglected and unloved.

Trouble may brew when expectations remain fully unconscious, because the feelings aroused by their disappointment cannot then be understood. How could she make such an unreasonable-sounding admission as to say that she didn't want her husband to go to work? How could she even know that that was how she felt? This woman's story is to some extent reflected in that of Pippa and Timothy below.

After the wedding . . .

The fantasy of being totally cared for is not an unusual one in early marriage. Many women admit to a period of depression following the wedding. Some of it may be due to the 'post-wedding blues', the come-down after the excitement of the wedding. Some of it may be connected with a sense of dislocation while old definitions are discarded and new ones have yet to evolve. And some of it is caused by the disappointment of not being a fairy princess after all, at least not full-time. The daily demands of work and cleaning and shopping continue; one's new partner for life is not constantly available, and there are limits to how interested and understanding he (or she) can be. It can be a shock to realise the extent to which one is still responsible for one's own happiness, even as a married woman.

Even less elevated expectations can lead to misunderstandings, if they cannot be identified or spoken about. He doesn't offer to wash the dishes after supper. She doesn't offer to massage his head when he has a headache. She always asks him how his day has been but he never asks her. She spends the evening on the phone to her mother when he wanted to be with her, and so on. If these things cannot be addressed directly in the early days, for fear of seeming silly or over-demanding, feelings of disappointment may get expressed in other ways – in outbursts about small things, in quarrels that escalate, in small retaliations, withholding of services and affection even. Both parties are bewildered, worried, and a little saddened. We love each other. It ought to be easy. Why are we having these stupid problems?

Everyday closeness and distance

Expectations also turn on the emotional colour and intensity of the married relationship – how close or distant to be on an everyday, workaday basis. How much do we talk – touch – show affection, for both of us to feel satisfied, but not suffocated? How much time do we spend together in the evenings and at weekends? Do we go out on our own as well as together? This is an area in which expectations can be particularly strong but also particularly difficult to voice, and therefore especially open to disappointment.

The level of emotional intensity tacitly agreed upon by newly-weds in their first year probably remains the foundation for the rest of their life together. Couple A may talk on the phone at least once during the day; tell each other all that happened when they get home, being well versed in their partner's office set-up and cast of colleagues; cook supper together, and kiss and touch each other intermittently throughout the evening, except on evenings when they quarrel. Couple B may hardly talk about what's going on in their lives at all during the week, but take a picnic and drive into the country at the weekend to spend the day together, though they may still not talk very much, and only very rarely quarrel. Of course patterns may change over time and are strongly influenced by circumstances: how busy people are at work, how far they have to commute and, of course, whether or not they have children. So perhaps it would be more accurate to say that at the beginning of marriage couples establish a *range* of emotional interaction within which they remain content. If the temperature drops too low or rises too high, they become uncomfortable.

In addition, couples have to acquire the flexibility to move gracefully between different points on the 'closeness/distance' scale. This may refer both to the long term, such as a period when one partner is deeply involved in some work project, and the short term, such as an ordinary day. It takes practice to make the transition gracefully from the 'genuine and incontestable experience of the Divine, whose transcendent force obliterates and consumes everything individual' (Jung) of the night before, to the 'morning that separates' (T.S. Eliot).[2]

Me and me-and-you

One aspect of closeness/distance regulation in early marriage is working out how to have one's 'self' and one's 'self in relation to partner' coexist comfortably: how to be close but still retain one's sense of self, how to be apart but not feel lonely.

As we shall see in the interviews below, some of the adjustments and anxieties of the first year of marriage have to do with this. Who am I now – and who are *we*? Are we *really* a couple? What is it that makes us so, apart from the marriage certificate?

For their book *The Beginning of the Rest of Your Life?*, Penny Mansfield and Jean Collard interviewed 65 young couples who had been married three months. One of their findings was that many of their subjects showed a concern with whether or not they were a 'proper' married couple and a 'proper' husband and wife, and sometimes looked to the interviewer for reassurance that they were.[3] For some people then, establishing themselves as a couple is the primary task at this stage: doing things together, going places together, being 'couply'; they are content to let their identity as individuals recede for a time. Others are anxious about being taken over by the couple, and feel the need to show that 'I am still me' – for example by seeing friends separately.

Virginia Woolf, in her diary, descr
being without her husband Leonard: 'S
right word; one's personality seems to
when he's not there to enclose all one's vi\
riage were a completing of the instrument,
alone penetrates as if it were a violin robbed
piano.'[4]

Felicity, a woman married five years, felt som\
ferently. She recalled how early in her marriage she was very
careful to guard her 'separate space'. She made sure she always
had part of the weekend to herself and took care not to neglect
seeing her friends. Her husband was sometimes hurt by her
apparently cool control of their time together. 'I hardly ever get
to see you,' he would complain. Felicity explained: 'I needed
time away from him to get back to my normal shape. I found
relating to someone for long periods very exhausting. I remember thinking I was like a sea anemone, always opening and
closing, opening and closing.'

Now, several years later, she felt more relaxed. 'I've come
to feel that I can be my "normal shape" when we are together
too. So I don't make a point of going away from him any more.
But if we are apart, there is this elastic bond between us that
stretches across the physical distance. I may feel alone, but I
don't feel abandoned.'

The capacity to be alone

Anthony Storr writes: Modern psychotherapists, including
myself, have taken as their criterion of emotional maturity the
capacity of the individual to make mature relationships on equal
terms. With few exceptions, psychotherapists have omitted to
consider the fact that the capacity to be alone is also an aspect of
emotional maturity.[5]

As an example of an exception, he goes on to quote a
paper entitled 'The Capacity to Be Alone', by the child psychoanalyst D. W. Winnicott. In it, Winnicott suggests that our adult

ty to be alone begins with our infant experience of *being* *e in the presence of our mother*. That is, a state of being in hich mother and baby are not directly involved or interacting – the baby is not being fed or changed or played with. The baby just is, or is doing its own thing, and the mother is there also, giving the baby the security, in Winnicott's words, to 'discover his personal life'.[6] The mother's unintrusive presence makes it possible for the baby to be absorbed in its own experience, playing, exploring, or looking at something and contemplating. If she were not there, the child would have to be preoccupied with her absence.

Winnicott's point is that in a situation of 'being alone with another', the infant or child can begin to develop and define his or her 'self' in a safe situation. A similar sort of process can be observed in marriages and couple relationships. Many people like to do their separate things in the same room as their partner – work, or read in companionable silence, or maybe one sorts through photographs while the other writes a letter. Occasionally one or other may make a remark, or not. The point is to be individually absorbed while still being together. As anyone who enjoys this kind of situation will agree, it feels quite different from being alone.

But Winnicott is also making the point that if as a child we have had a satisfactory experience of being alone in the presence of someone, we internalise this experience so that as adults we can be genuinely alone in the physical sense without feeling cut off from the world. We continue to carry the presence of the loved one inside ourselves. This is what Felicity talks about when she refers to the 'elastic bond' between her and her husband.

Me versus you
In addition to working out the parameters of one's self within the relationship, the first year or two of marriage, or of a committed relationship, is often also the time when one starts seeing one's partner's personality more clearly. The rose tints come

off, the mists clear, the projections are taken back – whatever one wants to call it. Increasingly, it is one's partner's real character and qualities and idiosyncrasies that give one pleasure, rather than the notion of 'what he or she can give me' which is so much part of falling in love.

Perhaps this is what one woman was getting at when she described how her attitude to love-making had changed since getting married.

'When we first got together,' she said, 'I couldn't really look at him while we had sex, so I kept my eyes closed most of the time. It was as if I had to be in a fuzzy magic mystic haze – if I opened my eyes and saw *him*, the real person, the spell would break. But now I can look straight at him, before and during and after sex, and still feel aroused. I don't need a spell any more. It's better this way. Before it was always so unpredictable, whether or not the spell would hold.'

Of course, people also fight against the parts of each other they had not reckoned on, and they fight to assert parts of themselves they may feel that their partner is failing to recognise. In arguments the underlying question is often: how far can we, as separate individuals, disagree about things, without threatening our coupledom?

Some people find that once they are married, or in other ways committed, their quarrels feel less threatening than before. The commitment is a 'container', a garden wall which keeps the fire from spreading out of control. The knowledge that 'we're together now so we've got to sort this out' encourages greater efforts to resolve disagreements. Sometimes the resolution is to agree to disagree – the garden is big enough to hold us both, and small enough to keep us from losing each other.

Others find quarrels much more frightening after marriage. Quarrels can bring to the fore the doubts hovering in the background: have I made the right decision? Have I married the right person? Can we make this work? Quarrelling can also feel less, not more, tolerable after marriage if disagreement is felt as a threat to one's unity as a couple, that still fragile new concept of oneself. Disagreement emphasises one's individuality, and a newly wed or newly committed couple may be far more concerned with strengthening their coupledom than asserting their separateness. For Linda and James, in the second of the case histories below, a major issue was their rows and what they might mean.

Building a future

All three couples in this chapter spoke about how they envisaged the future. A shared vision of 'how we will be' in a couple of years' time, or ten years' time, or 'when the children are grown up', is an important cement in a couple relationship. Simon and Frances, who already had a child, were thinking about his education and where they would like to be in ten years' time and even in retirement. As Frances said, 'I can see us growing old together, Daniel coming in with his wife . . .' Linda and James were looking as far as having children, while Pippa and Timothy weren't ready to think about children yet but were planning to move to London.

Visions sometimes conflict, and one partner may be keener on a certain plan than the other. Pippa was sure that moving to London would make her happy, but for Timothy it would be a move away from family and friends, and the business he had built up. Linda longed for a baby but James didn't seem in any hurry. How far they were aware of their differences in their hopes for the future, and how they dealt with them, is revealed below.

Pippa and Timothy:

'It felt like we were jinxed'

The interviews with Pippa and Timothy began some six months after their wedding, and it was Pippa's experience of early marriage which came across most clearly.

Pippa wrote in response to my advertisement for interviewees, saying: 'I have been married three months and I am finding everything very difficult! I have moved to be with Timothy in a city where I have no friends and no job. During the days I am very unhappy and spend my time waiting for Timothy to come home from work, but I can't talk to him about how I feel because I don't want to make him feel bad. Everything seems to be conspiring against a happy beginning for us. Perhaps if we talked to you it would help us work out how much is us and how much our circumstances.'

I wrote back explaining that I was not a counsellor, and that as she seemed to be asking for help she might be better off contacting Relate. If she and Timothy were still interested in doing the interviews, we could start them later on. Pippa wrote back after a few weeks and said that she had in fact already seen a Relate counsellor. She assured me that she understood that I was an interviewer not a counsellor, and said that she and Timothy would like to go ahead with the interviews. Some months after that I went up to their house in Norwich for the first meeting.

Pippa was 24, striking looking, and with a strong presence. She was quick-witted and intelligent and talked easily. Timothy was 29, tall and slim and much more withdrawn, though his face was friendly. As he explained several times in the course of the interviews, 'opening up' didn't come easily to him – though in fact, in his individual interview he showed himself to be both thoughtful and articulate. Together with a partner he ran a small desk-top publishing business while Pippa, having been unemployed, had recently started a part-time job in a bookshop.

How they met

They had met at a party in Cambridge less than two years ago, just before Pippa graduated from university, where she read English. Against the odds, among which were Pippa's professed contempt for men, and her longing to get out of Cambridge and back to London, they fell in love quickly. Timothy asked her to come to live with him in Norwich. So after a short period of separation, during which they passionately reunited once a fortnight, Pippa went back east, not to Norwich but to Cambridge again, where she found a flat and a voluntary job with an adult literacy project, and she also signed on.

At various times during the interviews she gave two different accounts of her post-graduation time in Cambridge. Sometimes she painted an idyll of early-adult independence, 'I loved my little flat', 'I loved the job, if only it had been paid'. But more often she described it as a period of intolerable struggle and fragmented meetings with Timothy. She was broke. Her flat was cold and grotty. Their weekends together were too short, and if Timothy drove over on weekdays he arrived tired in the evening and had to leave again early the next morning. She couldn't stand the journeys to and from Norwich. 'I seemed constantly to have this big bag on my shoulder going from one place to another.'

While Pippa had 'no money ever', Timothy's business was doing well and he was able to pay himself a good salary. Pippa found herself torn between the seductiveness of Timothy's ability to pay for evenings out and weekend pleasures, and standing on her feminist principles of financial independence – which in practice meant spending the evenings in.

Timothy had repeatedly asked her to marry him. She'd always said no; but now she decided to ask him to marry her. After some initial surprise, he agreed – indeed, he was 'overjoyed'. The date was set for just over a year after they first met. Timothy bought an enormous, near-derelict house on the outskirts of Norwich (Pippa had no capital to contribute), and started to do it up, in preparation for bringing home his bride. Family and friends were told, and wedding plans snowballed. Pippa accepted a church wedding to please Timothy's parents, though at first she was afraid she might be 'seduced by the fairytale princess wedding'. The wedding was certainly a great success in fairytale tradition: white dress, grand lunch for family followed by an all-night party with all their friends in the new house.

The aftermath was less wonderful. Timothy began to work overtime, gripped by panic at the debts incurred over the wedding and the house purchase. Pippa languished at home, having given up her voluntary job because it made no sense to spend money on the train fares when she wasn't earning anything. Being married, she lost her right to supplementary benefit. She was jobless, aimless, and increasingly angry as she found herself spending her evenings watching TV in the company of the lodger they had taken to help with the bills, while waiting for Timothy to come home from work. Timothy paid for mortgage, bills, food and treats, but Pippa couldn't even go shopping to amuse herself. She hated the house and she hated Norwich: 'It's small and provincial and boring, nothing ever happens here, the people are awful and narrow-minded and sexist and everyone has known everyone since primary school.' She became more and more depressed. She saw the Relate counsellor twice but didn't think she could help. Eventually she went to her GP, who prescribed antidepressants. She had just stopped taking the pills when the interviews began.

Pippa's background

Pippa came from a broken home. Her parents divorced when she was young, her father soon remarried and she saw him only intermittently until her teens, when there was a *rapprochement*. She still did not see him often, and described their relationship as stormy: 'We're very alike, so we bat off at the same things. It's all great fun, and a lot of hassle.' Her latter-day acceptance of her father did not prevent her from understanding her parents' divorce as being entirely his fault.

She was extremely close to her mother, drawing three lines to her on her geneogram. She described her as 'mostly being given over to helping other people, being selfless, being there for others'. Her mother remarried when Pippa started secondary school. Her new husband was a 'difficult man', prone to bad moods and sulks, but they had worked on their marriage and it had survived. In spite of her mother's selflessness, relationships in the new family were tempestuous all round. Pippa recalled family life as 'very loud, very chaotic, loads of arguments about issues, the whole family screaming at each other'.

Yet Pippa remembered very little about her childhood. She thought she was 'bolshy' and held her own in the family; yet she was also withdrawn, a bookworm who didn't go out to play. In her late teens she decided she was lesbian, joined a Young Lesbians' Group and went out with an older woman, though the following year she went out with a boy.

At university, Pippa belonged to 'a core of bolshy women. I was always very outspoken and stood up to male tutors. I always felt strong – but then it started to crumble a bit.' Her coursework was full of 'anger and pain and men stuff', which she had believed was political but which she now also attributed to personal experiences. She began to think that she treated men badly. 'I slept with men. I didn't have boyfriends.' She identified herself as bisexual, although at college she never actually had a sexual relationship with a woman. There was one with whom 'I imagined I was utterly in love. But it went nowhere.'

It was in this state, when she was confused, 'tired of dealing with all these personal things', and finding it almost impossible to revise for her imminent finals, that she met Timothy.

Timothy's background
Timothy's background presented a model of family stability. His parents' marriage was solid and, according to Pippa, they were 'sixtysomething and so in love'. His mother was the talkative one and had a habit of interrupting his father and not letting him speak, which irritated Timothy. Timothy's home life during

his growing-up years in Norwich was uneventful. All the members of his family on both his father's and his mother's side were from Norwich and lived in and around Norwich. Family gatherings and family anecdotes were so familiar and predictable that they irritated him too.

He went away to university to do computer studies but returned to his home town afterwards. He worked for a publishing company for a few years before setting up on his own, initially using his parents' basement as his office. When he met Pippa he was immediately attracted by her difference. 'I didn't want to be with someone local. Pippa had a nicer accent for a start . . . I found it attractive that she came from somewhere different, that she was brought up differently, had different friends . . . I wouldn't know everything by the second date.'

The couple, the choice

So what was it that prevented Pippa from treating Timothy as 'all the other men', that is, as a one-night stand? For one thing, he turned up the next night too, without an appointment, and insisted on seeing her. Until then, she said, 'I just wasn't used to seeing people again. I was used to just saying hello to people at college and thinking, ha-ha. So when Timothy came along I thought, this is ridiculous, I've been so horrible to men, I've got to give this one a chance.'

Timing

The timing of Timothy's appearance in Pippa's life was important. It was nearing the end of her degree. 'I was so fed up with work and college. I'd been dealing with all these personal things which I was tired of dealing with. So when Timothy came along it was almost a chance for me to see if I'd dealt with it all. I suppose I was ready to let someone in – to let a man in. And Timothy got in there, gently. He was sensitive and funny and generous.' When he took her away for a weekend at a 'posh hotel' in the country she found, for the first time in ages, that 'I was just having a nice time'. Her finals 'seemed to lose their importance'. And after finals, and newly in love, planning for the next weekend with Timothy was more important and much easier than planning for the rest of her life. Questions of where to live, what to do and how to go about it were allowed to recede a little into the background.

Timothy was a shy, serious person who was looking for a lasting relationship at the time he met Pippa. He had last been in love at the age of 21, so much so that he had wanted to marry his girlfriend. After that relationship broke up he had only short ones. But when he met Pippa he soon felt that he 'didn't want to be with anyone else', and that despite all the logistical problems he wanted to persevere. Quite soon, too, he proposed, but when Pippa said no, a sort of game developed whereby he asked regularly, knowing he would be turned down. Until, that is, Pippa turned the tables and asked him to marry her.

Why did she decide to propose? And why, after such euphoric beginnings, did everything become so difficult and Pippa so depressed?

This is how they told it themselves.[7]

'Just the shock of being married?'

PIPPA: After college everything went downhill. There was nothing happening, for me or my friends. My voluntary work with the literacy project was interesting, but it wasn't enough. It was, 'either I stick to all my guns and am really strong and cut off my nose to spite my face and stay in this cold little flat on my own and work voluntarily, or . . .' It was ultimately better to be with Timothy than to be striving for all the rest of it, so I asked Timothy to marry me . . . because I didn't think there was any other way . . . am I explaining this right?

TIMOTHY: Well, I just think you wanted to show commitment, didn't you?

PIPPA: I'd already agreed to live with you, but I didn't think I'd ever set a date. Right up until getting married it didn't seem real. I was worried I was being seduced by the fairytale princess wedding but that didn't happen. I tried to be so strong – at first I was a bit embarrassed to tell my friends I was getting married, and they did change.

TIMOTHY: It was probably a shock; we are both the only ones in our circle of friends to be married. But we did it for the right reasons, because we wanted to be together.

PIPPA: Everything was so mad it was the only way we could be together. Timothy has always been very stable, with his company and his car, and I was in a real mess, with no money or job and not knowing what I wanted to do. I was subsidised by Timothy for things like holidays, though I was always really stubborn about paying my way – but then that led to spending really dull evenings in. It was always this argument between feminism and socialism.

TIMOTHY: I thought, I want to be with you and we want to have a good time, so . . .

PIPPA: Timothy had too much money before he bought the house.

TIMOTHY: It was just silly.

PIPPA: I always wished I didn't have to . . . Now with my part-time job I just contribute to the bills. At the beginning, before I got the job, I was just alone here, with no money, no friends, nothing to do. It was revolting.

TIMOTHY: It was a strain.

PIPPA: Timothy was being Mr Responsible – 'Oh, I've got a house and a wife now, better work late.' That was around the time I wrote to you. Things got pretty bad for a while. But they changed dramatically between my first and second letter: we asked the lodger to move out, I got offered the job, so I thought, my God, everything is wonderful again . . . because I couldn't work out why I was feeling so bad. Well I could: I had no money, no job, this person living with us. I thought, if those things can change everything will be fine. And they did – and then everything got quite bad again. I went to see a marriage counsellor, I just wept the whole hour. The second time I saw her I said everything has changed, I'm fine, I'm fine – but it didn't work out like that. Eventually I went to the doctor and went on antidepressants because I had no control over my emotions any more and I needed something to stabilise me.

TIMOTHY: (*With a small laugh.*) It sounds well doesn't it!

PIPPA: It doesn't sound too good, does it? But now everything's fine – well, that sounds pat, but much better. The pills have stabilised me, our relationship has improved no end, the job in the bookshop is working out.

TIMOTHY: I think part of it is just the shock of being married all of a sudden, after the day and the honeymoon are over.

PIPPA: That was a disaster.

TIMOTHY: It's getting used to living with each other, at the end of the day. People handle stress differently, don't they, and I think it is a form of stress. At the beginning I kind of shut off. I'd be silent about my worries, for example, over money. Whereas Pippa came out with it another way. We've matured, haven't we?

PIPPA: I think we've got used to living together . . . and I haven't got time to brood and to dwell on how miserable I am, and how cold – because the house is so cold. I was just bloody miserable for three months and horrible to live with. We have got closer, I think.

TIMOTHY: I think so. We come from totally different backgrounds; mine is quiet, stable, but people are unwilling to talk about things and problems. Pippa's is totally different, everyone lets everyone know if they are pissed off.

PIPPA: I thought Timothy's silence meant 'shut up, I don't want to know'. At one point I thought he'd rather live with the lodger.

TIMOTHY: It's never been particularly easy – but that's made it stronger, it's increased my feelings. At the beginning I didn't know how to cope.

PIPPA: I think I was unhappy before the wedding. I was very stressed by the arrangements because of my parents being divorced . . . and the voluntary job and living on £30 per week. There was all this stuff coming down on me.

INTERVIEWER: Did you hope marriage would change that?

TIMOTHY: I think we're both fairly realistic, aren't we?

PIPPA: Yes . . . but obviously people have expectations which they don't consider really looking at properly.

TIMOTHY: Well, obviously you don't look at the black side.

PIPPA: For example, my expectations of how you would be when we first got married were completely wrong.

TIMOTHY: (*Laughs.*)

PIPPA: I expected him to be far more relaxed about money and not work till 8 p.m. very often – I thought he'd realise that it was far more important to spend time in the house and . . . with me, than working late to rush through an order when there was no need.

TIMOTHY: I was definitely very anxious about our finances.

PIPPA: And then when you came home we'd just sit and watch TV with the lodger. I was going insane.

TIMOTHY: Looking back I can see the problems . . . I was panicked in my own way. You take a lot on your shoulders. I'm pretty good at taking a lot on my shoulders, but it gradually wears you down. And when we got in the house – it was a small thing, but it was freezing, as Pippa said.

PIPPA: It was not a small thing.

TIMOTHY: That's right, it was no longer a refuge – I'd have been more comfortable in my office!

PIPPA: And I'd been here all day.

TIMOTHY: But getting the house and getting married was expensive. And I didn't want to be the couple who fell into debt and it all got taken away.

PIPPA: Timothy had said to me, when he was trying to persuade me to marry him – I was saying I'll have nothing, no money, no job – and he always said, 'Oh come on, I don't want you to get a job in a supermarket, I can support you until you get what you want.' But when we got married it didn't work out like that. There wasn't enough money. And Timothy was really worried.

TIMOTHY: I cared about her well-being and I didn't want her to worry about things, which is probably where the offer of financial support came from. I thought, we've got this money and we should share it till you find what you want. It's natural when you care for someone. I did feel quite badly when it didn't work out.

PIPPA: It did mess things up slightly.

TIMOTHY: The things we took for granted we could no longer afford. At the back of my mind I figured it would be a struggle for a while on all fronts. But I felt so strongly for her I felt no big barriers – I just thought there'd be wrinkles, no big problems. And we're coming out of it now, which is nice.

PIPPA: We seemed to have a run of bad luck. It started with the honeymoon: the ferry was cancelled, the hotel didn't have our booking, and then it seemed to go on and on. It felt like we were jinxed . . . the house hated us . . . it all got out of proportion.

TIMOTHY: Yes . . . it was a struggle. It all sounds very depressing, a catalogue of disasters – but it's never been a case where we haven't sat down and laughed or whatever.

PIPPA: I don't think I laughed for four months.

TIMOTHY: It's not as serious as we are portraying.

PIPPA: I wasn't in a position to handle things well.

Is it us or is it circumstance?

TIMOTHY: It's never been either one of us. Circumstances got on top of us.

PIPPA: Yes, I always felt if circumstances could change things would be much better. And they are now. Before . . . I thought, I can't be going mad, it must be something hormonal, chemical, that just needs balancing. During the week I could hold myself together – but then the thought of being here on the weekend, cold, with the lodger – and everything would go right down, and I'd break down on Friday night or Saturday morning and the weekend would be revolting. There was no point going to a counsellor when it was all circumstances, and talking to a counsellor couldn't get me a job or make the lodger leave. I just needed something artificial to make me feel better and help me get through it, so I went to the doctor who said it sounded as if I'd been clinically depressed ever since I got married.

TIMOTHY: The worst thing was to feel a bit helpless. I couldn't change everything instantly, sell the house, for example. It did make me feel bad, I didn't want to see Pippa so unhappy.

PIPPA: I always felt bad about being so upset because I knew he couldn't change everything: the house, and being in Norwich. But now I feel more positive about that – I have a job, a little money, and I'm enjoying the relationship more. I just needed the chemical boost to get me out of the rut.

TIMOTHY: I've been thinking about selling my share of the business to my partner and looking for a job in London.

PIPPA: Which I haven't pushed.

TIMOTHY: I didn't want to move before because I'd have had no one to share it with.

PIPPA: Now we could explore London together.

TIMOTHY: To tell the truth I've been looking for a way of making a change – I've been running the business now for five years. But I'd be sorry to leave the house because I have put so much work into it. But it's only a building.

PIPPA: I always held back on the 'we're buying it together, darling', because it was *his* money. We came to see it together. I thought it was revolting. It was thick with snow, the house was freezing, an old woman had been living here and it was smelly and empty.

I've always been very bolshy in my attempt at independence; financial independence is very important to me. Getting married, becoming a wife, being negated as a married woman – not being able to get dole money . . . I think I was so frightened of commitment it made me really reticent to take part in any decision about money or the house.

Contradictions

The themes of this first interview were repeated through the rest of the interviews – the prelude to getting married, the awfulness of the house, Pippa's depression. Pippa was confused about how much of her unhappiness was internal, attributable to 'me' or 'us', and how much caused by external circumstances. She wanted to think it was circumstance – but then she hadn't become instantly happier when she did get a job and the lodger moved out, so what was wrong? She couldn't work it out.

Pippa made powerful statements without apparently hearing the full meaning of what she was saying. She was painfully honest about one set of her reasons for getting married: it was either having no money, a cold little flat, and seemingly always going to and fro with a heavy bag over her shoulder, or asking Timothy to marry her. What did this imply about her expectations of marriage? Was it to rescue her from discomfort and shabbiness and take the weight off her shoulders? Far from Timothy's hopeful assertion that she married him to 'show commitment', it sounded as if she married with the hope of being transformed from a bag-lady into a princess, or at least a comfortably off woman with the security of her own house, warmth, and no money worries at last.

This was not to say that she did not love Timothy, which she surely did. At other times during the interviews she said, 'I'm living with the person I really love.' But she herself did not seem to notice, or at least didn't acknowledge, how much she contradicted herself when talking about her reasons for wanting to marry Timothy.

Given her emphasis on independence, it was not surprising that Pippa should have ambivalent feelings about marriage. Marriage, for her, had become the hole she bolted into when her stab at adult independence failed. She and Timothy regarded the institution of marriage quite differently. While Timothy was proud to be married, Pippa was embarrassed to tell her friends. She said that the priest who married them 'offended my gay friends with his talk of the sanctity of marriage'. That they also held different ideas about the nature of commitment in marriage was revealed in one exchange:

TIMOTHY: I've never wanted to be with someone I didn't really love. I don't see the point in playing at it. It was going to be with the right person for the right reasons.

PIPPA: It sounds very dewy-eyed . . . forever . . .

TIMOTHY: Well, I've always watched too many films.

PIPPA: No, what I mean is, sorry, I don't believe one can say this will be forever . . .

(*Pause.*)

TIMOTHY: Why are you so tongue-tied?

PIPPA: I think we both had a healthy realism about it: this is wonderful now, and I can see it going on for a long time, but for ever is a completely different thing. I don't think I

ever saw it like that; you never . . . I don't see how anyone
can think like that.

TIMOTHY: I disagree. I don't say one thing doesn't lead to
another – it's not just because we've got married – but I
can't see myself ever wanting to be with anyone else, so
in those terms it is forever. But things change; Pippa
might not choose to live with me forever.

PIPPA: I'm not saying I wouldn't. But I don't think you can ever
believe that.

The discomfort of dependence

For a feminist who had always been 'bolshy about independence', it must have been uncomfortable for Pippa to find herself
so utterly financially dependent on Timothy. Perhaps because of
this humiliation, she couldn't resist taking several little nips at
the hand that fed her. When Timothy said that he wanted to
share his money with her, she denigrated his generosity by saying that before he bought the house he had 'too much money'
anyway. When Timothy acknowledged that he felt bad about
the financial constraints after the wedding, and that he had not
managed to fulfil his pre-wedding offer of no financial worries,
Pippa kicked in with 'it did mess things up slightly'.

Pippa did not say that she expected Timothy to provide
her with money, a comfortable and adequately heated home, a
fun social life; but she was angry when he didn't. In many ways
her behaviour was reminiscent of that of the short story writer
Katherine Mansfield, as described by Claire Tomalin in her fascinating biography. Between 1912, when she was 24, and her
death in 1923, she had a relationship with the writer and editor
John Middleton Murry. From early on, Katherine confused her
friends by complaining to them about Murry and professing
her love for him at the same time. Later, she and Murry often
spent long periods apart as Katherine went to southern Europe
in search of a cure for her advancing tuberculosis. She wrote
him letters, in which, by turns, she berated him for neglecting

her by not coming to look after her, put him off coming when he proposed to, and doused him in fantasies of how perfect everything would be once he did join her ('tea in a forest, cold chicken on a rock by the sea . . . For we must be happy. Blissful happiness.'[8]) Claire Tomalin interprets her inconsistencies as 'a way of working out a fundamental conflict for a strongwilled person who resented dependence on a lover'.[9]

The same might surely be said about Pippa. If the side of her that was humiliated by her dependence was plain to see, the side that longed to be allowed to be dependent was more disguised, perhaps in the form of depression. To Pippa, Timothy's offer of financial security may have suggested a more total offer to take care of her which she, in her confused and unhappy state at the end of her degree, must have found very attractive. Her verbal lashings out at marriage and at the 'cosy hetero thing' may have masked an idealisation of marriage – marriage as a haven, a place of safety, a place where she would be allowed to rest from her striving for financial independence, to make a home for herself, and all the other challenges of early adulthood. In her unconscious fantasy, marriage, for Pippa, was somewhere she might be allowed to regress and become a cherished and pampered child-princess. Timothy would be mother and father and husband and caretaker and provider all rolled into one.

(A hint that this was how she did see him was contained in her remark that their sex life always 'revived' when they went to stay at her mother's house. When people invest their partner with too many roles besides that of husband or wife, sex understandably comes to feel problematic, sometimes even incestuous: who are you having sex with? Perhaps when Pippa was in her mother's house, where her mother took the role of her mother, and homemaker, Timothy was freed in her eyes to become a sexual partner again.)

Carer and cared for

Timothy, who confessed in his individual interview that 'if I have a fault it is that I do try to take care of Pippa too much and don't accept that she is a responsible adult who can take care of herself', was then the ideal person to become Pippa's caretaker. It is not surprising that when Pippa found that in marriage things were still demanded of her, and that her caretaker-husband abandoned her each morning and left her alone all day, she fell prey to a crashing depression born of crumbling dreams and disappointment.

This was compounded by the conflict between her principles and her actual life: she was a feminist, yet her day focused on Timothy's homecoming at night. She thought independence enormously important, yet was entirely financially dependent on her husband.

In his individual interview, Timothy described how Pippa used to greet him when he came home from work: 'At first she was quiet and sulky, then we'd talk and it would burst out, and there would be tears and she couldn't say why. Well, she could say "I'm not happy with having no job, or the lodger, or hanging around the house all day", but that didn't justify the extent of it. Sometimes of course I got fed up; we'd have a nice Saturday planned and then the tears would start, and you'd think "Oh God almighty". Just sometimes it slightly wore me down, because I didn't know how to combat it.'

This pattern of behaviour could be compared to that of a small child who feels let down by a parent, for example by being left. According to the child psychoanalyst John Bowlby,[10] ambivalent behaviour, such as first acting in a rejecting way and then clinging or crying, is typical of a young child unexpectedly separated from its parents, even for a short time. Of course, for Pippa, Timothy's absences at work were not unexpected, but one might say that the 'child in her' did not accept them. It was significant that she really broke down at weekends, when she knew Timothy would be there for a longer stretch. Rather than being happier when the attachment figure was there, this was the time when it was safe to give vent to rage and disappointment and protest at the prospect of further 'abandonment', which was what it felt like to her when she was 'left alone' in the house all day.

Pippa's disappointed hopes of being totally cared for in marriage were expressed especially strongly in her attitude to the house.

She allowed Timothy to buy a house she knew she hated because 'it was his money', and then opted out of homemaking right from the start. She was then angry with Timothy for providing a house that was not a home. It was cold, much too large, inhabited by a lodger until he was asked to leave, endlessly requiring repairs. As the plans for going to London became more firm, Pippa began to dream: 'I am really looking forward to being on our own,' she said in the last interview, even though by this time the lodger had already left, 'and choosing a house together, and getting to know London together. We'll start on our own, just us, no baggage. The place I want will be small and warm. We'll be making a home together, definitely; I feel if we go to London I have a total right to be involved.'

In her individual interview, which took place in her mother's large house in London, she said, 'It sounds awful, as if I'm always waiting for the next thing, but I am waiting to move to London now, and for a time when we'll really have a good crack at working on us – when we can sit back and think, right, it's us now, this is what we've got and this is what we have to work with.' What was stopping them from doing so in their Norwich house now that the lodger had left?

'Things just aren't as comfortable. I come home here for a weekend,' she waved her hand around the room, 'and I just love it. It's warm, a big nice house – even doing hand-washing in my mother's warm kitchen with hot water coming out of the tap instead of having to boil a kettle is fairly pleasurable. In Norwich it's a trek from the TV room to the toilet through half-done rooms, and I don't really want to be concerned with them.'

It sounded as if Pippa somehow expected to be taken to a ready-made home when she got married, rather than creating a new one. Her longings to start afresh in a small warm flat, 'just the two of us', even though they already were just two, could be expressions of a fantasy of 'returning home' to infancy and the warmth and safety of a mother's lap: 'Going to London' became idealised: '*then* we'll be able to be happy!'

What about Timothy?

This account has concentrated on Pippa's experience of early marriage. What about Timothy? He was certainly distressed by seeing Pippa so miserable, but he did not actually fall to blaming himself. His soothing words in the first interview, as he later said himself, were born partly of embarrassment that a stranger should hear such a woeful story of their first months of marriage, but they also reflected his genuine belief that these were adjustment pains, which would pass. 'In an earlier relationship I might have thought, "what have I done?",' he said, 'but I'm more mature now, and I thought it would pass. I also tried to think, "let's calm down and see how we can change things".'

Timothy was prepared to overlook Pippa's black moods and demanding behaviour for the pleasure of experiencing her good moods. He said, 'I like Pippa's personality as a whole, so when she is up it's marvellous, but I accept that there is another side to it and that she can't always be bubbly. She is very thoughtful, and feminine, and affectionate, both physically and mentally. She cares, and if she thinks I'm tired or worried she tries to drag out of me the problem, which is good because I'm not used to opening up.'

He hoped that his stability would act as a counterweight to Pippa's more volatile nature: 'I understand that Pippa may be in a bad mood for whatever reason so I try to take the opposite stance. Sometimes it works the other way but normally it's that way round. I try to gauge my moods and be more mature – I don't mean than Pippa but than I would be if I let myself go.'

Occasionally he felt his role was restrictive. He commented that he found Pippa's 'childish excitement' about things like Christmas and birthdays very attractive. But he acknowledged that this caused him to suppress his own excitement: 'I leave it to Pippa, so it does rob the moment for me slightly.' If they were both excited at the same time, he said, it would be like two children hopping up and down, 'and I couldn't handle that – you're living in a different world then.'

Timothy seemed to be saying he had to be the adult in the relationship to look after Pippa's child. Another way of looking at it would be to see Timothy as the container for all the disunited parts of Pippa's complex personality. She needed him to hold her together. Her sexual confusion at college, toing and froing between men and women, was brought to an end when she met Timothy. As she said, she was tired of dealing with all the 'personal things', longing for some respite from herself.

Pippa's geographical toing and froing in the year after leaving college can be heard not only as a literal description of rootlessness but as a metaphorical one. As she herself said, 'I thought if I marry Timothy at least I'll be settled.' What she hadn't bargained for was that 'settling' had to come from inside as well as outside. Her six months of depression after the wedding were caused partly by her disappointment at the imperfection of the man and the situation; and partly by the discovery that she was still responsible for her own happiness.

Looking ahead . . .

Nevertheless, Pippa seemed gradually to be coming to terms with her situation. Towards the end of the interviews she said, 'Maybe marriage *is* a big thing for me. Maybe I do rate it extremely highly, maybe I want to be the one to make it work.' She expressed wonder and pleasure that she was able to 'fancy the same person and be happy going to bed night after night with the same person'.

That Pippa had taken on some of Timothy's quiet optimism was also shown at the end when she said, 'I am very positive about the future.' She added, however, 'Though I have to admit that I'm now waiting to go to London.' This cast a slight shadow in the form of a question mark. Could London really fulfil Pippa's expectations, or would she once again be beset by disappointment?

Linda and James:

'We complement each other very well'

Linda, 30, and James, 35, were also just six months married when the interviews began, and another couple engaged in adjusting to married life.

They were interviewed in their new house, the pastel interior of which had been completed only the night before their wedding, so that they could move in immediately after the honeymoon for a 'fresh start'. She was blonde and rounded, he was tall and dark. She enjoyed cooking and making the house look nice, while James did the gardening and pursued his hobby of doing up old cars. She was open, talkative, and a little giggly, but also thoughtful about herself and her relationship. He came across as solid and unrufflable.

Linda and James themselves presented their attraction in terms of complementarity. James said he had been attracted by Linda's prettiness, her liveliness and also intelligence. She seemed a woman who had 'done something' in her life. He gave it as his view that women in general were 'the lifeblood' because they knew their way around the complicated and confusing world of emotions, and he indicated that part of Linda's charm was that she had access to feelings which were unknown to him:

'I just think of babies as babies, but to Linda any small thing is just so precious. For example, we saw a foal on TV; I thought, oh that's nice, but she really feels it, she wants to pick up the telly and cuddle it.'

For her part, Linda said she had been attracted by James's consistency, reliability, and kind and loving nature: 'I know where I am with him.' In contrast to her last boyfriend, James was 'without any hideous moods where I have to tread on eggshells.' He was a 'good husband', like her father: 'James has certain things in common with my dad,' she said. 'He is a dutiful husband, committed to caring for his wife and home. James would be the last one to go out and stay out with his friends, he would rather have a cosy evening in with his wife.'

Linda and James seemed to have adjusted to marriage easily. They said they felt settled and close. 'We do a lot of things together,' said Linda; 'we love our weekends. We go for a walk, or enjoy a meal at home and a film on TV, or go out for a meal together. I can't understand one couple we know who always do separate things on weekends, she goes to her mum. Because a lot of our feeling of closeness I think comes from spending time together and doing things we enjoy together. Of course you need space and time alone – but most of the time we are together.'

Much of their activity around the house was role-divided, and they said they were comfortable with this. Linda said: 'James's hobby with the cars fits in: he fiddles for a couple of hours and that is the ideal time for me to get dinner ready or go round with a duster – or write a long letter to my friend in America.' She continued, 'I like cooking, and James is a very appreciative person to cook for.'

'I like eating,' said James.

'We both do,' said Linda. I feel we complement each other very well. I do most of the housework and the bathroom and the cooking, and if James did nothing I'd probably feel resentful and want more help. But because he does a great job on the garden and DIY and we have a nice little house because of it . . . James will say "Come and have a look at what I've done in the garden", and I'll say "Come and look at what I've made", so it's turned out well. And if I want something around the house, for example an electrical socket in the kitchen, one will appear in a couple of days.'

How they met

Linda and James met through Dateline. When they joined, they were both on the rebound. Linda was trying to extricate herself from an on–off relationship with a man whom she described as 'the creative type'. She had been very in love with him, but he was unreliable: one minute tender and the next 'cold as ice'. 'I never knew where I was with him, one minute very happy and the next crying my eyes out and not knowing what day of the week it was.'

Meanwhile James had come to the end of a long relation-ship with a woman he'd met at college. He described it as 'a deep friendship', although he had not been in love with her. He had tried to break it off several times but always stepped down when she got into a terrible state and started 'foaming at the mouth'. When she began to press for marriage he hedged around until finally she left. The break-up had been messy and he had given her more money from the sale of their house than he need have, as well as the car, because he felt so guilty.

Linda and James's first date was at a pub. James described their meeting: 'We both came in cars and drove towards each other – it was quite romantic, like coming towards each other on a beach except we did it in cars. I thought, oh she's the best one yet.'

Linda said, 'Looks do matter. I'd had lots of phone con-versations with men I'd got on well with, but when I met them I wasn't attracted to them. But James was nice, not disappoint-ing.' They hit it off on their first date, and soon Linda was spending the weekends at James's house.

They got married two years after meeting. James was laying carpets in the new house right up until the night before the wedding because, in Linda's words, 'We were trying to tie in a fresh start as closely as possible. We didn't want his past hanging around us.'

Linda's background

Linda's growing-up years were unsettled and troubled. Her mother married at 18 because she was pregnant with Linda. At 20 she had Linda's younger sister Jeanette, and a couple of years later she was divorced. She remarried quite soon and had three more children. When Linda was 16, her mother divorced again, and was now living with a new man.

Linda adored her real father, but relations between Linda and her stepfather were conflictual. Linda felt that her stepfather favoured his own children over her and Jeanette. 'I always felt he saw the worst in me.'

Linda was quite close to Jeanette, although as children Jeanette was the pretty, popular one who got boyfriends, while Linda was the bookworm stuck at home. But she who laughs last . . . Linda now had a degree, a good job, and a 'lovely husband' and home, while Jeanette had no training, three children already, and a rocky marriage. And when James met Jeanette, he even thought that Linda was the prettier one.

Of her mother, Linda said, 'It wasn't roses all the way, we argued and fell out, but I was closest to her. She was a good mother, she cared about us and tried to do her best by us. She got on her bike (she couldn't drive) and came to parents' evening for every one of us.'

Linda readily identified James's apparent stability and calm as what she wanted; it seemed to promise something better than her own home, where she often saw her mother tense and worried or in tears, where quarrels were frequent, money short, and her stepfather, a self-employed businessman, so unreliable that her mother had to fend off irate creditors and customers from their doorstep. Eventually they had been forced to sell their house to pay his debts. She said, 'I have a great feeling that when James and I have children I will bend over backwards to give them a secure and loving background.'

James's background

James was the oldest of three children. His brother was conventional, careful with money, while his sister was a full-time mother and housewife. James always felt that his father was always far more approving of his brother and sister; he thought James was 'outrageous', particularly with regard to his hobby of buying and doing up old cars and selling, or intending to sell, them for a profit. On his geneogram James went so far as to draw a distance line to his father.

He said he was close to his mother, a lively, outgoing woman who loved parties and even went dancing now, at 60. She often became frustrated with her careful, precise, controlled husband.

Although James placed great weight on meeting a woman through Dateline who had 'done' something, he seemed to have relatively little to say about his own background. He grew up in a coastal town, went to college, and met the girlfriend with whom he lived for the next ten years.

It seemed that what he really meant when he said that Linda had 'done' a lot was that she had been through a lot: her background was high on emotion and turbulence compared with his, and this seemed to be an important factor in his attraction to her.

The couple, the choice

At this early stage of Linda and James's relationship, their attraction was still expressed through an exchange of projections: Linda saw in James the 'good husband', even-tempered and dependable, whom she had chosen to make up for her splintered past. James saw in Linda a woman with access to the wonderful world of emotions. She had been through a lot in her life and seemed equipped to offer him a passport to a livelier place. As he said in his individual interview: 'I don't think I'll ever understand how women work. For many years I found it amazing how girls can change, their moods! I am even-tempered, though I get angry sometimes, but girls are very responsive to feelings. I think it's wonderful, females are wonderful, they are the lifeblood, really. It's unnerving sometimes.'

Each seemed to offer the other one what they needed and did not have. As the Cole Porter song says, 'You've got what I lack in me.'

Fights: who is right?
In fact, by the time the interviews started, the smoothness of their exchange was interrupted by rows, which surged forth with a suddenness and passion that Linda found distressing and James bewildering. They could not understand these rows, and variously attempted to dismiss them as silly and unimportant, or to control them with 'written contracts' which they signed in times of harmony.

Both had strong visions of how they wanted married life to be, but their visions did not tally entirely. Linda was extremely keen to have children soon. James, however, had ticked the 'no' box on the Dateline form in answer to the question, 'Do you want children?' He felt the question was 'manipulative'.

Before they could have children, they agreed, they would need to build an extension for a nursery, and to get the money for it James would have to sell some of the five cars that were currently crammed into the front drive. By the end of the interviews he had sold one, but this had not brought in very much, and he had great trouble bringing himself to sell any of the ones he had done up.

His vision of the future included himself as a 'country boy' with a house in the Home Counties, a brook running across the bottom of the garden, and a stable full of horses, but he didn't mention children. When Linda said she was 'indifferent' to this and called it James's 'dream', he said firmly, 'It is what will happen.' When Linda said she thought they would stay in their present house for the next ten years with a couple of kids, James said 'I'm not sure about ten years.'

But these kinds of important differences were not what they quarrelled about, because as yet they did not fully acknowledge them. Instead, the subjects of their rows were 'silly things'. In the last interview, Linda said: 'I wonder if I have been too one-sided about how wonderful James is. After all, we do argue and get on each other's nerves.' As an example, they rehearsed the thread of their most recent argument. Not surprisingly, they found that they still saw things quite differently and almost got embroiled again.

The subject was weight loss, and it had been quite a long-player. After Christmas, they had agreed to go on a diet together. James began the story: 'We were having Sunday morning breakfast in bed, and I brought in the Cornflakes, and Linda said, "You've got too much."'

LINDA: Only because you said you wanted to lose weight and were going to make all sorts of sacrifices.

JAMES: We both have our ideas about how it should be done. Linda tends to just stop eating.

LINDA: I don't, James – after Christmas we both decided to lose weight.

JAMES: You realise you could start an argument here.

LINDA: James swore he was going to get in shape, swimming, eating healthily, and he did hardly anything.

JAMES: I lost three-quarters of a stone in three weeks.

LINDA: But he made no sacrifices – if you are on a diet you have to cut down.

JAMES: Stop eating.

LINDA: Not stop eating – James's idea of a diet is three slices of cake instead of about six.

JAMES: I lost three-quarters of a stone in three weeks. Linda eats nothing; then she has a big binge and eats every chocolate biscuit in the house, and then tries to get me to eat them and I don't really want them. I have a more long-term approach.

LINDA: Yes, permanent piggery. We have a different approach.

JAMES: And we are both convinced we're right.

LINDA: I don't think James needs to lose a lot of weight. He's flabby around the middle, his clothes were getting tight, weren't they, and he said he must do something about it. So we made an agreement to do it together and I felt he wasn't doing anything at all, saying he wouldn't eat this and that and then he did.

[*After a while they tried to move on to describe how they felt during these clashes.*]

LINDA: I feel incredibly angry. I could hit him for being so stubborn.

JAMES: I feel henpecked. (*Long silence.*) And annoyed, I suppose, and disbelief, as if I can't believe what I'm hearing, that she can be being serious in what she's saying about something where I know I'm right – ha ha.

LINDA: For me there's incredible frustration and anger at not being able to get myself understood. But it blows over quickly.

JAMES: Usually when I prove Linda is wrong.

LINDA: Oh shut up.

JAMES: I showed her the scales.

LINDA: That's a bad example, it's one where you can measure black and white and I admitted that yes, you had lost three-quarters of a stone and you had a great moment of triumph. But usually there is no right or wrong, and we just agree to differ.

JAMES: I must tell this one, about the washing machine. It really did get heated – I was virtually chased out of the house for suggesting that you put the powder directly in the machine, as we have a weak water supply – you were shouting and screaming that you knew how to do the washing because you always did it or something ridiculous. She was standing outside with soap in one hand about to thwack me.

LINDA: I didn't.

JAMES: You say—

LINDA: I was very cross about that. I felt insulted because I felt James was implying incompetence on my part when I do the washing however many times a week. But despite all that I don't think we argue very much: 80–90 per cent of the time everything is great, 10 per cent of the time we argue – we hate each other, don't we?

JAMES: Yes we do, for a very short period of time, because we both feel we are very very right.

LINDA: I get very fierce – I hate James at that moment. It's very painful at the time.

JAMES: Not painful – I don't take it as seriously as perhaps I should.

LINDA: I don't deny I get very heated and angry – I could hit him and I hate him, but then it's over and nothing has changed and we still have lots of good times and it's just part of living with someone. It probably sounds a funny thing to say, but having arguments and still being stable is a very reassuring thing, and the more of that you build up . . .

JAMES: Is this going to become more regular then?

LINDA: No, you know what I mean – that it hasn't actually changed anything fundamental, our love for each other. It almost strengthens things.

'The even-tempered one' and 'the emotional one'

There are surely many different ways of understanding James and Linda's rows. One subtext in their argument over dieting seemed to be about being a couple versus being an individual. To Linda, the important thing was to support each other, as a couple, in the unpleasant business of restricting their eating. To James, the important thing was to lose weight, which he went ahead and did successfully on his own, in his own way, without regard for the idea of doing it together.

In general, their quarrels may have been an expression of some resentment, on both their parts, for being slotted into each other's fantasy life plans. If James insisted on horses in the country even as Linda said she wasn't interested, and if Linda said how much she looked forward to having children without noticing that James failed to concur, then they were not listening to each other properly. Conflict had not yet been allocated a legitimate place in their marriage, and as long as this was so, it would continue to erupt like violent bubbles in a vat of hot sugar.

Another potential meaning of their quarrels was suggested by the nature of the topic which James brought up immediately after their dialogue above. Having made it clear that he did not take their rows 'as seriously as perhaps I should', he went on to talk about what really did make him angry.

'People pushing in in traffic, that really makes me angry,' he said. 'I quite often have slanging matches with people, I'll get out of the car.'

Linda said, 'To me you are not an angry person.'

JAMES: But that one thing.

LINDA: You say that and I suppose I've heard you swear in traffic, but you're not even in at the start where some people are concerned. To me you are a very even-tempered person. I don't think you really get angry.

JAMES: I haven't done with you.

LINDA: I think you get more depressed than angry.

JAMES: To some extent . . . but that traffic thing comes to mind because it happens every day. It sounds silly but it's one thing . . .

Linda did not want to hear that James could be an angry person. He was supposed to be the even-tempered and calm one, and she needed to continue seeing him in this way. She was not ready to re-own this projection. But James had never been entirely thrilled with his role as solid rock. When Linda praised him for being 'reliable and consistent', he said, 'Sounds really boring.' He emphasised that in his own family he was considered the outrageous, risk-taking one.

When he fell in love with Linda, James had hoped that through her he might step into a wider world of feelings. When he began to experiment with feelings of anger, however, Linda could not allow it. Thus while every day James was letting passions flow outside their relationship and into the rush-hour traffic, it felt too frightening to allow James to be emotional inside the relationship. Linda had too much invested in her choice of James as 'the good husband type' with whom she would *not* repeat scenes from her childhood.

In a way their rows became a way of reaffirming their original contract. Linda, 'the emotional one', could get more and more angry until she could actually say that she hated James. She could scream and shout with frustration. But as long as James never fully lost his temper, she could experience these episodes as ultimately reassuring: James was still the man she had married, relatively unruffled. They could feel that they were playing the roles they had agreed at the beginning, even if in extreme form.

At the same time, they had a lot unconsciously invested in changing the original projections. Had they not married with the hope of complementing each other, not just through projection but through actually absorbing something of the other? Had Linda's unconscious hope not been to find some of James's stability for herself? Had James not hoped to find a way, through his contact with Linda, to connect with a greater range of feelings inside himself? They found themselves in a Catch-22.

Their anxiety about these little volcanoes in the midst of their cosy new nest might have been increased by the fact that they met through Dateline, prompting the question: 'Are we really a couple? Did we really choose each other, or was it the computer?' At the end of the interviews this question was actually voiced, when Linda asked, 'Do we seem to you like the kind of couple where you can see what the attraction was?'

While no lodestar appeared to beckon them out of their dilemma by the time the interviews ended, their deliberate commitment to their marriage was strong. This would surely help them to overcome and accept a certain measure of post-marital disappointment – whether it turned out to be that 'you are changing too much', or 'you are not changing enough'.

Simon and Frances:

'We want to achieve a lot'

Simon and Frances were both in their late twenties. They were a good-looking couple, both tall and slim and attractive; he wore jeans and a T-shirt while she was usually just in from work and glamorously dressed in tailored skirts and high heels. They were the new parents of a baby boy, Daniel, aged seven months.

Frances was the breadwinner, the financial director of a communications and public relations firm, and by her own description 'a successful black person'. Simon was househusband and stayed at home looking after Daniel. He had a weekend job in one of the large DIY stores and was soon to start working full time, and Daniel would then go to a childminder. Their house in Bristol was spotless; there was barely a hint that there was a baby living in it. 'It's Simon who keeps it like this,' Frances said in a stage whisper. Indeed, Daniel himself was a fairly undemanding baby, apparently content to sit in his bouncy chair or lie in his cot upstairs during the interviews. Simon and Frances appeared calmly in charge of a well-ordered household.

How they met

When they met at a party less than three years ago, Frances was single, fed up with men, and determined to be celibate. Simon was living with his pregnant girlfriend. They started seeing each other occasionally. Frances invited Simon for lunch a couple of times and was impressed with his self-restraint. 'Some guys would try to grab a kiss but he came and had lunch, talked, played cards, and when he went he said, "see you".'

They made love for the first time on a Sunday in May, a few months after their first meeting. By then Simon's girl-friend, Dawn, was eight months' pregnant and he was still living with her. A few weeks later, Frances remembered, 'We were watching videos at about eleven in the evening and there was a phone call and Simon had to rush to the hospital. It was horrible, it was so horrible. And then I thought, "It's fine. I just have to live with it."' Latisha, Simon's daughter, was born. After the birth Simon gradually withdrew from his relationship with Dawn, but he still saw her and his baby daughter regularly.

Simon explained: I wanted us to happen, I wanted Frances and me to have a relationship, but I felt obligated. At the party Frances asked me if I had kids and I said, not right now, and she said, what, have you got one on the way? I said yes, because I thought I'd better tell her what's going on: "I'm in a bit of a stick right now and I need some time to get over it. I don't want to be the kind of guy who is selfish and leaves the girl with her problems . . ." But I wasn't overjoyed with my situation. Dawn was much younger than me. I couldn't really talk to her. If something was bothering me I'd get no feedback, just "Well babes, it'll be OK, it'll be better tomorrow," the kind of mundane shit you can get from anybody in the street. What I'm looking for is: "This is how you can solve it." We couldn't communicate – she was still young.'

Frances said, 'I felt in a Catch-22 situation. You think you love this guy but can't have him – so I was prepared to wait but also thinking, why should I wait? Why don't I leave him and get on as I was? It was a horrible time.'

Frances did wait, but not without a good deal of conflict over Simon's 'other family', at least in the early days.

'I don't know how the relationship has survived, I really don't,' said Frances. 'I got a lot of grief from Latisha's mother, well, I think I did. I felt as if she was trying to get at me. Silly things like one time she phoned early on a Sunday morning and asked Simon to fetch her because she'd gone out and couldn't get home from where she was, and asking Simon to bring up some nappies for his child, and he'd tell me the same day that we were having Latisha for the weekend, and there was conflict over him going over there.'

In her individual interview, Frances elaborated the story of what happened when Dawn rang them that Sunday morning.

'I mean, Simon jumped. He flung his clothes on, and when I said "Where are you going?" he said, "I'm going to pick her up." So I said, "I'm coming too." It was the first time I met her. She was there with a friend standing out in the street with a short tight dress on, high heels, no tights, and when she saw me she was shocked. She got in the car; Simon was driving my car at the time and she went to sit in the front and I said "Sit in the back!", and all the way to her place we argued. Simon was quiet. He didn't say anything to back me up. I said to her "How could you come out of your house, go to a party all night and not have money to get a cab home?" And I said, "Where's your bloody daughter?" And she said, "Is that your fucking business?" She was really horrible, she was so rough. She said to me "Simon and I have something you will never have, we have a child."'

We've achieved a lot together
Frances had been told that she could not have children. Not long after she and Simon got together she started fertility treatment, and when she found that she would have to wait at least

two years on the NHS, she decided to devote all her savings to private treatment. Within three months she was pregnant. Daniel was born in September 1992, when Frances and Simon had been together two and a half years.

'Simon gave me the will to believe that I can have kids,' said Frances. 'I thought, no, never, which was probably partly the reason we had such problems when Latisha was born. Simon was very supportive at the counselling sessions. They were very emotional: the counsellor would say, "You know there is an 80 per cent chance that you won't succeed" and I would burst into tears every time.'

'We never thought we could have a child and then bang, here he is,' said Simon. They both agreed that Daniel was their proudest achievement.

In the very first interview they emphasised that they had achieved a lot in the short time that they had been together. They had Daniel, they had bought a house, they had been to Jamaica together to visit relatives and friends. They shared a belief in the value of hard work, getting ahead, and self-improvement. They were both second-generation black Britons whose mothers had come over from Jamaica to work as nurses in the great wave of emigration in the late 1950s and early 1960s. They talked a lot about their ambitions. They planned to semi-emigrate to Jamaica: to have land and a house over there, and to send Daniel to school there, but to keep a house in England as well. As Simon said, 'The ideal situation would be to flip-flop between the two.'

Simon's career plans were hazy, but Frances's were more clear. She planned to continue in her job as financial director while doing a part-time degree in education over five years to become a teacher. She said, 'I have always visualised myself in front of a class teaching geography – I love geography. Plus I want to make a difference in the world, I want to teach people. Looking at myself at 11, you really need someone, a role model, and I think I could put that into education. There is a real need for black teachers. When I was at school and growing up all authority figures were white. I grew up feeling uncomfortable with black teachers, I always judged them more than white ones, and I've always had white bosses. I'd like to be a role model for black children – and white children.'

Her plan would mean evening and night study on top of her demanding career, not to mention her commitments as a mother. But, she said, 'It won't be a burden because I want to achieve a lot.'

Frances's background

Frances was the oldest of three girls born in Britain to Jamaican parents. Frances said: 'My mother says she saved up and came over when she was barely 20, and met my father here. One of the reasons she came was because obviously there were a lot of opportunities here and she wanted a piece of that because she is ambitious, and also she wanted to try to get some money to Jamaica. She sends money to her mother who is still alive, and to her brothers and sisters.'

Frances remembered her early childhood in 'a loving family, cosy, a warm home, Sundays round the table, you know, rice and peas and chicken, yum yum. We were really close.' But when she was 10, her parents separated. 'When it came to the time when Mummy and Daddy divorced it started to get a bit tense. They had arguments; I would side with my mother and my sisters with my father, so the split went right through the family.'

Frances's father left, and eventually returned to Jamaica and remarried. The three girls were farmed out to live with friends and relatives while Frances's mother worked and tried to save enough money to support them all. Frances's father made no financial contribution.

'It was a big shock when they split up, and especially the repercussions. I blamed him for a long time for doing that to us. My sisters kept in touch with him but I didn't, I didn't want to. I was very angry with him.' When Frances visited Jamaica with

Simon, she saw her father again for the first time in many years. 'It was very emotional, and we cried a lot. He really cried, it's the first time I've seen my dad cry. So I've forgiven him. My mum can't understand why, she is still angry with him. But I love him dearly.'

For two years after the separation Frances lived with the family of a close friend of her mother. 'It was a horrible time. I was very . . . deviant. I was rude all the time, and I used to mess up the house, spill flour and things, do everything to show that I didn't want to be there. I would go out to play and not come home till really late. I was always running out to look for my mother and my sisters. I was really bad, really bad.

'But they loved me! They were really good to me, plus they wanted to adopt me, and that is when I really, kind of, went mad, because I definitely didn't want that.'

Eventually her mother got a council flat and the three girls went to live with her again. Frances was very close to her mother, but their relationship went through a rough patch when Frances was a teenager. Her mother wanted her to do well at school. 'Mummy was really strict: "keep your head in your books and keep out of trouble!" She wouldn't let me into the kitchen, and I was really into my books. I lost a lot of friends that way because I wasn't into going to youth clubs.

'When I got to 16 I went to my first party and that was it – I went astray! I started going out with my first boyfriend, who was almost ten years older than me. Mummy went crazy, but I was in love and I moved in with him. Mummy came and took me home, I moved back with him, she took me back home, there were terrible rows. By the time I was 17 I'd left home. I ran away and Mummy eventually gave up coming to get me back. I did carry on going to school and I did my A levels, but I didn't pass them because I had my head in the air, I was too in love, I couldn't see in front of me.'

Frances stayed with her first boyfriend for four years, but it was not a good experience. He beat her, and dominated her emotionally. 'He tried to mould me into something he wanted . . . I had a really bad time with him. He was up there, I listened to everything he said, like a sort of teacher but a bad one. I was very frightened of him. For example, he'd come into the kitchen while I was trying to cook a meal and I'd freeze, things would burn . . . he'd be watching me, telling me I was doing it wrong, I couldn't do anything. I lost all my confidence, and I lost contact with my family and friends, it was just me and him.'

Eventually Frances managed to leave him by running away. To this day she had not told anyone in her family about her first boyfriend's violence. 'I told my next boyfriend, and then he became violent too! It was ridiculous. I did leave him, though. After that I was just really angry with myself, and with men, until I met Simon. There's no way that would ever happen to me again. Men shouldn't be allowed to dominate someone like that, especially so young. I'm stronger now, a lot stronger and more confident in myself. I learned a lot from talking to other women, especially friends who are older. I think my sis-ter's boyfriend beats her up, but she is in love with him . . . She is like my mother, very strong, but still she lets him walk all over her, she just lets him do what he wants. For example, he's got kids elsewhere and still sees their mother, and she just accepts it.'

Consequently, Frances felt it was safest not to tell Simon either.

'I feel I know him well enough, but then again you can never know anyone well enough, and you should never ever take anything for granted. I never do, I'm always aware of what could and could not happen . . . so I feel I'm prepared, if something really terrible happens. As my mother says, men are hunters.'

Violence against women was not a model Frances carried with her from home. She said that she had once seen her father be violent towards her mother, but that if anything it was the other way round. 'My mother was very dominant – we say all the women in our family are very dominant. She ruled her men; she tried to rule my father and it probably got to the point where he didn't want to take it any more, and that was the end of that.'

Rather, then, the lesson that Frances learned in her own home was that dominant women get left by their men. Perhaps by allowing herself to be dominated and abused in her first relationship, Frances was in some way trying to atone for her mother's dominance and for her parents' break-up. Her sister was still caught in the contradiction of being a 'strong woman' who nevertheless let her man 'walk all over her'. Frances had come further and was now a strong woman who had chosen the man she deserved: a good man, a supportive man, and a man who was a good father. With Simon, Frances had achieved a home and a family and the child she thought she couldn't have, and with Simon she could have plans and dreams for the future.

But she felt she trod a tightrope between being a strong woman and being a dominant woman. Her position as bread-winner could easily have made her dominant, and she was concerned that Simon should not feel undermined. She wanted him to feel that everything she earned was shared. 'I bought the house, I put his name on the deed but everything is mine and I can understand that he probably feels a bit uncomfortable sometimes. But I really go all out to make him feel everything is his, my salary is his.'

As a warning example of what can happen when women start dominating their men, she mentioned her friend Vivien who had just broken up with her husband. 'Vivien didn't read the situation. She would come home with the car full of shopping and bring the baby in and say, "John, go and get the stuff in the car!" At the end of the day women have to be a bit old-fashioned – you have to pamper your man, make him feel the most important man in the world.'

Simon's background

Simon's mother also came from Jamaica in search of work and opportunities some thirty years ago, but she left her husband behind. She was pregnant with Simon when she came to England, and brought him up alone. Simon never knew his father, who was now dead. His mother never remarried or had men around. 'She's on a Christianity thing now,' Simon explained, 'so she was like "I don't need any man because I've got God and I've got Jesus."'

'It was just me and my mum': they had no other family in England, everyone was in Jamaica. But when Simon went to Jamaica with Frances, he didn't feel able to look up relatives. 'When you go to Jamaica you've got to give them things, and I didn't really have anything to give, because I wasn't working and didn't have a lot of money. If it had been a case of going round and saying hello, I'm Simon, shaking hands and sitting down and having something to eat, that would have been fine. But you can't go and not give them at least something. My mother was always going on about that. So no, I didn't see anyone, but next time I'll get round to it.'

Simon did not mind growing up as an only child in a one-parent family, he said. He believed it had made him independent and content with his own company. 'I could be inside this house for a week and it wouldn't bother me. When I'm on my own I listen to music, and I think, I think a lot, about myself and how I would like to be in a few years' time.'

He knew that where he wanted to be in ten years' time was in Jamaica. He had persuaded his mother to return, and that had been a great success. His mother had lived on a run-down council estate in Bristol, notorious for crime, vandalism and the lifts not working, and the winters were taking their toll on her health. 'I was thinking about the sunshine out there. She lives in the country now, and she grows her own food. Jamaica is a very fertile country, everyone grows their own things. And she looks like a different person. The difference is amazing. She gets her state pension from here which they send over there. She's a rich woman by Jamaican standards; she's doing a lot better than me.'

On his visit with Frances, Simon had been very taken with the climate and the pace of life.

'In Jamaica life is laid back. I would like the time to appreciate things, to watch the sun go down and the stars come out, which you can't even do here: here you come home from work and just want to sit down in front of the telly, here you can't appreciate things and life is short – look, I'm almost 30 already. I want to appreciate things, watch yourself progress, look at yourself, sit back and take it easy, really, or even watch Daniel grow up.'

He didn't think it would be difficult to make a living in Jamaica. 'I would do an Arthur Daley, there is a lot of opportunity if you go with a fresh idea. Jamaicans are lazy, they don't like to work, they like to do things easy. The traditional thing is "soon come" . . . I mean, once they get up and going they are fine, but just to give them that initial push, because the ideas we have over here they would never think of. For example a travel agency, that's nothing to do really, all you need is contacts and a few airports and an office. Or a minicab service, something simple, they would never think of it.'

He also wanted the time and the chance to talk to his mother. He missed her enormously. Although their relationship was close, he said, it was also distant, 'because I don't really know my mum. Even though I have lived with her for years I haven't really sat down and talked to her as a man to his mother. I'd still like to know about my dad, how she was feeling at the time. I haven't just sat down and talked to her, but I will do one day, sit her down in a corner and have a couple of hours just to talk.'

Simon left school at 16, partly under pressure to start earning money and contributing to the household. 'The way my mother made it sound I was lucky to get any job at all,' he said.

He started out in retail sales, and made it up to assistant manager, but then left, impatient with not being made manager. 'I wanted to run my own shop, I was really running the show anyway. So I left. It was a bit hot-headed because if I'd stayed I might be running the place now. It went downhill after that really.'

He was unemployed for a few years, then did a course in business administration, had various office jobs, taught a course at the community college, then left his job to set up his own business, with Frances's help, but it didn't work. For a couple of years now he had been supported by Frances. He had mixed feelings about his financial dependency.

The couple, the choice

Money matters?

On the one hand, Simon did not feel that his lack of earnings caused friction between them, because, he said, 'Frances is not like that, the money side doesn't really bother her. I suppose if I was a different person and going "Frances, give me money" all the time, but I believe in making your own money – what is yours is yours, or in our case what is ours is ours, you've got to contribute in some way. I'm not really driven by money, I would rather be driven by the relationship and make that work and money can come later. Money can't make you happy. Money can't give your relationship stability.'

On the other hand, he did feel that being a non-earner meant that he had to take a back seat in the relationship. He said, 'When Frances comes home from work it's not to say that we sit down and have a conversation, more like reflecting on what she's done at work and stuff like that. We can't sit down and have a conversation about us, or hardly. I don't push her into that, because you've got to be understanding. She's the breadwinner, and I can't go, "Oh, what are we going to do next?" when she wants to sit down and get herself together and relax her brain. I've been in the house with the baby all day and I want conversation, but she's been working 12 hours and she needs time to relax. I never usually make suggestions until I get a vibe from Frances that she is willing to talk about a certain thing. So our relationship could be better, but I'm not really in control of it because she's working. If it was down to me she'd be here all day with me! But I have to understand that she's out there doing it.'

And he added, 'I don't really mind, because obviously she is in a high-profile job and to tell you the truth, I kind of look forward to when she comes home and we talk about her work and I go, "Well, babe, I think you should do this and this", because I see myself as that kind of person.

'It's not that I think I should be the man, the breadwinner, but I'd like to be doing my piece, because it's been bred in me that if I want something I'll do it for myself. I've always catered for myself as a one-parent child, and I don't want anyone to say, "All right Simon I'll help you out" – even though she doesn't mind, she loves it really. But it's just my self-pride, I shouldn't need anyone to do it for me. And it's about self-satisfaction, for myself, that I could dip into my pocket for anything we need. I feel a bit inadequate, in a way. And I don't have any money to give Latisha when I'm not working, there is that aspect as well: that I'm not fulfilling that side as I think I should.'

Frances said similar things.

'When Simon was earning I would buy him things, a pair of shorts or something, and he didn't mind, but now he's not earning he doesn't want it and I understand why. He can't do the things he wants to for Daniel and for his daughter. It's a man thing, he doesn't feel a "complete man", he wants something even if it's only a bit each month and not just to watch me tot up the figures, "Oh we've got enough today, darling." It has affected our relationship a bit in that he stays in the background now, but I think it'll be OK when he goes to work full-time. I'm not really happy that he's going to be working for the DIY store,

I wish he would do something that would push him mentally because he is an intelligent person. But it's important that he gets out of the house and I think that's why he likes the job.'

Sex matters

Despite this slight tension over earning capacity, Frances and Simon showed that they appreciated each other; Frances appreciated Simon's emotional support, while Simon appreciated Frances's hard work as provider. They spoke tenderly about each other, and were generous with praise throughout the interviews.

Frances said, 'Simon is just a good person. He's bordering on the spiritual so he could easily become a Christian, and he's so good with Daniel, and . . . last night, for example, we were at a dinner dance, and I was asked what wine I wanted and I said white, and then the waitress asked Simon and he said, "I'm going with what my woman wants", and it was just so nice and all the girls round the table went, aaahh!

'And he looks good . . . and he's understanding, he'll listen if I have a problem, and advise me. He gives me lots of love and attention. He makes me feel good, and confident, and he's really good, a good person and a good friend.'

And Simon said: 'Frances is unique. She looks after me, she'll go out on a limb for me. Like with the business plan, she did most of the groundwork for me, she would give up days at work for me. And every morning she'll say, "Simon, are you OK for money?" I mean bloody hell, people don't really do that for me – I find that very, very unique. And in a couple of weeks we are going away for the weekend, and she's organised it all, booked this and booked that, and made sure I've got the least amount of things to do.'

Their weekend away in a five-star hotel was to be child-free; Daniel was to be looked after by Frances's middle sister while Simon and Frances recouped some time for themselves as a couple. 'I sat down and thought, Simon and I need some complete time together, so I booked it, hired a car, and told him it was all arranged,' said Frances. 'He was over the moon, and we're going to really enjoy it. I expect we'll have a weekend of debauchery.'

Frances thought sex a very important part of their relationship. 'If he wasn't good in bed we wouldn't be together now.'

For Frances, sex with Simon was different from her previous experiences. 'My experience with my first boyfriend affected me in a funny way, actually . . . It wasn't like I went frigid or anything, it was the total opposite, I became a complete nymphomaniac. It was like, "I'm in control, I don't have to have sex with you if I don't want to" – and then having sex and using them, as was done to me. Damn, it was weird. It went on for a long time, and then I just had to calm down and look at myself and what I wanted. It wasn't like that with Simon, because it was a long time before we went to bed, and it was lovely, we made love, we didn't "have sex". But it also helped, being like that with him, a bit dominant. It got him going and made him decide that this is the woman I want. I think Simon was in awe for a long time.

'Now, having the baby, we have it less. It's difficult to find the time, and I come home from work tired. Simon is not the type to say, "I want sex tonight", he'd wait for me to approach him as I did at the beginning. I like making the advance, I still like being a bit dominant, it comes out now and again, and he loves it. But I don't feel comfortable when Daniel is there, I feel he might wake up and spoil it.'

Simon, too, was pleased with their sex life, and he didn't even think it had been adversely affected by having a baby. 'It's funny, because with Frances, the relationship always seems as if we just met each other. Things are very new, and even making love is still fresh, like a taste in your mouth. It's amazing really, because I've never come across that in anybody before. It's one of those mysteries, and I'm glad it's happening, and glad I can't put my finger on it because then it would be mundane and put in the pocket like everything else.'

Ambitions

Both said independently that they thought the relationship could last for the rest of their lives.

Frances said, 'I can see it lasting for ever and I hope it does. We've got so much to do together and it would be a shame to lose it. I can see us growing old together, Daniel coming in with his wife . . . Simon's the one, you know, he's the one.'

Simon said: 'It can last as long as we want it to. It can go the whole nine yards, really, yes, definitely. I'm comfortable – not because she's earning vast sums of money but because she makes me feel comfortable and I make her feel comfortable, and trivial domestic nonsense doesn't come into it. It's more, "What's going to happen tomorrow? and next year?"'

Their plans and ambitions for the future were an important focus for their relationship. On the one hand they wanted to achieve increasing material comfort – a new car, a bigger house, 'and I want to be able to turn round to Daniel and say, "Here's ten grand",' said Frances. 'My mother worked all the hours God sent and at the time it was horrible. But now I think it's good, because she bought a house and she is going to emigrate back to Jamaica, and she pulls money out of all sorts of corners. My mother is comfortable now. What upsets me is when I hear of friends whose parents are still in council flats. I think, "They worked hard, why haven't they got any money?"'

Frances, as we have seen, was not afraid of the prospect of working a full day as financial director and then going on to night school to become a teacher, because, as she said, 'I want to achieve a lot.'

Simon said, 'We've had it hard from day one, really. Your parents are strict on you, then school, then they're strict at work – so you know, life is not easy. You can incorporate that into going out and achieving your goals.'

Simon especially came across as an individualist, saying that he did not vote for any political party on the grounds that 'everyone should support themselves before they start supporting anyone else. Check yourself first.' He didn't much value having black MPs because, he said, 'I don't want anyone to represent me, I'll do it my way, I can't see how they are going to help *me*.'

Neither was politically minded and both felt that although they had experienced the racism institutionalised in British society, they had not felt it in a personal sense. Simon said, 'If you are looking for it you see racism everywhere and if you don't you don't.'

Frances said, 'We didn't really know about racism when we were growing up. What really changed it for black kids was when *Roots* came on, that was like oh, racism, racism. I do remember that all the white girls in my class did typing, but the teacher said it was not necessary for me to do typing, so that put me back a bit. When we left school it was easier for them to find a job than for me: all the white girls went into the typing pool. When I left I only had sociology, English and geography, and what can you do with that? I said to the careers teacher I wanted a job in sales.'

'I think sales was the only avenue open to us,' said Simon. 'I went into sales after school – it was the only place that would take you on. The way my mother made it sound, I was lucky to get anything at all. Her attitude did lower my expectations, yes.'

Now, with Frances, Simon felt able to raise his sights. If in practice she was the achiever while he was the supporter, it was a division of labour which seemed to work well for them. Their relationship was a fresh start for both of them, in which the choice of partner was crucial.

When Frances met Simon, she was reeling from two abusive relationships, which left her suspicious of and angry with men. Simon represented a new sort of choice: a good man, not into control and abuse, but loving and above all supportive: of

Frances as a worker, as a father and househusband; supportive emotionally; and supportive in their joint ambition to achieve a lot. By choosing Simon Frances seemed to be saying, 'This time I am going to treat myself well.'

For Simon, Frances was a new kind of woman in that she was a grown-up, someone with whom he could share serious conversation and planning for the future. His relationship with Dawn had not been a relationship of equals, they couldn't communicate. But with Frances he could talk, and he frequently emphasised how important talking was in their relationship. Frances also made him feel cared for, not least by providing for them materially. Far from resenting this, he appreciated it. His career might not have taken off, but instead he could take pleasure in Frances's successes and feel proud of her. Yet he was careful not to exploit her and felt strongly about making his contribution. So he chose to go back to work to a job that was not very challenging but which would bring in some money. 'We have a good balance going,' said Frances, and it certainly appeared to be true.

There was just one thing hovering over them which had the power to upset their family stability, and that was the existence of Simon's 'other family'. Frances had criticised her sister for 'just accepting' that her boyfriend had another family, but in fact Frances had little choice but to do the same.

She did not find it easy. She regarded Dawn with contempt, and felt uncomfortable with Latisha. When Latisha came to visit, said Frances, 'I do get a bit funny. I leave the room and stay upstairs with Daniel; yes, I do get a bit jealous. I don't know if I'll ever get out of that little bit of jealousy. Simon doesn't understand my feelings about it, he never has and he never will. Simon doesn't like conflict or anything to mess with his head and so if I say anything it's, "Oh you're being silly, you're being silly." No, he doesn't understand.

'And when I was giving birth I did think that Simon had been there before – but then I thought, I'm having a boy! I am glad I was able to provide a boy for him, because men have something about boys. But then Latisha is his only daughter . . . I want more children – but for the wrong reasons! I want a girl, so then we'll have a boy and a girl, and *that'll* be the family.'

CHAPTER FOUR

Crossroads

HOW does the original choice stay alive in the daily round of working, looking after children, cooking, cleaning and planning for the next day? And does it even matter?

As the relationship takes root and grows, and as the lives of the two individuals weave into each other and the network of family, friends, work and community, the original attraction may come to seem just the little acorn out of which a whole oak has sprung forth. In a good relationship, the liking and the love, the mutual support, and the daily sense of pleasure in a person whom one knows well, naturally overshadow the question of what it was that made one fall for the other at the start.

But at certain points in life the relationship may be called into question and the original choice re-examined. Well-documented times of stress are the birth of the first child, the time when children leave home, and retirement. Events such as redundancy or moving house can also cause great strain. A change in one partner, for example the development of a new interest, a change of career, returning to work, or a new friendship, can all give the relationship a jolt. Then old patterns of living and relating to each other have to be adapted. There is the practical renegotiation: for example, he has to be home to look after the children two evenings a week because she is on a course. There is also an emotional renegotiation; a new image and a new understanding of one's partner have to follow. She is no longer purely a wife and a mother but a worker, who leaves the house and meets other people . . . He is now passionately involved in local politics but when she met him he wasn't political at all, so is he still the man she married? These kinds of changes can be threatening and difficult to absorb but can also bring new life to a relationship.

At times of change the couple relationship comes into focus again. Tacitly, the question is asked, 'Is our original choice of each other still right, even though things have changed?' and, 'Can we adapt to the changes together, or will we grow apart?'

This chapter contains the stories of two couples who had been married fourteen and eighteen years respectively. Both stood at a crossroads, though not one occasioned by the standard big events of the life-cycle. The first couple, Cheryl and Michael, had just seen their youngest child off to school. They were both devoted parents; Cheryl derived her greatest confidence from being a mother. They now faced the question: what next for us as a couple, with the first and most intense phase of parenting behind us? As Cheryl said, she couldn't bear to go out into the street without the protection of a pushchair, because then people looked directly at *her*. Her lack of confidence as a non-mother made her afraid that her husband would start looking at her as a woman and a sexual being – but also just as afraid that he might not. Cheryl and Michael's crossroads was like an uncultivated patch of land where all manner of plants might be seeded. They made lively use of the interviews, bringing up all kinds of issue, as if trying to decide which plants to choose for nurture.

The other couple, Jane and George, had both recently turned 40. This signalled the end of Jane's period of fertility, and yet they had never been able to agree on how many children they wanted. They had a teenage daughter and for Jane, an only child herself, this was enough. But George had always wanted more – and now it was getting too late.

At a crossroads, people feel uncertain about which road to take. They may want to take the safe road, where they continue to relate to each other as they always have done. This may have been one attraction of taking part in the interviews: to have the chance to reaffirm the strengths of the relationship, to say, 'We share these things, and we do this and this together, and we work well together, and do you remember when . . .?' Or there is the more challenging road, where old patterns of relating that are no longer so satisfying can be looked at anew. By allowing themselves to be interviewed, people might also have hoped for the opportunity to air their dissatisfactions, as well as their inchoate hopes for change. But this road is dangerous, because, who knows, the relationship might not stand up to such scrutiny. Not surprisingly, people usually chose to make their complaints in their individual interviews when their partner was not present.

Cheryl and Michael seemed to be trying to set off down both roads at once. On the safe road they would continue as they were: comfortable with each other, plenty of laughs, but more parents than partners, which meant that their sex life was not very satisfying. On the challenging road, which Cheryl explored verbally in her individual interview, they would have adult time together and more satisfying sex. She might even wear sexy underwear.

Jane and George's safe road also meant continuing comfortable, in a low-key sort of way. The high-risk road would involve being more open about their real feelings and acknowledging certain disappointments and conflicts.

Cheryl and Michael:
'We just go together!'

Cheryl and Michael were both in their early thirties and had three children: two daughters aged 11 and seven, and a son aged five who had just started school. They lived in Birmingham in a slightly dark and crumbling flat which came with Michael's job as deputy nursing manager in a hospital. Michael gestured around the living-room and said regretfully that the three-piece suite belonged to the health authority while the TV was rented and the hi-fi on loan from a friend; their finances were not strong. But they appreciated what they had. They came across as a lively, warm couple, and they were a happy family. Cheryl said, 'We laugh a lot. If you ask the children they would probably say we were mad. We skate across the living-room and on Sunday morning we have discos in the house – the Sunday morning "blast".'

How they met
They were 19 when they married, just six months after they started going out together. They met when they were both working in a London hospital, he as a student nurse and she as a nursing auxiliary. Their wedding was precipitated by the threat of being parted. Cheryl was due to start nursing training in a hospital in the north of England. She had applied for a place there before she met Michael.

'The day came, my boxes were all packed. Mike took me to the train,' she recalled.

'We were crying like a couple of kids,' said Michael. 'So I said to her, don't go.'

They went to a coffee bar, where Michael proposed to her. Cheryl rang the personnel officer and told her she wouldn't be starting training after all. She continued her job as a nursing auxiliary for a couple of months. Then Michael qualified and moved to a hospital in another area, where Cheryl couldn't find a job. Her career came to an end and she settled down to being Michael's wife. Their first child was born a couple of years later. Michael, meanwhile, moved up the career ladder, and was currently studying for a degree in health management.

Many teenagers in Cheryl and Michael's situation would not have married on the strength of a six-month relationship but would have hearkened to the call of adventure and consoled themselves with the thought that there would be other fish in the sea. But for Michael and Cheryl this was not an option. Why not? Cheryl said, 'I wasn't like that. I knew from the beginning – I really do believe there is love at first sight. Mike had had girlfriends before, but I was quiet and had never had a boyfriend. Mike was my first and I just knew. Mike had all these plans not to get married until he was 28, and I hadn't even thought about it. It was just like that. But with Mike it felt right. I knew we'd get married as soon as I saw him really, we were so comfortable together. I can't imagine him not being there. We just go together!'

Michael added, 'We were so strongly attached by then.'

Michael quickly became very possessive of Cheryl. For him, 'It was the first time I fell in love. I remember being very scared of losing her, which perhaps was why it dawned on me that I did love her. If a man spoke to her in the hospital corridor I would make a beeline for them because I felt he was a threat to me and Cheryl.'

How did they come to make such a rapid and strong attachment that they were made desperate by the thought of parting after such a short time together? Partly, it seemed, they were just two youngsters away from home for the first time, clinging to each other for safety in the face of the unknown. As the story below will suggest, an important aspect of the psychological 'fit' between Michael and Cheryl was that each sensed that here was someone with whom they could delay facing some of the challenges of adulthood for a while.

On one level they were extremely adult. Michael worked

hard and took his responsibilities as provider very seriously (and suffered feelings of failure because his salary always fell short). Cheryl was a full-time mother, competent and caring and very much there for her children. But paradoxically, their strong investment in their family and parenthood protected them from the demands of 'growing up' in other important areas – particularly where relations with the outside world were concerned, and in the area of sex.

At the time of the interviews they had been married for fourteen years. Michael was about to complete a degree which would take his career forward in a leap. Their youngest child had started school, which meant that Cheryl was no longer indispensable as a full-time mother. Changes lay ahead for both of them. Was their original choice strong enough to adapt to this new phase of their relationship, in which they might grow individually – and together?

The interviews with Cheryl and Michael seemed to take place on the cusp of their old way of being playmates and parents, and a new way, still waiting to be formed. Both of them showed themselves pushing forward and then pulling back, just as adolescents who are tossed between drives towards independence and retreats to the safety of home base.

Cheryl's background

Cheryl was born and raised near Leeds, and she had one older brother. She remembered little about her childhood, but in adolescence was 'quiet', and never had boyfriends until she met Mike. 'I didn't go out a lot – it wasn't that I was sheltered, but I was so tall and gangly, and skinny then, and I had big feet. I was very insecure about myself then.' In fact, she was still insecure about herself; her insecurity became a major theme of the interviews.

Cheryl was extremely close to her mother. She had been deeply shocked when her mother died, quite suddenly, a few years ago. Even now, Cheryl could not talk about her without tears filling her eyes. Her mother had been her closest, and only real friend. Her mother, too, had been the only person to whom Cheryl would entrust her children.

When Cheryl's mother married Cheryl's father, his parents cut them both off because they disapproved of him. Gradually, too, Cheryl's mother became alienated from her own family, and stopped seeing her brothers and sisters one by one. Cheryl could not really explain this slow falling out, but suggested it had to do with money: all her mother's siblings did very well for themselves and grew richer, while her mother and father only grew poorer. 'I think they were afraid that my mother would ask them for something. But she would never have done that, she was very proud. She had a lot of self-respect.'

By contrast, Cheryl's father emerged as a weak man. He had been dependent on Cheryl's mother in many ways – she was the one who kept the home going, she was the one with the get-up-and-go. He was a travelling salesman but stopped working on grounds of ill-health when he was only 50. After Cheryl's mother died he moved into sheltered accommodation – the youngest resident there. 'He is happy to let everyone run around him, he wouldn't do anything if he didn't have to – it makes me mad really,' said Cheryl. Then she added, 'But he's very good really; if I needed him he'd come, if I needed babysitting, for example. He would have the children if I wanted to go away for a weekend. Mind you, I wouldn't let him have them.'

Cheryl was very fond of her brother Tom, and so was Michael, who regarded him as his own brother. Tom was a frequent and welcome visitor at their house, often arriving in the company of a new girlfriend. He was in the army and as he lived in barracks where he was not allowed to entertain women, he brought them to spend the night at Cheryl and Michael's house. He was twice married and twice divorced; a philanderer whose exploits Cheryl and Michael regarded with a mixture of disapproval and fascination.

The picture Cheryl painted of her background revolved

around a strong mother whose pride caused the household to become increasingly cut off from the outside world. Her father hovered ineffectually on the periphery, and as a travelling sales-man was often absent altogether. At 16 Cheryl left school and then waited impatiently until she was accepted to work in a London hospital. Perhaps she was so keen to get away from home because, in spite of their closeness, she needed to get out from beneath her mother's shadow. The prominence which Cheryl gave to her 'insecurity' in the interviews suggested that far from inheriting her mother's 'strength', she had been under-mined by it. A girl who grows up with a parental model of a strong mother and a weak father may pick up the message that strong women emasculate men. She herself may then bend over backwards to insist on her own 'weakness', for fear of repeating her parents' relationship.

Michael's background

Michael was born and brought up in the East End of London, the middle one of three boys. His father worked his way up to a managerial position and was now at last able to enjoy a com-fortable lifestyle. His mother was a housewife; a woman who, according to Michael, could be very touchy and 'blow hot and cold'. This was one reason why, in his late teens, he had wanted to leave home.

Both his parents drank heavily. His father always had done: Michael's childhood memories were punctuated by his father's violent outbursts on Saturday afternoons, and the rows between his parents on Wednesday and Friday evenings when he came home from darts night at the pub. More recently, Michael's mother had joined Michael's father in his drinking. She would try to hide it when Michael and Cheryl visited by bringing in a large glass of lemonade for herself, 'as if one couldn't smell the gin'. When she was drunk she became senti-mental and made great promises to Michael and Cheryl's children, which she had forgotten by the following day, and this was one of the reasons they didn't like to visit for long.

Michael was his father's favourite; the only one of the three sons to turn out well. The oldest brother, Mark, was an alcoholic, and the youngest, Martin, was chronically unemployed and lived at home. Michael and Cheryl would never think of leaving their children with his parents, partly because of their drinking and partly because Michael did not trust Martin around them.

As a teenager, Michael wanted to be a doctor. However, he did not receive much encouragement from his parents, and after coming to blows, literally, with a teacher, he dropped out of A levels and applied to do nursing. 'Typical frustrated doctor,' he called himself. His current degree course would go some way to making up for his frustrated ambitions.

These days his parents were very proud of him. Cheryl commented that Michael cared very much about pleasing his parents. Certainly as the only good egg in the family, it seemed that family responsibility rested heavily on his shoulders. 'I know when the time comes it will fall to me to make the funeral arrangements,' he said.

In his own family, too, Michael took the protective, caring role. He was acutely conscious of the dangers threatening from the world outside. 'There are some nasty people around,' he said. 'I see them in Casualty and Psychiatry.' As a consequence, all his children were sent to karate classes: 'No one is going to rape my daughters.'

The couple, the choice

A certain suspicion or fear of the world outside was a trait which Cheryl and Michael shared. Michael tended to express it in terms of the baddies out there, while Cheryl was more inclined to attribute it to her own 'insecurity'. She was reluctant to meet new people or go to new places because 'I'm not comfortable with strangers'.

In the last few years while Cheryl stayed at home as a

full-time mother, Michael had been forging ahead in his career by means of study. He had devoted evenings and weekends and holidays to it, and was now in his final year. Now that their youngest son had started school, Cheryl was left to spend a lot of time alone at home, somewhat bereft and aimless.

She said that in the four months since her son started school, she had only been out on her own twice. 'It's scary to go out on my own without a child or a buggy to push. People wouldn't have the buggy to look at, they'd look at me – it was very strange.' She had recently acquired a new buggy to push, by taking on childminding for two toddlers in the neighbourhood. In practice, then, Cheryl and Michael's shared distrust of the big bad world led them into opposite ways of dealing with it. While Michael grasped its challenges by the horns, even by the very nature of his work, Cheryl retreated into the home.

'I'm too insecure'

Her own career had of course come to an abrupt end when she was 19 and married Michael. Now she thought she might like to go back to working in a hospital, or perhaps do a course in childcare, as she was so fond of children. But there was always some obstacle standing in her way, as illustrated by this circular conversation which took place between her and Michael in the final interview. Michael was pressing her to do a course, and Cheryl was resisting on the grounds that she was too insecure.

MICHAEL: Cheryl doesn't have a lot of faith in herself and her abilities. It frustrates me.

CHERYL: Yes, it frustrates him.

MICHAEL: I write off regularly for lists of correspondence courses she could do, to broaden herself, but she won't.

CHERYL: I don't have the confidence. So.

MICHAEL: You won't know until you try.

CHERYL: It's like driving the car, I won't do that. But then I said I would never be able to learn my Highway Code and I did, so maybe the potential is there . . . [*She had passed her test, but would not drive.*]

MICHAEL: You're scared of looking silly.

CHERYL: I'd love to do a nursery nursing course, wouldn't I? Because I love children, I'd like something child oriented – but it's having the confidence, and the time. It all comes down to driving the car: independence.

MICHAEL: I'm convinced Cheryl has a lot of untapped potential to do things, for herself. But she won't do anything.

CHERYL: No.

MICHAEL: You'd rather sit and watch *Neighbours*. It drives me mad.

CHERYL: I know what he means. But it's having the time: I look after the children, I look after the home, when am I supposed to fit in a course, and revising? In the evenings I'm tired! I couldn't sit down in the dining-room and concentrate on books then.

MICHAEL: Unless it was something you were really interested in – then you wouldn't feel tired.

CHERYL: I don't want to go out in the evenings. I don't want to do a course – not yet. There are things I'm interested in, but to me, the time will come.

MICHAEL: Just something for yourself, even if it was cake decorating or basic car maintenance . . .

CHERYL: Mike has hobbies: bird-watching and cars. I do nothing. Mike wants me to have a hobby. What? The things I would like to do we can't afford. I'd love to join a fitness centre, for example. But we can't afford it.

MICHAEL: You could go to the aerobics class at the leisure centre.

CHERYL: I hate aerobics! And there would be men there and I wouldn't like that.

MICHAEL: The thing is, you don't know until you look, do you?

CHERYL: No.

MICHAEL: There are so many courses and things you could do.

CHERYL: I would love to do a nursery-nurse qualification, but it's a whole day a week, and it doesn't fit in with Mike's work. And there is nobody who will have my children for two hours till Mike or I get home – so you're stuck.

MICHAEL: I know the course she means, but the local tech doesn't do it.

CHERYL: Which would mean going further afield.

MICHAEL: Which would mean driving the car, which she won't do.

CHERYL: And the time.

MICHAEL: And the time – and driving the car, let's not get away from that. But there are childcare courses you could do by correspondence.

CHERYL: They cost a lot of money.

MICHAEL: You can pay monthly.

CHERYL: It's still a lot of money, isn't it? Three hundred pounds! It's a hell of a lot of money.

MICHAEL: But you gain something at the end.

CHERYL: And have to go without something else in the meantime.

MICHAEL: Perhaps I am being unrealistic about the finances. But for everything I come up with, you come up with something else.

CHERYL: Yes – perhaps I am just making excuses. But with the correspondence course it is the money.

MICHAEL: Evening classes cost £70–80.

CHERYL: But then it's driving the car.

(*Great laughter.*)

But despite his protestations that he wished Cheryl would become more independent and find something 'for herself', Michael's emphasis on *correspondence* courses hinted at his actual ambivalence about Cheryl going out into the world. To Michael, a correspondence course may have seemed a good compromise. Cheryl would 'broaden' herself, and thus take a few steps towards catching up with him, without leaving the home. He still needed her to stay more or less where she was so that he could continue to feel that she needed him. This polarisation, where Cheryl was almost paralysed by 'insecurity' while Michael completed a degree course at the same time as he held down a full-time job, provided for his family and took part in all the social activities connected with his job, was surely an example of a 'projective exchange' between them. Cheryl was probably carrying a 'double load' and expressing both of their feelings of insecurity, while 'handing over' to Michael her capable part, which he put to use in his own endeavours.

Looked at in terms of 'growing up together', this exchange over what was billed as 'Cheryl's insecurity' was an example of a dynamic working both between the two of them, and between them as a couple and the outside world. 'Let's go and explore the world!' 'No, let's stay here where it's safe, it's scary out there.' Young children alternate between clinging and letting go as they venture out into the world – it was as if Michael and Cheryl were experiencing the same as their son who had recently started school. Later, on a bolder scale, adolescents go through the same stage of alternate forging ahead and retreat.

Us against the big bad world

If Michael was often allocated the role of the bold one who seemed to say 'let's go', while Cheryl was the timid one who said 'let's stay' this was not always so. They were not always polarised. In some of their relations with the outside world they seemed very much to share a *contra mundi* streak – us against the world. Their relations with their respective families were wary; the only trustworthy person had been Cheryl's mother. The same was even more true of friends. Cheryl had no close female friends. Michael had one close male friend with whom he liked to spend the day bird-watching. But, he said, 'I quite like sitting in the hide on my own'.

Cheryl said, 'Michael would be happy on a little desert island, wouldn't you, without people?'

'Sometimes.'

'So long as I'm there,' Cheryl added.

'And the immediate family,' said Michael. 'Sometimes I find other people intensely irritating and selfish – it's all me me me.'

Cheryl concurred. 'Mmm. We'd like to go and live somewhere quiet,' she said. 'The ideal would be a little farm in the country, with a cow, a couple of chickens – aren't we boring!'

Michael said, 'I have often thought I could retire from nursing and take part-time work as a warden on a bird reserve and live in a little cottage.'

'It might happen,' said Cheryl. And later she added, 'Our time will come. We will move to the country later.'

Cheryl and Michael's *contra mundi* attitude was a streak, not the whole canvas of their lives. It somewhat inhibited their friendships and relations with family. But on the positive side, it enhanced their investment in their family. They derived pride and pleasure from being loving parents and creating a happy and safe home.

Having said that, something had recently happened which brought the outside world right into their living-room like a burning fireball. Cheryl had discovered, or thought she had discovered, that Michael was having an affair.

'Why would a man say no?'

Some months before, Michael had worked on a study project with a group of other students, which took up several evenings a week. Cheryl thought she began to notice the name Sandy cropping up a lot whenever he talked about it. Once when she rang him in the evening the person who answered the phone said she would get him from 'Sandy's room'. So by the time Cheryl actually met Sandy at the end-of-project party, her suspicions had been aroused, and when she found Sandy to be a young, slim, blonde, pretty and intelligent woman, she 'flipped'.

She made a scene at the party, and was upset for long enough to ring the local council asking to be rehoused as a single mother.

Michael denied categorically that he had ever contemplated an affair, let alone had one. 'I have no inclination to have an affair with anyone, I'm not that sort of person – that's me.' After a big argument they had managed to talk about it and Cheryl had eventually believed what Michael said and calmed down, attributing her 'flip' to pre-menstrual tension. And so within a day or two, the fireball doused in cold water, everything was once again 'tickety-boo – that's us', in Michael's words.

And yet things were not back to normal. Cheryl could not let go of the thought of the affair: why had Michael *not* had an affair with a woman as attractive as Sandy? What was wrong with him that he didn't want an affair? Again, a to-and-fro exchange took place between them. It began with the question of how Michael dealt with working in a predominantly female environment.

MICHAEL: They're mates – friends – the gender is not important. I would be lying to say I didn't see them sexually, but that is not the same as seeing them as potential conquests. I've been in this field for sixteen years, it's like working in a chocolate factory, you stop wanting chocolate. The temptation isn't there. The first thing is, I wouldn't do it to Cheryl and the kids. And I'm not really interested.

CHERYL: You see, I don't understand that. It can't be right. I can't imagine any man, Mike, *any* man, being offered something on a plate and not taking it. Why say no if a tall leggy blonde threw herself at him?

MICHAEL: It would depend on the strength of the relationship behind you – and I see no reason to do that. Why?

CHERYL: And I don't understand that. I just . . . I can't understand it. Why would a man say no? Why wouldn't he want to try others after fourteen years? Wouldn't you like a change? I know he had girlfriends before but . . .

MICHAEL: Why? What is to be gained from a quick one-night stand?

CHERYL: You must fancy other women.

MICHAEL: I don't view other women as potential conquests. I think they're attractive, but not, 'I have to get her home and into bed'. Perhaps I'm unusual.

CHERYL: I don't know, because I don't know that many men, but I don't understand it and wonder if he says it because it's what I want to hear.

MICHAEL: I could turn it round: what about you?

CHERYL: What?

MICHAEL: With other guys.

CHERYL: No one would want me so it makes no difference.

INTERVIEWER: Have you never asked yourself if you are attracted to other men?

CHERYL: No, I don't think so . . . I'm quite happy as I am.

MICHAEL: So you've answered the question you are asking me.

CHERYL: I think it's different for a man.

MICHAEL: You are making assumptions.

CHERYL: Yes I am, I am generalising and I shouldn't, but you know I do that kind of thing. Why would someone give up someone else for me?

MICHAEL: Turn it round; why would I give you up for someone else?

CHERYL: I've had three children, I'm overweight, I have lumps and bumps where I shouldn't have . . .

MICHAEL: *We've* had three children.

CHERYL; A ruined body!

MICHAEL: That's why we've got the fitness plan tape, isn't it? You've just got to take me at my word, kid.

CHERYL: I know. See, this is us.

Michael said he would not have an affair because he wasn't that sort of person and because Cheryl and his family were too important for him to risk losing them. But he did not say, 'I don't want an affair because Cheryl is the one who is attractive to me and I'm sexually satisfied by her.' Perhaps he wasn't sure how attractive he did find his wife. If so, it was surely understandable that Cheryl went on pushing the way she did, because nothing Michael said was fully reassuring.

And Cheryl had a further concern. If Michael was really telling the truth when he said he was not interested in having an affair with such an attractive woman as Sandy, then what was wrong with him? Was his sex drive abnormally weak? Was he not a real red-blooded man?

In addition, Cheryl's prodding – 'Don't you fancy other women? Don't you wonder what it would be like with someone else?' – must also be seen against the background of her individual interview, in which she asked exactly these questions of herself, in spite of her denial in the joint interview. Indeed, although she came over so timid and unconfident in her and Michael's discussion about courses, in her individual interview she showed that she was quite boldly thinking about change – not change by means of a correspondence course, but change in their sex life and her own sexuality.

'I would love to take him away for the weekend'
Cheryl said she had sometimes thought of going to a sex therapist, 'to find out why I am like I am – why I'm not overly sexed, and are other women like that? Sometimes sex feels like a chore, and it's not always just because I'm tired. If something happened and I could never have it again I don't think I'd be bothered. Some part of me holds back, and it feels as if something's missing. Perhaps it's not, perhaps everyone feels like that. Sometimes over the years I wonder, am I missing something, what do other people do, what would it feel like with someone else . . .?'

She said she didn't often have orgasms. 'I do feel – not always satisfied, because it would take longer, but I don't know how long. I can't tell Mike what I want, because I don't know. So perhaps if I saw a sex therapist she would be able to sort out what holds me back. Do other women feel the same? It would be interesting to see someone who knows how other women feel.' And if she found that plenty of other women felt like her, would it then be good enough? 'No, it's not good enough, if things can be improved.' Was her 'holding back' in sex in some way linked with the idea that strong women emasculated men? If she were able to enjoy sex robustly, might she not frighten Michael, if he was not very confident in his own performance?

She said that sex had got better since she started taking oil of evening primrose for her pre-menstrual tension: now she was more willing to 'experiment'. She said she would love to wear beautiful underwear. 'But look at me! I saw a woman undress on a games show, and she looked grotesque – she had stockings, basque, the lot – and I thought, that's how I would look. I don't talk to Mike about it because I know what he would say – that I was being silly.

'And we don't spend enough time on our own. I would love to take him away for the weekend. But we can't afford it, and it's getting someone you trust to look after three children for you. So perhaps as we get older . . . I don't remember the last time we had quality time together, not since we had children.'

In this part of her interview, Cheryl seemed to be expressing a wish for a satisfying adult sex life as an adult couple. But how might Michael react? Michael was not to know what she was thinking about – at least not yet. Her insistence in their discussion that surely every man would want to get into bed with a sexy woman who came within his reach, and surely there was something wrong with a man who did not, can be seen as a kind of preliminary probing of what Michael's attitude to a sexier sex life might be. If he really didn't think of Sandy in sexual terms, then perhaps he wasn't very interested in sex. Perhaps he was actually content with their sex life as it was.

Michael did not talk openly about his feelings about sex. There were just hints that he was uncomfortable with the subject. There was his ambivalence about the sexually charged figure of Cheryl's brother Tom walking in and out of their home: he thought he should stop him, but found it hard to say no when he brought his girlfriends back.

There was also the matter of having his pre-adolescent daughters karate trained so that they might know how to resist rapists. A running joke whenever they saw youths with multi-coloured Mohican haircuts in town was to warn their oldest daughter that if she ever brought one of those home, the door would be shut in her face. At the same time, he said that whenever his 11-year-old mentioned the name of a boy at school he would joke, rather pruriently, 'You haven't kissed him have you?'

It seemed that a certain discomfort about sex, and a sense that neither would demand too much of the other sexually, had a place both in Michael and Cheryl's early attraction and in their subsequent relationship.

Wanting and fearing change

But now their marriage had reached its teens. Cheryl had begun to wonder what an adult sex life might feel like, one in which she might enjoy orgasms and dress in beautiful underwear. Of course she was ambivalent. Part of this had to do with her collusion with Michael: what if he wasn't ready for an 'adult sex life'? So she relied on her much-paraded insecurity to protect them both from any steps that might lead to change:

'I'm very insecure about how I look. I look in the mirror and I think, yuk! I feel fat – I would like to lose this tummy, it's like a football – but I don't have the willpower. So do I really want to lose it? If I really, really wanted to lose it all I would, wouldn't I? I think about it a lot.'

Many women express their ambivalence about their sexuality in terms of fat and losing weight. It's the paradox that was pinpointed by Susie Orbach in *Fat is a Feminist Issue:* women dream about being slim and sexy and alluring like magazine models – but if they really looked like that, what would the consequences be? If scores of men were attracted to them, might they not leave their husbands and children and go on the rampage? Being sexy is dangerous – and so it's safer to leave those extra pounds where they are, along with the slumping, slouching self-image.[1]

Because *if* Cheryl were confident as a person and as a sexual woman, might she not be tempted to find out what she had been missing by marrying so young – were there other men who were better lovers than Michael? Might she find she was no longer satisfied with him? Might she be faced with a terrible choice between her family, her children and everything they had built up over the years, their fun, their laughter – and her own fulfilment? And, on a more prosaic level, would she not have to stop being somewhat lazy about the world, and start to make an effort – face challenges – and the fear of failure? And did not Michael, for his part, sense the danger inherent in Cheryl gaining confidence?

Through the interviews, Cheryl said she was 'insecure' so often and so stoutly that it suggested that her insecurity was somehow precious to her. The potential consequences of a confident Cheryl could be terrifying – for both of them.

Cheryl may have had a dual purpose in mind when she responded to the advertisement for interviewees. On the one hand she may have aimed to reaffirm her and Michael's original choice of a partner who would be a not-too-sexual playmate and a buffer against the big bad world beyond. On the other hand she may have wanted to speculate about what it would be like to 'grow up' and become a sexual adult. She was just not sure whether Michael would be able to keep up with her.

Meanwhile, Michael's commitment to his degree and his career were irresistibly taking him further out into the world, and Cheryl was the one who was in danger of being left behind. Michael's eagerness for her to do a course too was the expression of his wish for her to keep up with him – on his terms, which were not Cheryl's terms. Her insistence that she was 'too insecure' may, in this context, have been a strategy to get him to stay by her side and stick to the unspoken contract of their original choice. Although Cheryl was speculating about the possibilities for change in their sex life, and even about sex outside their marriage, these speculations took place inside her head, and so were not visible threats to their original choice – at least, not yet. Which way would they go?

Jane and George:

'We've got by this far so there must be something there'

The light in Jane and George's house was gloomy, and they themselves did not alleviate this first impression. In the first joint interview they sat side by side on the sofa, without looking at each other or responding to what the other one said. Both measured their words carefully and often corrected themselves, as if anxious to avoid creating the wrong impression. But as the interviews progressed they relaxed and talked more freely.

Jane was a brown-haired woman of average build; the deputy head of the local authority housing department. George was tall and blond and quite handsome. He was a product development manager in a software company, although he had begun his career as an archaeologist. They had recently celebrated their fortieth birthdays which fell within a few days of each other, and they had one teenage daughter.

In the joint interviews, it was difficult to keep to the subject of their relationship. Or rather, it was easy enough to talk about its facts and circumstances: how they met, how long their courtship lasted, and what happened next – in short, to trace the course of their lives in the twenty years that had passed since their relationship began. But the discussion flickered and faltered when the conversation turned to their relationship, to what they found attractive about each other, what they shared and what kept their relationship alive. The talk flowed best when it concerned their families rather than themselves; indeed, the most animated interview of the series was the second one in which they drew up their geneograms and focused attention on parents and grandparents, aunts and cousins. They also talked about their work, and their hobbies. Most prominent among these was ballroom dancing, their shared hobby to which they devoted several evenings a week.

They said frequently how well they got on because they enjoyed the same activities and were alike in their emotional attitudes. But on closer scrutiny, these attitudes seemed to diverge. And, apart from dancing, their interests also turned out to be different: George liked hiking and walking, in which Jane preferred not to join him, and he would go alone on outdoor weekends. He kept up his interest in archaeology, which Jane didn't share. Jane liked classical music concerts, which George was not so interested in. George liked gardening while Jane liked pottery. Perhaps the similarity which they emphasised as their base for 'getting on so well' had been there earlier on in their marriage, and their perception of themselves as a couple had not kept up with changes over the years.

'It's a good job we do get on so well,' Jane once began, and told a story of their visit to the Well Woman/Well Man clinic the previous week. The nurse had assumed that each would have their examination with their partner present in the room. 'It's a good job we get on so well, because many people might have been intimidated into saying yes.' But George contradicted her by pointing out that the nurse did ask; and anyway, he chose to walk into the room where Jane was having her examination. The gist of Jane's story seemed to be that getting on well was synonymous with keeping one's partner at a certain distance, away from too-intimate situations. George's walking in on her might suggest that this was no longer his definition of what it meant to get on well.

How they met

They met when they were 18, as part of a group of English teenagers working on an archaeological dig in France and supposedly learning French – George was there for the archaeology and Jane for the French. Although brought up in England, they were both Welsh, and they agreed that what brought them together in this bunch of English kids was their shared 'Celtic sense of humour', which they described as 'half based on insult'. This shared humour was still an important part of their relationship. They said, 'sometimes people feel we are being quite sharp with each other when it's only in jest. For example, one of us might say, "Can you hand me that book" and the other one would say "No", but do it anyway.'

They spent the summer in each other's company, 'a holiday fling', but in the autumn they went off to begin their studies at separate universities. George explained, 'I'm fairly easygoing so it almost fizzled out because I didn't bother to write. But then I got a letter from Jane telling me what she'd been doing.' The upshot was that George was invited to spend a part of the holidays with Jane's family and their courtship started from there. 'If we hadn't done that we would never have met up again,' George said. He continued, 'I was at an all-boys' school but it wasn't that I didn't go to places where I would meet girls if I'd really wanted to find another girlfriend – it's wrong to say it was the easy way out – but I felt comfortable knowing that Jane was there.' From that first visit at New Year he remembered 'a strong sense of how right it was'. Jane said similarly, 'It was comfortable and comforting. It just seemed to have been the right thing to have done.'

A four-year courtship followed, carried out mainly by correspondence, although holidays were spent with each other's families, and sometimes travelling. Towards the end of their time at university George began to get impatient, and pressed for marriage. 'I had this stable relationship which wasn't going anywhere and I got a bit . . . troubled. I couldn't see a way out. So we got engaged.'

When they married they were still young, just 22. Jane found a job and supported George through his PhD. Three years later Fiona was born. When she was still a baby, George was offered a lectureship in archaeology at a German university. Jane didn't work during this time. Fiona was five when they returned to England and, said Jane in her individual interview, 'I felt I had given up quite a lot and a number of years in terms of my career. I felt the need to get back to work and, I suppose, to assert myself as an individual.'

This was one of the reasons why they never had more children. It was a subject which, in Jane's words, tended 'to raise rather strong feelings'. Jane and George gave their separate versions of this conflict in their individual interviews, but it was not mentioned in any of the joint interviews. As we shall see below, they said different things, as they did on other subjects when interviewed individually – without showing that they really knew about their partner's differing point of view. It seemed that one of the ways in which they ensured that they got on well was by preventing certain issues from ever receiving a full airing.

Jane's background

Jane was an only child, born to working-class parents nine months after their marriage. 'I don't think they knew much about family planning,' she commented. Although her parents never said so, the idea hovered that she rather scotched things for her parents by arriving so soon, for they never had another child. She said she had been content to be an only child.

George commented that Jane's parents did not behave affectionately towards each other. Jane replied that they were affectionate to her. Jane was close to her mother, a lively, alert woman with whom she enjoyed long chats over the phone. Her father was ill and might die soon. He had always been 'unassuming and quiet' and, since his illness, increasingly withdrawn and inward looking. These days Jane had difficulty in finding anything to talk with him about.

As a child Jane had a particularly close relationship with her grandmother, her mother's mother. She was the only grandchild, and recalled with evident pleasure how her grandmother used to pick her up after school and take her to a cake shop.

The impression Jane evoked of her background was that her position as only child was a privileged one: the focus of her parents' affection and grandmother's doting, she grew up quiet but self-assured, and didn't much miss the company of other children. Her confidence allowed her to go into higher education, the first in her whole extended family to do so.

At the same time she came across as somewhat insular, a bit of a loner. She was not emotionally expressive, either as a child or as an adult. While drawing up the geneograms, George commented, 'By all accounts you were a passive child', and Jane concurred: 'Yes, I wasn't given to bouts of bad behaviour.'

George's background

George was the third and youngest child, with a sister and a brother ten and twelve years older than him. Some time before his birth, his mother had started a training in midwifery but had had to give it up because of George's father's 'immoderate jealousy' of her having a job. So she had George instead. Jane commented that he might as well have been an only child, like her.

George did not like thinking of himself as an only child, perhaps because of the implication that 'only child equals lonely child'. He emphasised that he made friends easily and that his family was very close. As an illustration, he told a story of an occasion in his childhood when his father walked in the door and demanded that everybody stop fussing, since poor George seemed to have two mothers and two fathers! Which sounded rather like a confirmation that he was indeed an only child.

George's father was a vet for a sprawling rural area, and George did not see him much during his growing-up years, because he worked so hard. His mother was a very good-looking woman, who showed herself extremely competent on the few occasions when she was allowed to have a job, but she was also 'very insecure'. George and Jane together offered the interpretation that his mother had married his father as a substitute for her own father who died when she was young, and she depended on him for everything, but also he on her, because he could not bear her to have interests outside the home. It was not just full-time jobs that he was jealous of; he even complained when she became head of the local Women's Institute.

As a child George was very close to his mother. In adolescence, however, they began to experience conflict. George said, 'I realise now that she went through her menopause when I was 13 or 14, when I was at my most rebellious and she was very low. She was extremely touchy then. I am fairly passive, or defensive, when people have a go at me, so I would always cave in. I still do in personal relationships. I don't like conflict and have never seen the point of it.'

One might conjecture that by the time George met Jane in his late teens, he felt just about ready to escape from his mother's orbit. In contrast to his mother, Jane was calm and quiet and seemed to make few demands on him. Like him, she too disliked conflict and avoided it. If she got angry, she would rather go quiet for a long time than let it out.

The couple, the choice

Perhaps we may picture Jane and George at about 18: she a somewhat withdrawn, careful, only child, who wasn't finding it very easy to make friends at university; he by nature more lively than Jane, perhaps, but also the baby of the family looking for a way out of home which would nevertheless allow him to continue to feel safe. Jane wrote to George when she began to feel lonely in her first term at university thinking, perhaps, of their friendship formed in the congenial circumstances of the camp in France: every evening they had gone to the café in the local village and a 'pattern developed' of being in each other's company.

It was not a grand passion, and neither of them mentioned the word love. It was a kind of coupling up for comfort. George recalled feeling in the early days 'an incredible warmth and insulation from everything else – the knowledge that there is always someone there'.

Jane said, 'A lot of the initial attraction was that I felt he was someone I had known for a long time.'

So what was it that fuelled this sense of recognition and allowed them to feel so comfortable so soon with each other?

Shared defence

When a couple joins together to keep certain uncomfortable emotions or experiences out of their relationship, marital therapists speak of a 'shared defence'. Clulow and Mattinson write about extreme cases of a shared defence:

> There are people whose early experience of bodily closeness, intimacy and care has been so uncomfortable or so traumatic that they dare not risk a repetition of such pain. If, despite this, social and economic pressures lead them to marry, they may find a partner who also needs to avoid close involvement, emotional or physical. They may even marry quite young to escape the pressures of the courting scene, but in these cases choice of partner is based more on the need for a mutual defence against a mutual problem than in hope of a mutual problem being resolved.[2]

A desire to 'escape the pressures of the courting scene' certainly seemed to be a factor leading Jane and George to make an early commitment to each other. Of course, we cannot know what Jane and George's 'early experience of intimacy' was like, and I am not suggesting that they needed totally to avoid 'close involvement, emotional or physical' – only somewhat. The 'defensive alliance' which it seemed that Jane and George sealed in the early years of their relationship was by no means of an extreme kind. It was more like saying to each other, 'Let's be low-key together.' It was a covenant to support each other in avoiding the expression of too strong emotion, negative and positive. For example, while most of the interview couples liked to pay tribute to their partner's enchanting personality traits, neither Jane nor George complimented each other as an individual. The words 'love' or 'falling in love' were not mentioned in the context of their marriage.

They also avoided strong negative feelings and overt conflict – no rowing or arguing. This may throw some light on the place of the 'Celtic sense of humour' in their attraction and marriage. After all, a sharp sense of humour, 'half based on insult', can be a valve that allows a certain amount of conflict, annoyance and even hostility to escape into the atmosphere in a controlled way. And in addition to its function as a pressure valve, a shared sense of humour is playful: a way of being intimate that is not too emotionally demanding.

Another way of minimising conflict is simply to omit to find out that one's partner has important views and feelings that differ from one's own. Judging by the separate interviews, one area in which Jane and George limited their communication was the contentious question of children.

One child or more?

George had always wanted more children, but Jane had resisted. She felt she had sacrificed her career enough while they were abroad, and that when they got back to England it was her turn. In addition, she said, 'I never felt strongly maternal. I never went gooey-eyed and weak-kneed at the sight of a baby. I enjoyed the one we had, but feel that I've "been there, done that". I don't mind small children but I don't particularly feel the need to have another one of my own.' She knew, she said, that George wanted more children, but she suspected his motives. 'I think George will tell you this too, that he really wants a male. He fears that the family will die out. I don't have that same sense of dynasty and my family has effectively died out, so I don't have that sense of wishing to perpetuate a name.'

But George himself said nothing about wanting a son and heir. He said that he had always wanted more children and regretted not having them, and that in his 'lowest moments' he felt he had given up his career as a lecturer in archaeology to have more children. The switch from archaeology to computers had been made when they returned from their years in Germany and the university job which George had been promised in England fell through at the last moment. He decided not to look for another one. 'When I'm irritated about things, especially in my present job, I feel I gave up my academic career to provide a stable economic background to be able to have a second child. We came back from Germany to Thatcher's university grim reaper, and I didn't want to have to find a new job every three years. I didn't think that was a way to run a lifestyle and a family.'

He continued, 'But Jane hasn't wanted more, for various reasons, which is fair enough, I respect her feelings. That doesn't mean that I don't . . . I wouldn't say I feel bitter about it, but I regret it – but one has to make compromises in a relationship if one wants it to go on.'

One way of understanding their conflict over whether or not to have more children might be to focus on their respective positions in their own families. Jane, content as the only child in hers, might have felt threatened by a sibling, in her identification with Fiona. George, for his part, might have longed for the siblings close in age which he never had, and this wish might have been vicariously fulfilled by having a brood of children of his own.

'Unexcitable' or 'hypermanic'?

A striking discrepancy in their individual interviews emerged in their answers to two of the standard questions: 'How would you describe yourself?' and 'How would you describe your partner?'

George described himself thus: 'I'm more mercurial than Jane. I suppose I'm hypermanic or close to it; I don't have very great highs or clinical depressions but I'm up and down more than some people.'

Jane described George as 'even-tempered, in some ways like my father'. She believed, she said, that 'we are both fairly calm; excitable is not a word that strikes me as appropriate to either of us'.

And yet in his individual interview George spent considerable time describing his behaviour in his office, which did not at all accord with that of an unexcitable personality. He was prone to 'short, sharp outbursts' and 'shouts of joy'. When he got angry, he said, 'I don't shout at people, but afterwards I will blow up.' If, for example, he spoke to one of his superiors on the phone and they disagreed, 'People hear me shouting after I've put the phone down. I'm known for it. But I prefer it that way, it will do me no good to shout at senior management.' He would argue his corner, but if he came up against opposition he would generally back down – as he had done as a teenager with his mother.

With Jane, he said, 'We can get snappy with each other. We back away from blazing rows, but that doesn't mean we can't say hurtful things to each other. I know I can say hurtful things which I regret later, but it's better to get them out of my system and as far as I'm concerned it's over afterwards. There's no point dwelling on it: once it's said it's said.'

He conceded, however, that his approach did not produce good results with Jane. 'If I have really annoyed her she will clam up – for days. She finds it very hard to talk it out.'

Interestingly, although they never shouted at each other, they both acknowledged shouting at Fiona, especially during a particularly difficult period some years back when mornings often erupted into 'shouting sessions'. Jane also said that she sometimes shouted at her staff when things in the department became tense.

'Shouting' seemed to be the way they both conceived of expressing anger, but it was eliminated between them. Yet they both shouted at others: at their daughter, and in their respective places of work. George described a rather stressful way of handling frustration and anger, whereby he avoided confrontation but exploded afterwards. If there was conflict with Jane he wished to be allowed to 'snap' at her and then to forget about it, without having to take account of the effect of his words on her.

The discrepancies between Jane and George's individual interviews did not receive an airing in the final, joint interview. They said that they had not felt the need to compare notes after their separate interviews, as many couples did, 'because we have the same thought patterns'. If they *had* talked about what they had said, and discovered that they differed, conflict might have been brought in. Feelings might run high. In order to maintain tranquillity it was better simply to trust to 'the same thought patterns' and not try to find out too much.

Of course, 'a shared defence' was not all there was for Jane and George. But it seemed to apply to the 'emotional minimalism' they exhibited. What exactly did they have between them? On some level Jane must have wondered this herself when she ended the last interview with the words, 'Well, we've got by this far so there must be something there.'

It should be emphasised that the interpretation of a shared defence is speculative. This is because a psychological defence by its nature is something which its owner does not know about and therefore cannot hold out for inspection to an interviewer. A defence is an invisible barrier erected to keep out of sight the problem or fear beyond. Defences protect us from feelings and experiences that were painful once, and would be so again. With Jane and George, it is a speculation that it was some kind of shared defence which kept the emotional tone between them so muted, and that part of their attraction to each other, at the beginning, was the feeling that

---

neither would make very great emotional demands on the other. But now, more than twenty years on, was this still a satisfactory reason for being together?

Disappointments – and shared pleasures

Jane said at one point, 'So much of our relationship has been about looking forward.' Courtship, engagement, completing their education, marriage, having a child, going abroad, establishing themselves in careers. Now, aged 40, they were standing on the threshold of the second half of life. Jane's decision to have no more children would soon be irrevocable. They may have replied to the advertisement for interviewees because they were at a temporal crossroads, needing to evaluate their past before being able to decide on the next move.

George expressed disappointment with some important areas of his life. He was disappointed that they had not had more children. And he was disappointed in his career: that he had not been able to pursue archaeology, which, as he said, happened partly because he expected to have more children. 'A senior lectureship pays a pittance,' he said, 'but now I am doing a job not even vaguely comparable in terms of expertise and value to the community.'

Finally, he hinted that he was no longer quite satisfied with Jane's emotionally subdued nature. He said a little sadly: 'Jane has an ability which I cannot comprehend. After a long day at work she can make the effort to be vivacious with others, but when we get home she flops, and I sometimes feel, irrationally, I wish she would spend some of that energy on me.'

Jane may have begun to sense George's dissatisfaction, especially now that her wish not to have more children had won out, and she may have felt anxious. Was he going to start challenging their way of being, which suited her so well? How should she deal with it if an emotional whirlpool suddenly surfaced in her husband when she had little experience of it in herself? Perhaps, as both of them were so uneasy with conflict, and open discussion did not present itself as a feasible approach, the interviews may have seemed a controlled way to acknowledge the changes they were undergoing. Their differences were only allowed to emerge when they were separated, in the individual interviews. Jane may also have hoped that the interviews might serve to reassert their original contract, and this was one reason why she insisted that George was 'even-tempered' in the face of evidence to the contrary.

Again, both these interpretations are speculative. When asked why she had responded to the advertisement, Jane shook her head: she had no idea.

Jane and George's defence against emotionality did come with breathing holes. One such was their Celtic sense of humour, which allowed them to express some negative feelings safely, as well as simply bringing them the enjoyment of a shared sense of humour.

As for the pressure valve for positive emotion, perhaps it resided in their shared hobby of ballroom dancing. It was a serious hobby, occupying them several evenings a week and taking them to competitions in different parts of the country. 'It's very friendly,' said Jane. 'There is a warmth in the whole group.' 'It's a good way to meet people and to have a laugh,' said George. Sometimes they danced 'quite outrageously, jumping in the air and spinning each other around in all the wrong places'. Perhaps a good part of passion and excitement in their relationship was located in their dancing, and for them, that was a good place for it to be.

CHAPTER FIVE

Conflict

CONFLICT isn't just about fighting and arguing. Conflict can be expressed through silence, or through talking too much about things that don't matter. Conflict can be banished altogether from the couple relationship, in which case it usually surfaces somewhere else: in relations with one's children, or work colleagues, or other family. This chapter tells the stories of three couples and focuses on their attempts to deal with different kinds of conflict.

In the context of the couple relationship, we may look at two areas of conflict: conflict *within* the individual, and conflict *between* the partners. In practice these two distinct areas can become utterly entangled when aspects of the inner conflicts of one partner are projected on to the other. Since it is often very painful to feel at war with oneself, one may use projection as a way of ridding oneself of one's inner conflicts. If a part of oneself is attributed to one's partner, then one need no longer fight it in oneself – though one may well fight it in one's partner.

Initially, projection brings great relief as it feels as if one's inner conflicts have been solved; this feeling is part of falling in love. Later on, projection can become the source of conflict between partners, when one partner cannot tolerate in the other the projected characteristics any more than he or she could stand them in himself or herself. Projection also brings conflict between partners when one partner's projections become too heavy for the other partner to carry, and when it becomes clear that projection was not a long-term solution to inner conflict. A civil war is not ended by taking the aggression outside the national borders and attacking one's neighbour, although at first the two sides in the civil war may unite against a new enemy. But soon the tensions within the country will flare up again. Peace in a civil war only comes when the two sides try to accommodate their differences, and similarly with psychical conflicts. The sender of projections has to reabsorb them and make an internal peace before there can be harmony between the partners in a couple.

For example, Connie had always fought against her own tendency to be lazy. She felt that if she didn't always urge herself on – 'come on, go back to your desk, come on, get it done' – she might never get out of bed in the mornings. When she met Jack, a placid sort of man who quite happily allowed himself to flop in front of the telly all evening, she projected her lazy part on to him, and initially felt filled with a spurt of energy and efficiency, which she attributed to falling in love. But it was not long before she found herself irritated by Jack's habits and started telling him to get off his backside, as she used to tell herself. He told her to stop nagging him, and they started having quarrels. In this way Connie's unresolved inner conflict caused her first to fall in love with, and then to fight with, Jack. (For a fuller discussion of projection, see Chapter 1.)

According to Danish couple therapists Poula Jakobsen and Steen Visholm, people tend to fall in love just at the time when their old way of dealing with an internal conflict is losing its effectiveness, and they need a new focus for a projection. For example, as long as someone lives at home, her or his parents may be the recipients of projected feelings that are difficult to deal with. But when a young person leaves home this outlet is no longer so readily available, and the projected emotions threaten to return and to cause internal conflict. Falling in love is a way of deflecting this process. This can also be a reason why some people need to find a new partner immediately after the break-up of a previous relationship.

Jakobsen and Visholm write:

When people fall in love, their fundamental inner conflict is reorganised so that that which they used their energy to repress and keep out of their life is now allowed into the light, to be lived out – not by themselves, but by their love object. In other words, the repression is transformed into a projective identification, where the fundamental internal conflict still remains hidden but a mass of energy is released, giving the process of falling in love its euphoric character.[1]

Patricia and Peter, the first couple in this chapter, experienced the kind of conflict that springs from unacknowledged projections. They were very different in character, and although they appreciated their differences in some contexts, they also fought them.

The second couple dealt with conflict by banishing it from their relationship. Janet and Robin both carried with them from their childhoods a feeling of being unloved and unlovable. Together they had done a great deal to overcome this legacy by making each other feel needed and appreciated, and by supporting each other in their dealings with the outside world. But to be able to remain united, they could not allow conflict to enter their relationship. Their relationship was founded on the premiss that they were emotionally alike: 'I am a neglected child and you are a neglected child, and therefore I know what you feel like inside, because you feel the same as me.' The admission of conflict would signal that there were also differences between them, which would threaten their unity and their relationship. So conflict within their relationship was banished, but instead it was located outside, especially in their relations with their respective families.

Sometimes conflict erupts over one issue only, and this was the case for the third couple in this chapter, Gaspar and Helena. The subject of their conflict was an explosive one: Gaspar's infidelities. What it meant to them, and whether it could be resolved, will be examined in their story below.

Patricia and Peter:

'We're a happy, successful family, though as a couple we are obviously not perfect'

Peter and Patricia's relationship appeared a union of opposites. She was black and he was white. She had lived all her life in the city while he grew up in a rural area. She was forceful and out-spoken, while he was reserved, shy, and prone to monosyllables. She had an 'evil temper' and got angry several times a week while Peter was quiet and gentle and never lost his temper. She was houseproud and neat while he was untidy. Not surprisingly, their differences were a source both of interest and pleasure, and of conflict.

What they held in common, Patricia emphasised in their first interview, were certain basic values. Most importantly, Peter was not racist, and Patricia explained that she did not just mean overt racism, but also the covert kind:

'For example,' she said, 'I heard the entertainer Patti Boulaye talking about her husband who is white, and from what I could gather, when she talks about her experiences of racism he brushes it aside or tells her that she is being over-sensitive. If Peter wouldn't listen to me or take my experiences seriously, he'd be out the door. But he does listen.'

Patricia also respected Peter for his job in a local authority home for children with 'challenging behaviour'. 'Not many men would do that,' she said. Above all, Peter was 'not sexist, not macho', but a kind and gentle sort of man, who would never try to push her around: 'I have always felt passionately that I never wanted to be in a relationship where I felt dominated or had no say or control.' If anything, she was the dominant one in the relationship, both by being the major earner and the bolder personality. 'But I'm comfortable with that.'

Peter had been attracted to Patricia for her outgoing, vivacious nature, if somewhat overwhelmed at first: 'When the relationship started I wasn't too sure how to take Patricia,' he said. 'She was very forward: she made the first moves, and she was forward in what she talked about. She keeps nothing under wraps, she just basically tells you what she thinks. It took a bit of getting used to. For example, on our first date she wanted to know if we were going to have sex.'

On the other hand, Peter found Patricia easy to talk to, which he felt was one of the things that oiled their relationship.

Discoveries

Their stark temperamental differences – the underside of the very ones that had drawn them to each other in the first place – also brought conflict. Patricia liked quiet-mannered men – but expressed frustration that Peter was so difficult to talk to. 'I think he finds it very hard to express himself. Getting Peter to talk is very hard, on any level, both deep talk and just chatting. I want more than just "mmm"! It was difficult getting him to talk about sex, to say what he does and doesn't like, and to acknowledge what I like and don't like. He's much better than he was, though, because I wouldn't give up, because sex is a very important part of the relationship.'

For his part, Peter had been taken aback by the discovery of Patricia's volatile temper. He hadn't seen it at the beginning, and, he said, 'It's quite frightening sometimes, she loses control a bit, sometimes she throws things. I know what causes it – the kids, Joel and Amy make her lose her temper, and the state of the house. And sometimes me, normally when I'm not keeping things tidy. I'm tidy in a different way from her: I tidy things up so I can find them, whereas she likes things to look good. I wouldn't disagree with her losing her temper, but sometimes she loses her temper for things I don't think are worth it.'

Patricia was more brutal in her assessment of Peter's tidiness, or lack of it: 'He's disgustingly untidy. He doesn't put anything away, he just drops it on the floor, there are heaps of papers everywhere from his writing, he doesn't close drawers, which I hate . . . and when he cooks it's an explosion, drips and spills everywhere. It's just maddening!' She added, 'But he does make an effort, and he has changed a lot since I met him.' And importantly, Peter shared the housework and the childcare – especially the childcare. 'There is no question that he does not pull his weight,' Patricia acknowledged.

She also acknowledged her 'evil temper'. She said, 'I worry, because I think Peter must be outraged by the way I behave sometimes. I said to him, "If you sit on it it's not a good thing" but he just went "mmm".'

How they met

Patricia and Peter met through a mutual friend at a time when Peter was unemployed and at a bit of a loose end, having recently returned from odd-jobbing his way around Australia. He had trained as a carpenter but didn't want to be one, and so he had held a variety of jobs in his life, including one as a dustbin man. He was in his mid-thirties and he hadn't had a relationship for a while.

Patricia, on the other hand, had just split up with her previous partner, Andrew, who was also white. Their relationship had been a serious one, meant to last: they had bought a flat together, and they had a child, Joel. At the time she met Peter she was in turmoil, trying to cope with the loss of her home, her partner and her child's father, as well as holding down her fulltime job as a publicity officer.

Peter and Patricia's relationship moved ahead rapidly. From the moment they started going out they spent every day together, they bought a house, and within a year Patricia was pregnant. At the time of the interviews their daughter, Amy, was almost two, and Joel was six.

The transition from a courting couple to a 'reordered family' had been surprisingly smooth, they agreed. Patricia had been careful to take her son's feelings into account. 'Joel had a choice in the matter,' she said. 'I remember saying to a friend that I wouldn't go overboard hugging or kissing Peter in front of Joel because I didn't want him upset. My friend said, "Oh no, that's wrong, you've got to go with your own feelings." I said "Yes, but he's my son and he's more important than everything else." I wanted to give Joel a chance to get used to it, so I took it at a pace that suited him. That might have been harder on Peter, but I made it clear from the beginning that it was 'love me, love my child, and if you can't do that then go".'

'I thought that was quite reasonable,' said Peter. 'I wouldn't have expected Patricia to behave in any other way.'

'And that's probably one of the things that made me think that I would like to stay with him,' said Patricia. 'Most men have a hard job accepting their own children, never mind anybody else's.'

Peter and Joel now had a good relationship, and as for Peter's relationship with his daughter, he was in many respects the primary carer, because Patricia worked such long hours. She went out early in the morning and returned when the children were almost ready for bed. Peter would pick up Joel from the school bus, give him his tea, then a neighbour would bring Amy home from nursery and Peter would give her tea. When Patricia came home from work Amy wouldn't cuddle her but turned her face away. 'She would go to Peter and only come to me as a last resort if Peter wasn't around. I felt she never forgave me for going back to work, even though I did spend the first nine months with her full-time,' Patricia said.

But over the recent Christmas holidays, Peter observed, 'Amy has grown a lot closer to Patricia, because she was seeing her much more.' Partly as a result of this Patricia had decided to leave her job to go freelance. She would take a month off to begin with, and she was really looking forward to spending more time with the children. The last years had been hard. 'I'm really tired. I've had enough of commuting every day. Joel is six years old now, and it's been very draining physically and emotionally. I feel I've been through so many traumas, losing my home with Andrew, and I was ill for a while as well. I feel, when have I ever sat at home and *vegged*?'

At the time of the interviews, then, Patricia and Peter faced an uncertain future. Patricia wanted some let-up from the tough demands of working full-time, commuting, as well as looking after the children and the house. Peter, however, was fearful of losing her income and had strongly urged her to stay on in her job. Perhaps Patricia felt, now that she had settled with Peter, and, as she said, they were 'really happy as a family unit', that she could afford to relax a little. This was not something Peter had bargained for: he had neither the capacity nor the will to suddenly take over the role of breadwinner. How would they resolve their conflicting agendas?

Patricia's background

Patricia grew up with her mother and younger brother Vincent in a predominantly white area of north London. Her mother left her middle-class family in St Lucia and came to England some thirty years ago, where she met and married Patricia's father, who was from Trinidad. He turned out to be a bad egg.

'Basically my father was a liar, and a thief, and a cheat. He stole all my mother's jewellery and pawned it, even her wedding ring, and all my christening money. He never paid bills, even when they were married, and he had affairs. I recently discovered I have a half-sister. My father left us when Vincent was a baby, and the first time I remember seeing him was when I was seven. That was when he came out of prison, yes, he was in prison for fraud.'

Home alone

Patricia's mother supported herself and her two children by working night shifts as a residential social worker. During the day she was at home, and at night she left the children in the care of various childminders, but after a series of bad experiences with childminders, she left them on their own. Patricia said, 'Most people would condemn her for doing that, you can imagine it all now, home-alone stories. But I remember saying to her, "I don't want strangers living in the house any more, I'll look after us." She said, "But you can't", and I said, "Yes I can." We had friends across the way in case there was anything. Mum cooked, made sure we were bathed, then I watched a bit of TV and then we went to bed.' Patricia was six at the time, and Vincent four.

'My mother had a phone installed so she could ring and check we were OK or I could phone her, but there never was anything, because I was a really sensible kid. I took myself off to school by myself from the age of five, Mum showed me the way on the first day. I was very independent.

'Mum has said to me: "The one thing I will always treasure was that you were so good, and that you did everything I asked you to, and that you didn't argue." She said that she trusted me.' Later on, however, Patricia sometimes felt resentful that so much was expected of her. 'I was jealous that Vincent was allowed to do much less around the house than I was, because Vincent didn't want to and Mum didn't push it. I helped out because I realised that Mum had a lot to do, she had a hard life and worked very hard. My brother was more blinkered and was treated as the baby of the family. So in the end, because I did more in the house, Mum would expect more.'

Experiences of racism

Patricia's memories of her schooldays were not happy. She was one of only a few black children in a large comprehensive school of 900, and she had to fight to keep her end up. 'I got physical and emotional abuse, really cruel stuff, that I looked like a monkey and that I was ugly – but I never believed them! I was a really good fighter. I never fought unless I was provoked, but I was good at defending myself. I beat up a boy in my class for calling my brother names, and I have to say I licked him good!'

Racist treatment didn't come only from the other children at school but also from the teachers. 'One teacher wrote in my report that I antagonised all my classmates. My mother asked him to explain how one girl could antagonise thirty pupils and he said, "Well, Patricia is bright and ambitious and they don't like it." As a black girl I was expected to be dumb and stupid and not have any expectations.' But there were also some encouraging teachers, and Patricia passed her A levels with good grades. 'I liked learning,' she said, 'though I was called a snob for it.'

Patricia felt she had suffered from growing up without a black community. 'I think that was the one mistake my mother made, moving us to an all-white area. I think she thought we would have a better education and a better life than in the inner city. Don't forget the sixties were a time when a lot of black children were taken away from their parents and very quickly labelled educationally subnormal.'

Further experiences of racism awaited Patricia at the hands of the parents of her white boyfriends. The parents of her first boyfriend put pressure on him to end the relationship, Patricia said, to which he eventually succumbed. Peter's father had been literally dumbfounded when he first met Patricia: he would not speak to her, and turned his back on her in the sofa. He had since come round, having been 'worked on' by Peter's mother, but Patricia remained angry about it: 'I have never forgotten it, and people's views don't change overnight. That barrier will always be there and I will proceed with caution. My position is very clear: white people are racist and until they can show me otherwise that is how I will proceed.' She was also disappointed that Peter had not confronted his father. 'Like everything else in his family it's never been mentioned, never been raised, never been discussed. They act as if it never happened.'

On the other hand, Patricia's mother had not been pleased with Peter either. 'My mother disapproved of Peter because he had no job, no career prospects, he was over 30 and still unsettled. But Peter's parents never considered that *he* might not be good enough for *me*.'

Patricia's mother had grown to respect Peter because he worked hard and was so good with the children. Peter's parents also appeared to accept the relationship, though it had taken them a long time to tell other relatives about it. When Peter's aunt was finally told that Peter was living with a black woman, she commented, 'I hope to God they never have children.' No one told her they already had one.

'It infuriates me,' said Patricia. 'It's disgusting. I don't like myself and the children treated like some grubby little secret, because we're not.' Peter's aunt only discovered the truth when she stumbled across a photograph 'accidentally' left lying around Peter's parents' house. Things tended to get said in a roundabout way in his family.

Peter's background

Peter was the younger of two children. His older sister, Ceri, was something of a rebel. She left home at 16, or rather, she was kicked out by their father for having a boyfriend he couldn't stand, staying out late and other adolescent behaviour. Although Peter did not actively rebel, he too experienced conflict with his parents and also left home at 16.

The family moved several times on account of Peter's father's search for work as an aeronautical engineer. Peter felt his childhood had been unsettled, and said frequently during the course of the interviews that his wish, as a father, was for Joel and Amy to be settled at home and at school. Overall, Peter described his childhood as 'fairly happy, except for the last few years'. That was the time when he and his sister Ceri were adolescent and conflict erupted. 'I think the main tensions were me and Ceri wanting to live our own lives, and Mum and Dad not really approving.'

The main conflict between Peter and his parents, especially his father, was 'the fact that I took a long time to settle down. He thought I should get a trade.' At 16 Peter 'ran away' and went to work as a carpenter's apprentice. This did not satisfy his father.

He said, 'To a certain extent I did feel I was disappointing my parents, yes, and that did feel bad. But I never made a conscious decision . . . I knew there was a pressure there but I just ignored it.'

Peter remembered going with his father to fly model aeroplanes as a child. Patricia commented, 'Your dad told me he always wanted you to be interested in planes, and I deduced from that that he wanted you to follow in his footsteps. We were talking one time when we were shopping. He asked me about you and the kids, and I said you were terrific, very close to both of them. And then he said, "I would like to have had a better relationship with Peter".'

'Yes,' said Peter, 'he's getting to that stage where he's looking back. I think my dad tried to be a good father, but because of all the things going on with his work it made it quite difficult. He was away quite a lot.'

Dad's temper

Peter's father had a volatile temper. 'Dad was quite authoritarian. He has mellowed as he's grown older, but he was not as easy to get on with as Mum. I was, I suppose, not exactly scared of my dad, but he's got a powerful temper. You wouldn't want to get on the wrong side of him. He wasn't violent, but when he loses his rag he really does lose his rag. I can remember going on holiday to Cornwall and the car breaking down, and he actually attacked the car. As children we were a bit scared.'

Patricia commented: 'The impression I get is that he is the master of the house. Ceri said that when she went up for a visit her dad had gone out and locked her and her mother in – that's what he normally does!'

Peter, of course, grew up the very opposite of his father in temperament.

The couple, the choice

As a black child in an all-white environment, and as the daughter of a single mother struggling to provide, Patricia had grown up a fighter. She fostered in herself independence and survival skills. She placed great importance on being financially independent, for example, because 'if our relationship got into crisis I could say, get stuffed, I don't need you. I don't ever want to feel trapped, to feel that I had no choice because I couldn't pay the bills. My mother brought me up to take care of myself and that's what I do.'

In choosing Peter, Patricia may have been hoping, unconsciously perhaps, to make room for her needs for gentleness and even dependence – not always to have to view life as a struggle, but to dare to rely on someone else for support. It seemed that now, by giving up her job, she was testing whether this would be possible. Her vision of the future was somewhat ambivalent: she said she was 'going freelance' and she knew she had to earn money, but it seemed that what she really longed to do was spend more time at home and with the children.

Peter was attracted to Patricia because she was vivacious and outgoing – 'the opposite of me'. Further, he had found it quite difficult to make his way in life and settle to a career, while she excelled at coping, working, running a home. Peter's character appeared to have formed partly as a reaction to his father: his father was violent-tempered, so he would be gentle; his father placed great value on having a career, so Peter would not. Peter needed Patricia to give a bit of backbone to his life.

He also needed Patricia to be emotionally expressive for both of them. A by-product of his repression of any angry feelings in himself was that he found it hard to express feelings altogether, including positive ones. He was emotionally withdrawn, and when he first met Patricia, he felt both overwhelmed and liberated by her forthright way of talking. What he had not counted on was that Patricia also had a violent temper, just like his father.

Emotional violence

Emotional violence was an issue for both Patricia and Peter. It would be inaccurate to say that Peter chose Patricia for her violent temper; indeed, he said that he had not seen it at first. Nevertheless, it brought him into contact with the unresolved problem from his childhood, and his hope was surely to resolve it in some way through their relationship. As long as Patricia regularly lost her temper, Peter could remain vicariously in contact with the repressed anger inside himself.

For her part, Patricia was aware that violence, both in herself and in men, was an issue for her. She had very strong feelings about men's violence to women, and talked a lot about how she was trying to bring up Joel to be 'the kind of man who is gentle and caring and does not want to beat women'. At the same time, she was fully aware of the violence in herself. Patricia could see 'a real similarity between Peter's father and myself in terms of temper. I am quite explosive – I'm better than I was, as I get older I am calming down, but to Peter I probably seem murderous, I am terrible. It is something I recognise in myself, the way I react, and shout, and the things I will say, and I have to think about it a lot because if it's out of control it can be a form of abuse, actually.'

As we saw, Peter admitted that sometimes he felt quite

scared of Patricia because he thought she did get out of control sometimes. 'The only thing is, she is smaller than my dad so she doesn't do quite as much damage,' he said humorously. To which Patricia replied, 'Mind you, I did manage to break our chair, didn't I?' By always choosing 'gentle, non-macho' men, Patricia may have been trying to deal with the violence in herself.

Who will be the provider?

Peter showed deep anxiety about Patricia's plans for the future. Around the time that Patricia left her job he developed stomach pains and nausea and couldn't eat, and when he went to the doctor he was told he had the beginnings of a stomach ulcer. Patricia interpreted: 'He's nervous as hell about my going freelance. He is worried sick, to the point where it is making him sick.'

Peter himself said in his understated way, 'I'm not bothered as long as the money is coming in. I'm not bothered who is the major earner since it all goes into a joint account. I was content with the situation where the money was coming in every month.' Now, of course, the money would not be coming in every month, since Peter's work in the children's home was low-paid, and he had no prospect of earning much more. He could do extra work at weekends, but he didn't like to, because 'I don't like being away from the children.' Further, he was worried that a drop in their income would have repercussions on the children – that Joel might have to change school and Amy nursery, since both were private and fee-paying. 'I'd really hate for them to have to move when they are settled.' As we saw, he himself had suffered from being moved around in his own childhood.

As long as Patricia was the major earner, Peter made his main contribution as a father and carer. What would happen now that Patricia was stepping out of role? If Patricia was to spend more time at home being a mother, what would become of Peter as a father? He would not be able to compensate by providing more financial support – so would he become altogether redundant? Or would he have to work all hours and not see the children, a potential scenario that made him very unhappy? Patricia may have been looking to nurture some soft values in herself, but Peter did not appear quite prepared for the repercussions, namely that he would be called on to correspond by bringing out some of the traditional man, the provider, indeed his own father, in himself.

White men

There was an added component to Patricia's choice of Peter. She always chose gentle men, and she always chose white men. She believed this had mostly to do with 'where I socialise'. She had lived all her life in a white area; she met her first boyfriend at college, Andrew and Peter through white friends. She acknowledged that choosing only white men was 'very paradoxical' for a woman who felt so strongly about racism in British society, yet she explained it in non-political terms.

'I was talking to a colleague of mine, a black man who is having a relationship with a white woman. We were both having difficulties at work, with the way we are often treated by white people, and I said that sometimes I really wondered how I could have a relationship with a white person when I think how much we have to put up with in terms of racism. He said he thought so too, and that he must be really screwed up. I said, "You're not screwed up – you know, love, however it comes, is a positive thing, and you can't just define love in terms of race and gender, love is an emotion, it's a feeling, and if someone stirs those feelings in you, that's the important thing."'

In fact, though, by choosing to live with a white man and have children with him, Patricia was placing the issue of race relations right at the centre of her life. In that way she could keep the question alive and could keep fighting about it – for example by probing Peter on his understanding of the nature of racism, by scrutinising his friends for signs of racism, and above all by fighting the prejudices of his family. Although she said simply that the right black man had never come along at the right time, and that love transcended questions of race, her choice of white men as long-term serious partners was probably no accident. With a black partner, the question of racism might not have had to take centre stage in the same way. Patricia had grown up fighting in a white area, and that was how she continued to live.

In another sense, Patricia's choice of white men may have been a negative one, that is, actively not choosing black men. Her father, as she said, was 'a cheat, and a thief, and a liar' who never made any provision for his family. 'There is definitely an issue for me about how black men view their responsibilities to their children, a powerful issue. While I feel very positive about being black, I can't ignore the fact that many black men have children and don't look after them. It's not something to be ignored, it's a fact.' She added, 'which isn't to say that white men don't do the same'.

'Sex has been a pleasant surprise'

Peter and Patricia's shared conflict on the issue of violent temper might never be fully resolved, but there had already been changes which hinted at their ability to reclaim some of their projections. For example, Peter had become much more open about sex.

Patricia said: 'That is one thing which is really good about our relationship. I wouldn't say that Peter is the best lover I've had – I was probably most in tune with Andrew. But I enjoy sex with Peter: it's the one time I really feel he lets go, he is totally relaxed, very warm and very affectionate. Yes, sex has been a pleasant surprise in the relationship, that it has remained good, and how rampant he was when we went away for weekends at the beginning. Even though he is quite repressed and not very communicative, he is fun for sex, and he is always very complimentary to me. He would tell me I looked good even if I was wearing a sack. We make room for sex, definitely, and it's not just a physical pursuit.'

Peter also thought that sex was important in their relationship, but felt that their sex life, indeed their whole life as a couple, was suffering from the demands of working and looking after children and being tired.

He said: 'We don't really have very much time together at all, because by the time the kids go to bed we are completely knackered. Before Amy was born we had more time, we could get away for weekends, and Joel could go to Patricia's mother. But having Joel and Amy is quite a lot of work. I think our relationship is very much on a practical level at the moment: running the house, holding down jobs, looking after the kids. I think the more romantic aspects have been pushed to one side, which is a pity.

'Just being tired has affected our sex life – after looking after the kids all day you sometimes just want to flop into bed. But it is still an important aspect of our relationship; it's something we still want to explore more. We are going for a weekend to Bath together in a couple of weeks' time, and Patricia's mother will have the children. It's going to be the first time for so long that I can't remember when the last time was. We'll forget about the kids for the weekend, and probably just talk about us, and we can stay in bed all day if we want to.'

Changes for the better

In general, too, Patricia felt Peter was becoming more open.

'It probably sounds cold and analytical, but it has been interesting watching how Peter has changed. He is a lot more communicative – he is! Peter is never going to be a very overt personality. There is nothing vivid about him. But he is a good person, there is no malice in him, and he has a spark for life. He is youthful, and joyous, and he wants a life, a good life, and I like that.'

Peter appreciated the greater emotional openness that life

with Patricia brought. 'I think we talk about things a lot more than we used to at home. It's good, because then we know how everybody feels.'

In the short time they had been together there had already been positive changes. Peter had been able to reclaim some of the expressiveness that he originally projected on to Patricia, and had become more open. Patricia felt safe enough to go freelance in the hope of having more time to devote to the 'soft values' of home and children, originally more Peter's province, even though she thereby risked losing some of her financial independence. Even if they never fully solved the issue of 'emotional violence', their relationship seemed to offer other important satisfactions.

Janet and Robin

'You must be my long-lost twin sister'

We briefly encountered this couple in Chapter 1, where they were presented as an example of an attraction based on the principle of 'like seeks like'. Their similarity rested on a shared lack of confidence and feeling of self-worth, the legacy of childhoods which had not provided them with the certainty of being loved. In this chapter the focus is on how they dealt with conflict. Being together had done a great deal to repair any early damage: they were very close, and they gave each other encouragement and praise – as people, as parents, as workers. However, their closeness depended, to a certain extent, on not allowing conflict in their relationship.

Janet's background

Janet was the daughter of very young parents who found family responsibilities difficult to cope with, and who divorced when she was 10. Until that time there were many quarrels: her father had frequent affairs, while her mother regularly threatened to leave and walked out of the house, staying away for several hours, to Janet's acute distress. Her unhappiness was compounded by her older sister Sarah and her father 'ganging up' on her and teasing her while her mother wasn't there.

Janet's childhood was marred by her rivalry with her sister, from which she emerged the loser. Sarah usurped all their parents' attention because she was difficult, loud and demanding. 'I was quiet and helpful and a good girl. And also it was said that she took after my mother in good looks, and that she was intelligent – so what was there left for me? I was ugly and stupid – a bit much. As I was a plodder, I plodded away at school, A levels and college. I felt my sister was so much trouble they paid no attention to me, and I didn't want to give them any more concern. And I felt as I wasn't any trouble they didn't encourage anything in me.' With such evidence of her inability to hold her parents' affection and attention, Janet grew up without much belief in her own lovableness. She retained a sense of being wronged, and a powerful yearning to be wanted and needed by someone.

Robin's background

On the surface Robin's background was quite different. His parents were quite old when he was born, the youngest child by ten years. 'I was an afterthought,' said Robin.

'An accident,' said Janet.

'An accident,' Robin concurred.

His mother had him in defiance of his father's wish not to have any more children. When Robin was born, it seemed his father determined to show himself sticking to his guns by taking no interest in him; often, indeed, addressing Robin indirectly through his wife. Thus Robin grew up exclusively Mummy's boy – his father would not even join them on holidays. Robin repeatedly told of his sad belief that his family was much happier before he was born. 'I've seen holiday snaps with everybody together and smiling, my mother and father and brother and sister. But I never went on holiday with the whole family. My father never came, it was just my mother and me.'

In spite of her determination to have him, his mother undermined him by being 'negative' and critical and full of snide remarks: 'My mother always puts me down.' She would not tolerate shows of independence; until he met Janet he had never held an opinion of his own, he said.

With adult hindsight, Robin had come to believe that his mother had him merely as a pawn in her marriage. Janet had helped him to re-evaluate his family: 'I've seen my background and what made me how I was – I've almost started again and rebuilt myself if you like, seen what was wrong and tried to work on it, and you've helped me,' he said to her.

The couple, the choice
Janet and Robin had done a lot to make up to each other for their not very loving backgrounds. Robin actually felt that through Janet, he had become a person: 'Before I met Janet I was nothing,' he said, 'just a puppet of my mother's, I suppose.' He added, 'We both have very low opinions of ourselves – we are both amazed we found each other and like each other.' When Robin met Janet, he experienced, for the first time, what it felt like to receive praise and encouragement. Janet, for her part, now had the certainty that she was needed. 'I know that Robin needs me emotionally, which is nice, because I've never felt that, it's always been "Oh she's all right, she can cope on her own".'

They encouraged each other to take on the outside world in their careers: after many years in the same retail company Robin was finally advancing towards junior management, while Janet had recently got a job with a women's organisation that she really wanted.

Joy

But the pinnacle of their joint achievement had been the birth of their daughter Joy. Now 20 months old, she was intelligent and advanced and lovely looking, and a source of wonder to them both: 'the best thing that has ever happened to us'. As Janet said, 'We feel very privileged to have her because we never thought we could produce anything that good, really. When I first saw her and she was so beautiful I thought, where does she come from? Because we're not beautiful.'

Janet and Robin's leitmotif, in their own words, was 'individually we are not up to much, but together we are strong' This strength had not come to them easily, or immediately. The first few years of their relationship were difficult. Having met in their early twenties, they began to live together after six months, and then followed a depressing time after Janet graduated, when she was unemployed and had so little money she 'experimented with economical recipes for potatoes and baked beans'. Often she passed the day lying on her bed in a sort of daze, just waiting for Robin to come home from work. They saw few people and contact with home was patchy too – Janet attributed this to their having no phone. Finally she got a job as a clerk and their finances improved, but they still preferred spending their evenings at home with each other rather than going out. They were 'wrapped up in each other', Janet explained; Robin expressed it as being 'stuck together'. They made it sound as if they had no one in the world but each other, and perhaps this was how they felt.

Some seven years later this had changed in so far as they now also had Joy. They seemed to have made the transition from a twosome to a threesome remarkably smoothly. Joy was not excluded from anything. She went to bed at the same time as they did, and she slept between them in their bed. Their sex life was on hold, but this didn't seem to matter to either of them because, they said, they now had something 'more important'.

Janet said, 'Sex is not really an issue, because we are both tired. It has not been a major part of the relationship – maybe at the beginning, but never the most important by any means. There are too many things to consider now: work and getting things organised. I think we both think, we're going to stay together for ever, so there is no rush. If we don't have sex for a couple of years it's all right.'

And Robin said similarly, 'Having Joy has affected our sex life, but it doesn't bother me because in its place I have this other fun game, playing at Daddy, which is just as much fun. Well, not quite, but I don't resent it.' And he added, 'I like her sleeping with us because she cuddles me, as well as her mother.'

Joy brought them such great pleasure and pride that she amply compensated for the loss of their coupledom, it seemed. At the moment the three of them were all together 'in Arcadia', in the paradise of the first-born, most special child. Through Joy, both Janet and Robin were able to experience vicariously that glorious state of grace which neither had had in their own infancy. No wonder they did not feel ready to push Joy out of their bed and shatter the idyll.

Their identification with Joy brought them happiness and compounded their earlier work as a couple in helping each other feel good about themselves. But therein might lurk a danger. The following exchange took place towards the end of the final interview, when Joy was brought in:

ROBIN: So what do you think of Mummy and Daddy, then, Joy?

JANET: What's Mummy like? She's . . .

JOY: . . . bootiful.

JANET: And what's Daddy like?

JOY: Bootiful.

JANET: Also beautiful – and he's also . . .

JOY: . . .

JANET: That's right, Daddy works in a shop. And where does Mummy work?

JOY: Offiss.

JANET: And where does Joy work?
JOY: (*Named her childminder.*)

Robin then said, 'We want her to have as much confidence as possible.' Yet the fact that Joy was also beautiful seemed to get left out of the conversation. The danger, then, was that they might transfer too large a share of the task of making themselves feel better on to the pliable shoulders of their Joy.

On the other hand, the very fact that they had replied to an advertisement asking for couples to interview might suggest that they were thinking about reasserting the twosome within the threesome again. Robin said he had enjoyed the interviews: 'It was nice to spend all the hours just talking, getting it all out again, remembering – we have been so preoccupied with Joy.'

Being alike

Although Janet and Robin emphasised some of their differences, these related to the time before they met, especially that Janet had been a 'pacifist feminist left-wing student' (Robin's words) while Robin had never held a political opinion before he met her. Mostly they felt they were alike.

Janet said, 'Robin always used to say to me, "You must be my long-lost twin sister" because we were so in tune.' Robin said about their initial attraction, 'I felt we were similar. We still say or think the same thing.' They didn't feel they had learned anything new about each other in the interviews, because, said Janet, 'We knew everything there was to know about each other already.' In their final joint interview, they were keen to point out that they had said the same things in their individual interviews.

The absence of conflict in their relationship was something they valued highly. Robin said, 'I feel almost guilty to say we don't have rows when I hear other people talking about their relationships. I feel really lucky and amazed.' He partly attributed this to never having seen his own parents row, even though he thought their marital relationship was so poor that they would probably have divorced if they had belonged to a later generation. Janet attributed their lack of conflict to the opposite: 'My parents argued a lot and I hated it.' She herself fought tooth and nail with her sister: 'We often had to be pulled apart, or we would have killed each other.'

Janet later elaborated a little on their avoidance of conflict. She said, 'We'd be too frightened of hurting the other one to get worked up like that, because it destroys part of the relationship. We'd be afraid of losing each other.'

'Babes in the Wood'

By contrast, conflict did enter their relations with the world outside their twosome/threesome. They explicitly saw themselves taking on the world together in an adversarial manner: 'It's "Us United vs Them Lot",' said Robin. 'If we're down in the dumps it brings us together.'

'Isn't everyone else rotten, good job we've got each other,' Janet added.

'When we are both depressed it's us versus the world – when we're up, it's ha-ha, we can take on the world!' said Robin.

'Conquer the world,' said Janet. 'I think with us the whole is larger than its parts. Individually we are OK but together we are stronger.'

'Individually we are introverts, but put us together and we are – stronger introverts, but we can face the world,' said Robin.

'The world' might be anyone from Robin's intrusive and undermining mother to the towering bureaucracy of British Gas, with whom they had successfully fought over a bill. Robin had written angry letters, which he said he would never have dared to do before.

Robin actually had no friends at all apart from Janet. He admitted that his attitude to people was one of suspicion: 'I suppose I assume at first that people are horrible and wait for them to prove that they are nice – instead of the other way round.' In his work, too, he regarded clients as adversaries, and for him one bonus of being promoted was that he was in a stronger position against them. He said, 'I like getting my own back on customers at work. Having more power at work to retaliate against customers means perhaps that I feel stronger in my personal life, knowing what I can get away with saying back to them. As assistant manager I am the first to have to sort something out with a customer – I couldn't have managed that years ago.'

Robin's mother featured frequently as a focus for angry feelings. In the very first minutes of the first interview Robin mentioned that his mother always put him down, and Janet repeatedly talked about her snide remarks and her sneaky way of disguising criticisms as innocuous remarks. Robin complained of her interference in their way of bringing up Joy, especially with regard to her bedtime. Janet, of course, reserved a passionate and unshakeable hatred for her sister Sarah. She went as far as to say that 'she ruined my life'.

Where a couple uses 'us against the world' as a prominent dynamic in their relationship, marital therapists have dubbed them 'Babes in the Wood'.[2] A kind of projection takes place, not between the two individuals in the couple so much as between the couple as a unit and the outside world. All the bad is seen to belong to people and institutions on the outside so that the 'babes' may continue to see themselves and each other as good. They cling to each other for comfort and safety while all around them in the big bad forest bloodthirsty wolves, cunning foxes and all sorts of other dangerous animals prowl.

The reason the two partners in a 'Babes in the Wood' type of relationship need to see each other as simply good and kind is because they are both afraid of conflict and unable to handle it. Anger frightens them; they share a fear that anger, and even disagreement, will blow the relationship apart. Of course, a great number of people are uncomfortable with conflict and not very adept at constructive conflict. But often a relationship can be a safe place in which to experiment and learn: as Greg said in

Chapter 2, it was an important turning point in his relationship with Elaine when he found that they could row without it meaning the end of everything. And Linda, in Chapter 3, said that she found it reassuring that she and James could have their rows while knowing that they still loved each other.

'Babes in the Wood' have not acquired this confidence. For whatever reasons, they have not dared to put to the test the containing properties of their relationship. Unity is the most important thing, conflict is especially threatening because it might expose differences between the two of them and cracks in their unified front against the world. They fear they might lose each other – a fear which Janet expressed openly. Losing each other would indeed be something to fear, for as we have seen it would mean a return to the state where 'individually we are nothing'. It would also mean losing the person who instinctively understood and shared that core of worthlessness inside, and who was the best equipped to help.

'Babes in the Wood' are often more like brother and sister than husband and wife. One reason why Janet and Robin's sexual relationship was not very important to them might have been that sex demands that a fundamental difference, the difference between a man and a woman, is not only acknowledged but actively enjoyed. Janet actually said that on their first date, 'I really had fun – there was no nervousness of wondering what to say like there usually is with the opposite sex. It was just like going out with a girlfriend.' She clearly meant this as praise. And Robin, for his part, did call her his 'long-lost twin sister'.

Janet and Robin's story shows how an attraction based on emotional similarity can initially be enhancing and comforting. In many ways they had wrought wonders with each other. They rejoiced in their own and each other's achievements: having Joy, buying their own house, Janet finding a job she wanted at last, Robin doing well at work, separating from and standing up to their families, and so on. From what felt like meagre beginnings they had together created a good relationship and a good life for themselves. The danger was that if their fear of difference were to continue as strong, their relationship might gradually become impoverished. In the long run, if differences cannot be accepted and enjoyed, neither partner will dare to grow or change.

Gaspar and Helena:

'This relationship has made me blossom inside'

Helena was twice Gaspar's age: she was 52 and he was 26. He was a young scientist and she a former ballerina and now dance teacher. They were both Portuguese, although Helena had settled in England when she was young. Gaspar had come over to be with her, and also to study. They had known each other for four years and been married for two. Helena had been married twice before and had a daughter, Ana, from her first marriage and a teenage son, Antonio, from her second. Ana was older than Gaspar.

How they met

Helena and Gaspar met through friends while Helena was on a trip to Portugal, where she often had work. Helena rapidly became quite obsessed with Gaspar. 'I kept insisting on finding him – there was a force within me that really wanted to see him,' she said. 'My friends were slightly shocked: "Calm yourself, you're just up to your old tricks again," they said. But I persisted, it was so strong, I knew I had to get to know him. I was obsessed – I didn't know if it was love or what, but something very strong. I knew he had something that I wanted . . . to get to know.'

One day a group of them went to the beach. In the sea, at swimming distance from the shore, was a large rock, which Gaspar swam out to. 'My friends were being very noisy, and I looked at Gaspar and thought, I must get there, so I swam there. He was looking at the sea, and . . . I was completely taken by his tranquillity, taken over. I thought, "I want to be there too." I think that would be the main thing . . . this tranquillity.'

A few evenings later they met again at a party. Helena described it: 'I was all keyed up, because I already knew that Gaspar was someone I wanted to be with physically. After the party we stayed overnight at our mutual friend's house, in different rooms; Gaspar was sleeping on some cushions in the living-room. I said, "Oh no, I'm not sleeping alone", and I went and took hold of his hand and said, "Come with me," and we went to a room with a very nice view of the sky and the stars – and I said to him, "Just lie with me, I want to talk to you." I knew perfectly well that I wanted him, but I didn't want him to feel I just wanted him for my own pleasure. And it happened . . . but . . . he didn't take me nor did I take him. It was mutual: we started talking and . . . we made love. If I hadn't done it I would always have regretted it.'

For his part, Gaspar remembered, 'I just wanted to give myself. When Helena took my arm I was quite sleepy, but I went and lay down with her and I realised something was going to happen, so I said to myself, well, just relax and fly away!' Only several years later did he tell her that she had deflowered him that night.

At that time Gaspar, in Helena's words, was 'shy, introverted and reserved' and somewhat intimidated by Helena's renown in the dance world, not to mention the age difference. He was thus the passive, if willing, partner in the seduction.

For the next year they were apart, although Helena went to Lisbon three times to see him. 'I remember thinking, I know all this is going to change. I wanted to be with him, but not for him to come to England. It was an intense love affair, away from home and away from all the problems with my son, Antonio. So I was hanging on to it, even though Gaspar was prepared to come any time. I said no, wait, I have to prepare Antonio and

Ana, but it wasn't that, it was so intense, looking forward to a reunion, being together *alone,* which is what I really miss sometimes. Everything changes once you have to share your home with your child. I was afraid we wouldn't be able to stay together.'

Eventually Gaspar came, having arranged to do a course in London. At first he spoke no English, but by the time of the interviews he had more or less mastered the language; he flavoured it with idioms and words of his own, which often gave his speech a startling and fresh quality, and a feeling of sincerity. Helena, of course, spoke fluent English.

Helena's small flat, in a crumbling council block in west London, was light and airy with its whitewashed walls, furnished in a youthful, makeshift style, which one might associate with a couple just starting out in life: a futon on the floor doubling up as a sofa and covered with a soft Peruvian shawl, a simple wooden table and chairs to eat at. Along one wall was the cooking area, and outside, the balcony was crammed with pots and plants. There was nothing in the flat to say that Helena had two marriages and thirty years of adult life behind her.

As Helena had predicted, the troubles did start as soon as their relationship was taken out of the realm of fairy tale and plonked down into the reality of Helena's life, with her money shortage and her 'problem son'. Antonio's aggression, rudeness and failure to attend school pre-dated Gaspar's arrival, but were aggravated by his jealousy of his ten years older 'stepfather'.

'Look,' said Helena, pointing at an area of the wall, by the doorpost, where the white paint had crumbled away revealing the plaster underneath. 'Antonio kicked that, though he was aiming at me.' Gaspar said, 'Yes, there is a dent in the wall in his room where he landed a blow intended for me. And today he pushed me as if I didn't exist in this house.' They were now considering living apart until Antonio was old enough to leave home. But, said Helena, 'I can't stand the idea that I would have

to give up such an important part of my life because of my son!
It makes me so angry sometimes.'

Helena spoke lyrically about the happiness and confidence
that her relationship with Gaspar had given her. She said it was
the best relationship she had ever had. 'I feel I can communicate
almost anything to him and he will just accept it and we'll discuss it. Whereas before I was afraid because I was married to
people who were like policemen. They were judging; I had this
fear I was going to be judged, and because of being brought up
Catholic certain things were not accepted, I couldn't admit to
certain things. But this relationship has made me blossom
inside. I feel completely at peace with myself. I don't have to
regret being myself. I am becoming more of a whole person.'

Gaspar said that through his relationship with Helena, 'I
have enriched myself a great deal. Helena's experiences, what
Helena has to express is – just beautiful. She is someone who in
certain ways has lived what she wanted. I like Helena because
she just goes ahead, something has happened to her. I don't like
a plain, unflavoured life.'

In addition, he seemed flattered that Helena confided in
him. 'I feel really pleased when someone can talk with that
openness to me. I think that is really important in a relationship.
Part of the growth in our relationship is talking and communi-
cating every day: "I really like this or I don't like this." We
mustn't think, "If I say this to her I will be abandoned."' He
went on, 'There is a fear in this world that you are going to be
abandoned, it's always present. But the more you say, "I'm not
going to abandon you, open yourself, express yourself, bring
out everything from the past, explode – why not!?"'

Alongside the shared joy, however, were certain troubles,
quite apart from the strain of sharing a flat with Helena's son.
Foremost among these ranked two affairs that Gaspar had had
since their marriage, with women his own age.

Both Gaspar and Helena showed considerable confusion
about how to treat these. On the one hand, their marriage did

not stipulate fidelity but included 'permission to make those kinds of decisions ourselves'. 'Freedom' was immensely important: to Helena because it was what she had not had in her previous marriages, and to Gaspar because he was young, and Helena was his first sexual partner. For example, they did not tell people they were married, said Helena, 'because it would put too much pressure on Gaspar'. The idea seemed to be that he must be given a certain length of leash, a licence to experiment, or he might leave altogether.

On the other hand, for Helena, 'the affairs were devastating'. We will see below how they attempted to deal with this painful dilemma.

Gaspar's background

Gaspar looked even younger than his 26 years. He was quite short and dark, and had a vulnerable sort of air.

He drew up a geneogram with a short written description beside each member of his family. He described his mother as 'loving, extremely supportive, also quite domineering and sometimes possessive', and all of these adjectives recurred in varying permutations in his characterisations of his older sisters, of whom there were five. His father was a reserved man. Gaspar felt tenderly towards him, but he was not a great presence in his childhood.

The five older sisters were presented as an overwhelming force. Family legend recounted how, in the mornings, he was often bathed three times by different sisters, each one scooping him up and exclaiming, 'The poor little boy hasn't had his bath!'

Gaspar made some private space by keeping himself to himself and a lid on his feelings. He recalled, 'As a child I could not cope with emotional expression. If someone bothered me with hugs I would get a newspaper and hide behind it, even though I could not read.'

From an early age Gaspar made attempts to go his own

way: at 13 he decided to leave home to go to a special boarding-school for science prodigies. His mother tried to stop him, but his father told her to let him go. He became the only professional scientist in his family of mainly artists and teachers. He was also the only one in the family to live abroad. His parents and his brothers and sisters all still lived in and around Lisbon.

He had two attempted relationships in his late teens, both with older women. Neither came to much; in both cases the women quickly backed off and failed to reply to his letters. 'Maybe they thought they were perverting me,' he said. But Helena made it easy for him with her ardent suit, and with her he entered his first serious and first sexual relationship.

Helena's background

Helena was also small and dark, and looked more or less her age. She spoke forcefully and emotionally in a slightly husky voice.

She said, 'I didn't have a very happy childhood.' Her parents divorced when she was eight. Her mother was a 'nice simple woman' and a cook by profession. Her father, a journalist, was a 'sensitive, intelligent, educated man', but he drank and was violent to the point where Helena once saw him almost kill her mother. She and her little sister used to wet their beds when they heard their parents quarrelling at night. Helena seemed torn between respect for her mother for supporting herself and never accepting money from her father, and sympathy with her father for growing bored with such a simple woman, who could hardly spell. 'But he liked his women like that,' she said. 'Years later he went to France and married another cook – she was even worse than my mother, quite lacking in sensitivity. But he liked to be superior, to read to his women while they sat at his feet.' He died of his alcoholism relatively young when Helena was already living in England.

After her parents' divorce, Helena was sent to boarding-school where she suffered cold showers at 5 a.m. and glutinous cold food on tin plates. She said of her schooldays, 'I lived all the time in fear, because every Friday the headmistress presided over "the hour of truth". She sat high up with a list of all the people who had misbehaved. If you were on it you couldn't go out on weekends or have visitors on Sunday. So I spent my life at school praying on my knees to be allowed to go out on the weekend. Every night you had to pray a whole rosary.'

Helena loved singing and dancing and performing on stage, and with a like-minded friend managed to bend the regime enough to set up a school dance company which flourished and actually became famous. 'I was very afraid,' she said, 'but also resourceful: nothing stopped me from doing what I really wanted to do.' In her teens in 1950s Lisbon, this meant having boyfriends and gaining a bad reputation. The young men she dated had two girlfriends, one for marriage and one for fun. She was the latter sort. 'I liked sex, oh very much, but I always felt there was something wrong with it, but that didn't stop me from meeting my boyfriend and kissing at the cinema. That has been a constant with me: I have always done things, even though I have felt guilty about them. Only now, with Gaspar, am I beginning to be able to feel myself, without the guilt.'

In her early twenties she married an Englishman and came to live in England. He was also a dancer, and competitive with her. Two days before she was due to open in her biggest show to date, he announced that he had fallen in love with someone else. Helena interpreted this as a bid to shock her into passing up her great opportunity. During rehearsals she had struck up a friendship with a 22-year-old violinist in the orchestra and after her husband's bombshell she began an affair with him. By this time she herself was 32. She left her husband, and eventually remarried, not the violinist but another dancer, also more than ten years younger than her. By then she was 35 and her second husband 'begged' her to have a child for him before it was too late, and Antonio was born.

This husband was violent and brutal, yet Helena felt she

was 'sexually addicted' to him, and believed this contributed to her inability to leave him. 'He domineered me sexually, it was the most incredible thing, he was totally domineering in bed, in an exciting way, but in the end he used it to blackmail me. He could punish me, for example by withdrawing as I was about to reach a climax. He would call me a whore ... When he was himself he would say how much he enjoyed sex with me, but at other times he told me I was dirty, a bitch – I couldn't put the two together.'

Now, she said, 'Sex is best with Gaspar – better than with my second husband. No one is domineering, no one is controlling.' Gaspar never judged her, never made her feel a bad woman. Where she saw her other husbands trying to control her and making her feel bad through their criticism, her relationship with Gaspar was conceived as one of mutuality, equality and free will. But her sexual jealousy did not fit into this framework and consequently was enormously troublesome. At the same time it seemed impossible to reframe the relationship to exclude sexual encounters with others.

The couple, the choice

Helena had always had relationships with younger men; while she had aged, her partners had remained around 22. Gaspar had always sought out older women. It was not just chance that Helena was old enough to be Gaspar's mother and Gaspar young enough to be Helena's son – the age difference was clearly an indispensable factor in their attraction.

Helena: the hope of renewal

Why do middle-aged men fall in love with 20-year-old girls, as is the more usual way in our society with relationships spanning age gulfs? The commonplace answer is: to defend against the draining away of their youth – and to assure themselves that they are still sexual and attractive and powerful.

Jung writes about the mid-life crisis, when, he says, we

'become conscious of the possibility of an inner integration'.[3] Until this point Jung, presenting the subject mainly from the male point of view, sees life as driven mainly by biological and social imperatives – to find a mate, to procreate, to establish himself in the world. But now . . . what of his self? According to Jung, many men are content, in the first half of their lives, to live with their emotional side projected in their women, first their mothers and then their wives and other important women in their lives. These women are 'the bearers of the soul-image'; they express the 'feminine' side of a man's nature. If men fail to reclaim this part of themselves, says Jung, they will remain forever immature and susceptible to domination by women.[4] For a man, in his view, the mid-life crisis is an essential part of becoming, or rather discovering, his self. But if at this stage he falls in love with a young woman and allows himself to get caught up in a love affair, he is sidestepping the process of becoming himself, and simply transferring his soul from one 'bearer' to another.

The 'feminine' side which Jung wished middle-aged men to take back and make their own he called 'anima'. He also invented the 'animus' for women, but it does not correspond directly to the anima. The idea of women's 'masculine' side was far more problematic for him, with his time-bound beliefs and biases about how women should be. Nevertheless, his idea that in mid-life we may begin an urgent search for our 'real' selves can be useful for women too.

Polly Young-Eisendrath, a Jungian and feminist couples therapist, thinks of a woman's animus as containing that which she has the potential to become. If a woman is able to repossess her animus in mid-life, she develops competence, independence and authority.[5] This idea could certainly be seen to have some application to Helena's powerful attraction to Gaspar.

Helena had behind her a traumatic childhood, several broken relationships and two failed marriages, one of which duplicated the violence in her childhood home. All her life she had been burdened by sexual guilt and the belief, apparently reinforced by her two husbands, that she was a bad woman. She had an adolescent son who brought her mainly worry, she was short of money, and she was long past her prime as a dancer. Gaspar, when she met him, possessed youth, sexual innocence and, it seemed to her, an inner tranquillity which she had never had and which she coveted. She was almost 50, he 24: on to him she could project her longings for a fresh start. With him she might, perhaps, leave behind the unhappinesses of the past, her guilt, memories of ugly scenes, and violence. Within moments of meeting him, there was activated in her the passionate hope of renewal. Hence the urgency with which she sought out and wooed him.

In the interviews she made it clear that she did not much like to talk about the past, but preferred to concentrate on the present. This may have been a reason why she particularly resented her son Antonio at the moment: as a tangible legacy of her past and her unhappy second marriage, he seemed by his very presence to sabotage her attempt to start anew. 'In some ways we have excluded him,' she acknowledged. 'If he's being a pain we just have to shut the door.'

The things that Helena said about her relationship with Gaspar suggested that her hopes of renewal were in many ways being fulfilled. She felt she was blossoming, she was able to be herself, she felt whole. 'In my relationship with Gaspar I'm living all the things that I wanted – now. Things I wanted before which weren't possible with other partners, for example my dancing: I never had the peace of mind before to concentrate on work, and both my husbands competed with me. Gaspar is in a different field and doesn't compete with me. I am at the beginning of a very exciting time in my work,' she said, meaning as a teacher and choreographer. 'I have several new contracts and I know I'm going to have loads of work.' With Gaspar at her side she had even begun to repair relationships with her family back home, especially her mother.

It was not only Gaspar's tender age which fuelled Helena's

hopes, but also his personality. In choosing a tranquil, pacific, unpossessive, non-judgmental man, Helena was attempting to turn her back on the mistakes of her past.

Gaspar: leaving home

While Helena hoped for a second lease of life with Gaspar, his hope, perhaps, was to get started on life at all. At the time he met Helena it was already high time for him to emerge from the shadows of his mother and sisters and become independent. Why, then, would he choose someone rather like his mother, not only in age, but in character – emotional, expressive, sometimes overbearing – to assist him in his endeavour? Perhaps because with her he could first repeat, and then rework, his way of being in a relationship with a woman.

Helena was a good choice precisely because she possessed for him a certain familiarity. Because she was like the women in his family, he could 'act out' with her the process of growing up in a way he could not have if he had chosen someone, say, of his own age and temperament.

The trouble was that part of 'growing up' appeared to involve 'betraying Mummy' and having affairs with girls of his own age, as indeed it should – if Helena had been his real mother, which she was not. This may have been why Helena displayed such confusion about how to handle his infidelities. She could not simply tell him that he must stop, because on some level she sensed that part of the point of being with her, for Gaspar, was to enact his growing-up process. If this dimension was lost, might he not leave her altogether? She did not want to lose him, because of the great good that she felt their relationship did her.

Infidelities

Gaspar's first affair happened on a trip to Portugal where they were both combining work with holiday and seeing family and friends. While Helena was away touring with a dance company,

Gaspar had a brief affair. This was how he told it in his individual interview:

'Helena was my first sexual relationship, but I didn't want to tell her I was a virgin because I was scared of being rejected – she is well known in Portugal – I didn't want to lose her. An older person might assume a patronising manner: "You shouldn't be with me, it was nice to have met you, bye bye." I didn't want that. So I had my secret until last year. But I always wondered how it would have been with someone else, how it might feel, but I was scared to tell Helena.

'So I had an affair last year with an old friend from the past. She was in love with me ten years ago. She scared me then because she was very extrovert and energetic, and also very possessive. We met again in Lisbon. I wasn't in love with her but I liked her and felt physically attracted by her. So we had an affair. It was very traumatic because I didn't tell Helena – I struggled in my mind for three or four weeks – to tell or not? She got to know it from one of my sisters and I thought: thank God she knows, because I wasn't able to tell her.'

The tears and recriminations that followed were then interpreted by both of them as having to do with Gaspar's secrecy and deception – not with the act itself. It was Gaspar's cowardice in not *telling* Helena that he had slept with someone else that was the problem. 'It was not the actual sex but the way he conducted himself which upset me most,' Helena said, 'the way he deceived me.'

Gaspar felt that he had learned a valuable lesson from this episode: to be open and honest. 'Helena was suffering over my changed way of being. I was passing through a nightmare and she knew something was not right. I made her suffer a lot, all for my fear and insecurity. I was afraid of her leaving me. But she has told me, "I wouldn't leave you because of that". So afterwards I thought, well, it's not worth causing oneself and someone else such suffering, all because of one's fear.'

Importantly, Gaspar felt that since his affair there had

been a great improvement in their relationship. He felt more able to say how he felt and to stand up for himself. It was as if he had completed some kind of rite of passage. 'The affair has strengthened our relationship because since my experience we can be very transparent with each other, she doesn't have to hide anything from me, nor me from her. I have become stronger. This friend I had the affair with was very domineering. For example, she might ring and say let's meet somewhere, and even though I didn't want to I would say, oh yes! I didn't learn to say no – all the time I was pleasing people.

'I started thinking, what about myself? Now I can say "no" much better to Helena. It's about little things – I remember I didn't like to be interrupted when I was studying or reading, but I couldn't tell Helena, "Please don't interrupt me." Once or twice is all right but not all the time. I was thinking she wanted my whole attention and I felt absorbed very much, losing my own personality.' In Gaspar's mind his infidelity was clearly linked with his gain in assertiveness and self-expression within their relationship.

Gaspar pursued his struggle to achieve emotional openness a little naively, however. For example, he thought that next time he fancied someone and wanted to sleep with her all he need do was apprise Helena of his feelings, and it would be fine. So he had another affair, this time in England. It turned out not to be fine.

Helena explained that this second girlfriend 'was very supportive to him while I was going through traumas about the first girl'. She continued, 'I knew Gaspar was with me but I didn't understand which way to go in order to cope with the problem, and save my relationship with him. I knew he loved me, and I knew I loved him and didn't want to break the relationship because of sex, but I didn't know how to cope, how to do it. The feelings of jealousy were very hard to cope with.'

Gaspar ended this affair too, but his ex-lover would not leave him alone and kept contacting him. This time it was this intrusion which was made to account for Helena's distress. 'She couldn't accept that *I* was his partner, his woman.' And she said about both Gaspar's affairs: 'The reaction of the women has been really difficult to cope with. They feel excluded because they know I come first – they have wanted to push me out of the way – they have become very possessive, bombarded him with letters and calls, interfered with our lives, which has been very upsetting.'

Helena and Gaspar displayed confusion about the question of the legitimacy of infidelity altogether. As we saw, they gave elaborate explanations for why Helena was upset – it was not the sex, but the deception, or the fact that these women insisted on continuing contact with Gaspar afterwards. They could not acknowledge that infidelity by its very nature involved deception and exclusion. Gaspar seemed to take Helena at her word that openness was what mattered, and was then quite bewildered to find her upset once more over his second affair.

Underlying this fudging of the issues around infidelity was first, their conscious 'deal' that they should be free within their marriage, and secondly, their unconscious deal that Gaspar should be enabled to 'grow up' and 'leave home' through his relationship with Helena. And third, there was the matter of their age gap.

Staying together?

As Helena said, thoughts of the future were 'a painful thing – it's natural to think that by the time I'm 70 or something I will be too old for Gaspar.' Therefore staying in the present was 'a way of coping'. Gaspar too said, 'I don't know about the future, only the present.' For example, 'I know that Helena can't give me a child but it hasn't crossed my mind yet. When the feeling comes to me, I'm going to tell Helena, "There is a paternal energy coming out from me, we must do something about it."'

His way of protecting himself, or both of them, against the possibility or even likelihood of future separation was to indulge in a certain degree of vague and wishful thinking: 'We are always going to be together, by friendship, to respect that sacred quality of human being – wherever we are living. Because I cannot understand someone you have been living with saying, all right, I would like to be on my way, and disappearing and never being seen again. I would never cut off from someone, it's an illusion, it doesn't exist.'

Helena concurred: 'I remember the first time Gaspar said to me, "Don't worry, I am not going to abandon you." I think that's really wonderful – that even if we are not together, not having a relationship, he's going to be someone who is always there, someone I can write to or ring up and say, oh Gaspar, you know, this happened and that happened – that he'll have time for me and me for him.'

The age discrepancy meant that they had to be following different agendas in their marriage. Gaspar was at the start of life and through his relationship with Helena was being helped to launch himself into it. Helena, meanwhile, was engaged in starting afresh through her relationship with Gaspar, in all areas of her life: the way she related to men, her feelings about sex, her self-esteem, and even her career. As she said herself: 'I don't have that much time – really I can't make many plans.'

CHAPTER SIX

Ways of Being

ONE couple's problem is another couple's way of
living. For example, Janet and Robin, in the previous chapter, could not tolerate rows; in this chapter we meet a
couple who could not live without rows. A good sex life is considered an indispensable bond by many couples; in this chapter,
a couple tell how sex had disappeared from their joint life and
why they didn't need it.

The couples in this book are 'happy couples', as defined
not by psychologists' tests and scales but by themselves; at
least, they all felt their relationship was good enough to be
presented to an interviewer. Yet the ways of life established by
these couples differed enormously. Some spent a lot of time
together and others less; some talked a lot about their feelings
and others talked little; some had open conflicts and others
didn't; some had satisfying sex and others less so. Despite these
wide variations, the couples in this book were staying together
and coping with all kinds of situations, changes and challenges. The interesting thing was not whether the couples had
problems and dilemmas, but how they tried to deal with
them – sometimes trying to solve them and change things,

sometimes simply making them a part of their joint lives.

This last chapter tells the stories of two couples, two long-term, strong and committed relationships, which flourished despite the presence of what in conventional terms would be considered serious problems. Malcolm and Lindsay lived with frequent arguments of a ferocity that most couples would not be able to tolerate; Caroline and Kathleen lived without sex. Their respective problems were a problem for them – and then again they were not, because they lived with it, accommodated it, and in the end it suited them to live the way they did. This chapter, then, is intended as a celebration of the great range and variety of the 'happy couple'.

Malcolm and Lindsay:

'You can only attack someone you love'

Malcolm and Lindsay met when she was just out of college and he, fifteen years older, was going through a divorce. They got together slowly and casually, bumping into each other through friends, meeting now and then for a drink over a period of more than a year. Then Lindsay needed somewhere to live because her flat lease had come to an end, so she temporarily moved into Malcolm's and insisted on paying him rent. When she finally said she would like to stay, Malcolm went to a drawer and got out all her rent money, which he had saved, and gave it back to her.

They then lived together for seven years, much of that time sharing the flat with Malcolm's two teenage children from his first marriage. When Malcolm and Lindsay finally married, it was for reasons to do with life insurance. They were never ones for emotional declarations of commitment.

At the time of the interviews they had been together thirteen years. They had recently bought a house in the 'green belt' outside London and were spending a lot of time doing it up. Malcolm's children were grown up and had left home, and it was really the first time that Malcolm and Lindsay had lived together, just the two of them. They didn't plan to have any children of their own.

Emphasising their differences

At first meeting they appeared an incongruous couple. Lindsay, now in her mid-thirties, was blonde and well-groomed. She was passionate about the environment, and had recently left her well-paying job in a large multinational company to pursue a lifetime's ambition, a degree in geography and environmental studies, after which she wanted to go into environmental campaigning as a career. She had a fast and forceful way of speaking, repeating her point up to three or four times. Usually she liked to emphasise the positive, but sometimes Malcolm intervened to remind her of the negative, and then she might end up contradicting herself, leaving the listener quite confused. Did she hate her mother or love her? Was her father a mild-mannered animal-lover or a brute who beat his children? Although Lindsay might present both the black and the white, she never made the synthesis into any shade of grey. Sometimes she ended up like a pendulum, swinging to and fro between the two extremes, giving the impression that in the end she was not entirely familiar with her own mind and her own feelings. 'Don't get me wrong' was a favourite phrase of hers, with some justification.

Malcolm was now almost 50, rather shambolic in appearance and wearing thick glasses. He was a Liverpudlian and spoke in a thick Scouse accent which conceded nothing to the last twenty years spent in the south. In his youth he held a variety of manual jobs, but since coming south he had been carving out a career in the building industry: having started work as a night watchman for a large construction company he had risen to managerial level. At 20 he had married and, some fourteen years later, he was divorced with a son and a daughter. He was a shy and withdrawn man although, as the interviews progressed, it became evident that he did in fact communicate far more than he appeared to in his short, mumbled sentences. Unlike Lindsay, when he had an opinion about something he didn't change it.

He was proud of his origins in the Liverpool slums where five families shared one loo. Lindsay's mother came from a similar background – she was one of eight children 'all living in one room' – and an awareness of poverty, and their good fortune in climbing out of it, was a strong uniting bond between Malcolm and Lindsay. When Lindsay introduced Malcolm to her parents, her mother was horrified. 'I dragged you away from all that, and you've gone straight back into it!' she said. It took Lindsay's family many years to accept Malcolm.

Lindsay and Malcolm came across as a strong and committed couple, despite their early and vague beginnings. In social terms, each knew where the other one came from, even if in Lindsay's case the experience of the Liverpool tenements lay one generation back. In personality, they seemed to complement each other: Lindsay's cauldron bubbled over while Malcolm's simmered quietly, almost imperceptibly.

Lindsay was excitable and enthusiastic and, as she said, 'I give myself 150 per cent to everything – for me nothing is nice but it's wonderful terrific super, nor is anything bad but it's horrific.' Malcolm favoured a quiet life and said that most of the time he was not exactly happy but not unhappy either.

Malcolm's first wife had accused him of neglecting her in favour of the television set. With hindsight he recognised that this might have held some truth, but he hadn't changed his ways and still watched television every evening, during which time he didn't want Lindsay to talk.

'I want to talk when I feel like it,' he said. 'It's selfish maybe, but that's me. If I wasn't like that I wouldn't be me. I don't make a lot of allowances for people. Lindsay is generally the one to start conversations, and she arranges our social life and holidays. It suits me until she comes up with something I don't want to do. Then she can go ahead on her own if she likes.' This Lindsay did. It was important to her to have an independent life; they often took holidays apart, and she made a point of frequently going out on her own, and of keeping her own name after marriage.

'Humdingers'

Lindsay and Malcolm seemed to value their separateness. Paradoxically, the one time they really got entangled was during their arguments, 'humdingers' which usually began with a political difference and then escalated. It was often Malcolm who started them, Lindsay 'rose to the bait' and then, she said, 'I can get out of order, vicious, really vicious, I start attacking everything, I wish him dead every ten seconds and tell him so, that he'd drop dead from a dreadful disease like cancer, that's nothing, that's mild.' She said that she only apologised after the very worst quarrels: 'You have to know me to know how bad it's been if I say sorry.'

Malcolm said in his individual interview, that during their arguments, 'I can feel the hate coming from her'.

The last interview took place the day after a row. It had begun with a discussion of the rights and wrongs of civil disobedience: is the law always to be obeyed regardless, or can one break laws that are unjust? Malcolm took the position that laws must be obeyed, and Lindsay argued for the legitimacy of civil disobedience. Their argument ended with Lindsay telling Malcolm that he was a good-for-nothing and he might as well eff off.

Lindsay commented, 'I would never attack friends like that.' Malcolm said, 'You can only do it to someone you love.'

Perhaps it was love that Lindsay and Malcolm were showing each other in their awful rows, or at least a passion that was otherwise absent from their relationship. For Lindsay and Malcolm, it did not feel safe to express feelings of tenderness and attachment in a more usual and straightforward way.

Some couples take great care to emphasise their likenesses as a means of defence against the feeling of separateness which comes from acknowledging difference; for example, Janet and Robin in the previous chapter. Other couples who, like Lindsay and Malcolm, emphasise their differences – and where more so than in frequent and ferocious political argument? – may be defending against the feeling of becoming merged and thus losing their separate selves. If one's sense of identity is slightly fragile, one may choose a partner who seems obviously different, whom one can trust not to get in too close.

Lindsay's background

Lindsay was the youngest of four children. She and her next brother up, Luke, were close in age; then there was an eight-year gap, and then her oldest brother and sister. She described them as almost 'two separate families'. Apparently the two older ones had been severely beaten by her father, who had also beaten her mother, but she had never witnessed any of it, and her father had never laid a hand on her. It was Malcolm who brought up the subject of Lindsay's father's violence, and this is what Lindsay said about it in her characteristic way:

'The fact is my father is an older man, he's a very nice man, a very soft man, a very funny man, and I would defy anyone not to like him, defy anyone – dogs, children, everyone loves my father. The only one who dislikes him is my mother. He's a northern man and was very heavy-handed with the first two children, under provocation from my mother, saying "Hit them, Arthur, hit them", but that's very northern. My mother was brought up in a very close family but her father hit them all, you know, belted them. My father did the same with the first two – I think he discovered the errors of his ways, basically – I think he just stood back one day and said, this is ridiculous. I mean, he never struck me, never. He hit Luke, but never in the way my oldest brother and my sister talk about. He has beaten my mother – again, at a time when I didn't know this – quite severely, apparently. But again it's very difficult – no woman deserves being beaten up, but a lot of people say my mother deserved it, she's an extremely provocative person . . .'

'She's a nasty, vicious person,' said Malcolm. She hasn't any warmth and her sense of humour is hard to find as well, whereas Arthur laughs a lot. You can't joke with Ellen.'

Lindsay said her relationship with her mother now was 'really good, excellent'.

'Except you hate your mother,' said Malcolm.

'I hate my mother,' said Lindsay. 'I love her to pieces but if she were a friend I'd drop her tomorrow.' She laughed, and acknowledged that perhaps her geneogram should also show a conflict line to her mother, 'but only slight, because of her attitude – the relationship between anyone and my mother has a conflict line'. The relationship between her mother and her father was characterised as 'daggers drawn'. 'Her dad can't say white without her mother saying black,' said Malcolm. 'White, Arthur, *white*!' said Lindsay by way of illustration.

'My childhood was actually very good, I had a very nice childhood, but my brothers and sisters would say a different thing,' Lindsay continued.

'Some of their experiences are pretty horrendous,' said Malcolm.

'They're not horrendous,' said Lindsay. 'It was volatile, a very volatile family – I remember my father at the dinner table throwing his dinner at Annie, my sister, and me and Luke just going tee-hee and carrying on – my sister was provoking my father. Everyone was hitting everyone, it was all going on around me.'

Only Lindsay was surrounded by an invisible shield because, 'I was the favoured one. I was very close to everyone. My mother likes me the best and my father likes me the best. And Annie favoured me too, she was like a surrogate mother to me.'

How would it have felt to be the 'favoured one' in a family

as tempestuous as Lindsay's, where favoured meant not being hit; that is, paradoxically, left out? Why was she the only one to be spared her mother's urgings to 'hit them' and her father's belt? Was she really favoured or was she overlooked? Somehow Lindsay was different and separate from the rest of her siblings, and yet not – she was 'very close to everyone'. She still saw her mother every week, she got involved in her parents' quarrels, she helped her parents financially, and she saw her brothers and sister regularly.

We cannot know why Lindsay was treated differently but the result, perhaps, was that Lindsay grew up not knowing where she stood in her family, not knowing whether she was part of it or somehow simultaneously privileged and excluded. In late adolescence she developed anorexia, an illness which is often understood in terms of a girl's, or young woman's, struggle to carve herself an identity. By her own description, her illness was quite severe. Her periods stopped, her breasts disappeared and the bones in her back jutted out so that someone commented that she had her bust on her back. She remembered always being cold, shaking with cold. But her parents never commented on her condition. Her mother never tried to make her eat. 'No one named it anorexia, not even our family doctor – only Annie.'

A few years later Lindsay began to binge and ballooned to 14 stone. She went travelling, she said, 'in one of those desperate hopes of finding oneself, which of course one can't'. She had lots of boyfriends but no one significant. At 21 she went to college, and her life and eating habits began to improve. At 22 she started going out with Malcolm.

Malcolm's background

Malcolm was the third of six children and grew up in a Liverpool slum although, he emphasised, 'we didn't think they were slums – we didn't know we were deprived, we were happily deprived'. His father was a sailor, away at sea for all but a few weeks of the year, and the picture he painted of his childhood was dominated by the colourful figure of his mother. When his father went off to sea she moved herself and the children up to Malcolm's grandmother's, and there were always lots of aunts around, and friends of his mother's with whom he remembered going shopping. His mother was 'a livewire', a gatherer of parties around a bottle of whisky: 'life never stood still for her till the day she died,' was how Lindsay described her mother-in-law. 'She'd always be the centre of attention. She wouldn't be in a room and you not know she was there. She wouldn't be in a town and you not know she was there! Malcolm has lived his life among matriarchs.'

At 20 he got married to his girlfriend because she was pregnant: 'Our first son was born five months prematurely,' he joked. He did not regret the marriage at all: 'I loved her, I was delighted to be married to her.' But he found young parenthood too much. They had two children and, he said, 'It was a tremendous responsibility – from the minute they were born there was this great worry added to life. Before I just had to worry about the rent.'

The thought of having children with Lindsay and going through all that again was 'unthinkable. I've been through all the nappies and crying and sleepless nights and worrying – is he sleeping or is he dead? And now I'd be an old man and still having young kids, I couldn't accept that. It's a lot of pressure to put on Lindsay. But it was the agreement from the start. I told her before we got together. I always was a bit selfish.'

The couple, the choice

If Lindsay was engaged in a painful struggle to establish her own identity, to 'find herself', in her early twenties, Malcolm would have been a good choice as partner. He could be relied upon not to swamp her, given as he was to emotional understatement and silence. In addition, he had two children to occupy a good part of his thoughts and affections and therefore might be expected not to focus too much on her or make too many demands. Malcolm was not going to push for an intimacy which Lindsay, with her fragile boundaries, could not handle.

It might look as if Malcolm, far from having a fragile identity, knew exactly who he was and what he wanted. He presented himself as if his personality was fixed, his habits and world view unshakeable, and he was generally neither very up nor down. He was the anchor to Lindsay's bark tossing in a raging sea; as long as he was static, Lindsay was free to enjoy her contradictory feelings and opinions, her wild enthusiasms and occasional doldrums. Certainly this was how they seemed to view themselves. 'I like it that Malcolm is his own man,' Lindsay said.

But a somewhat rigid personality. such as Malcolm displayed, can also be a defence against a fragile sense of self. If Lindsay's pendulum thinking was an obvious demonstration that she didn't know her own mind, Malcolm's 'firmness' may have been the reverse of the same coin: 'If I am one way then at least I can't be the other way.'

'People let us down'

That Malcolm and Lindsay actually shared an uncertainty about their personal boundaries was illustrated in their stories about their dealings with other people, when they often ended up being taken advantage of, 'walked all over'. In the first interview, Lindsay said: 'He is very kind, very, very giving, sometimes to ridiculous lengths, and this has been one of the problems with our relationship, because I am somewhat like Malcolm in that respect.'

For example, Malcolm told how when he acquired a video camera he gave his top-quality Pentax to a colleague at work who didn't have a camera, only to find that his colleague had sold it through a photography magazine – for his own profit.

Lindsay told a story about how she had offered to sew her friend's wedding dress. They agreed that they would spend £500 on the fabrics (without any profit to herself, of course), and then she spent days and nights at the sewing machine, stitching button holes and embroidering by hand, producing a glorious creation just in time for the day. But she had still not been reimbursed because, her friend claimed, she needed the money to pay other outstanding bills. This would be fine, said Lindsay, if her friend had not also had two holidays since her wedding.

Lindsay said, 'It upsets us, people letting us down, because we give so much. We do give our all for a friend, the input is major, so the let-down is a bit chronic.' Malcolm said, 'It used to bother me, people letting me down, but not any more, because everyone does.' It seemed that they were not able to put boundaries on their own input, to say, 'I'll give this much but no more because then I will be taken advantage of.' Instead, they gave too much and were let down.

Staying safe with each other

'On one level, then, Malcolm and Lindsay were very different. On another level, they were alike: they shared an uncertainty about their own identity and their own boundaries. One way in which it expressed itself was in their joint trait of over-generosity. In their personalities, it expressed itself in diametrically opposite ways: while Malcolm appeared firm and fixed, Lindsay flowed out 'all over the place'.

The ability to be intimate with another person requires a strong sense of self: 'If I am sure of who I am, I won't be threatened by the feeling of merging with my partner when we are close, because I know that I can get back to myself afterwards.' People who are afraid of intimacy may unconsciously fear that if they get too close, the boundaries of their self will melt for ever and they will never be able to find themselves again. 'Fusion, like separation, brings the fear of losing oneself.'[1] So it is safer to choose a partner who is obviously different from oneself, whom one can trust not to want to get in too close.

Malcolm and Lindsay's shared defence against overt

intimacy offered protection against unconscious fears of losing the selves they had. That they were strongly attached to each other they showed in other ways, for example in their shared commitment to their house: in the interviews, they really came together when talking about their plans for it. Their decision not to have children could also be interpreted as a commitment to themselves as a couple. Their passionate 'political' quarrels had the paradoxical function of expressing their emotional involvement with each other while simultaneously maintaining a safe distance. While it might not look very comfortable to an outsider, Lindsay and Malcolm had found a *modus vivendi* that suited them.

Caroline and Kathleen:

'What you do is so good'

Caroline and Kathleen met when they were in their early thirties, and they became each other's first woman lover. Both had had boyfriends before; indeed, Caroline was on the rebound from a break-up with the man she thought would be 'the one', when she took the job as leader of a London women's writing workshop of which Kathleen was a member.

Their feelings for each other grew steadily over the following months. Caroline saw Kathleen as the centre of the group: 'Where she was was always a party – she was so magnetic, I just had to be near her.' Kathleen, for her part, was drawn to Caroline for 'her mind'. Now, seven years on, she said, 'Her mind still fascinates me. I'm for ever asking her, "What are you thinking, love?", which I'm sure irritates her. She is so creative. She can take nothing and turn it into something – like a blank piece of paper.'

Kathleen and Caroline began to meet in the pub after the group, ostensibly to discuss their respective writing projects.

Then Kathleen was moved out of town for three months by her employers, a market research agency. She and Caroline carried on their conversations by phone – one time they talked for five hours and at their separate ends of the phone, watched the dawn come up. When Kathleen came back to London they got drunk and declared their love.

The relationship quickly established itself as permanent. Within months they began thinking about having a child. Yet it was not easy for either of them to think of themselves as lesbian. Kathleen had never really considered the possibility of having a relationship with a woman, she said. In addition, she was aware that 'I might lose my family when I told them – they are working-class people and this was definite no-no.' In fact, her family turned out to be very supportive. Caroline, having moved in feminist circles all her adult life, was more used to the idea of lesbianism, at least intellectually. 'But I had a great resistance to it because I wanted to have a man my parents could approve of. Feminist though I was, I was very nervous without a man. I wanted to look normal.'

Caroline's family, middle-class and conventional, did not take easily to the fact of her relationship with Kathleen. For some years relations between her and her parents deteriorated sharply. When Kathleen became pregnant, her mother asked. 'What's it to do with you?' But the birth of their son Rufus, two years ago, had done much to reconcile her parents to their oldest daughter's set-up. 'There's nothing like a baby for bringing people together,' said Caroline. This year Kathleen and Rufus had even made it into Caroline's parents' Christmas letter to relatives and friends, which had made Caroline cry.

Really Caroline was the one who wanted to become pregnant. But her efforts at artificial insemination via a clinic failed, so Kathleen tried artificial insemination with the sperm of a friend. The process was excruciating. Caroline described it: 'What happened was that I would examine Kathleen with a speculum to see if her mucus was ready: when the neck of the womb is cloudy the sperm won't swim up with any vim, but as soon as it's clear and shiny around the neck of the womb . . . so Kathleen would be ripe, call up her friend, he'd come round, have a chat . . .'

'Hand him a little jar,' Kathleen filled in.

'He'd come back, have a little chat and go off.'

'A very little chat, because you have to keep it warm,' said Kathleen.

'And then you inject it with a two-millimetre syringe,' Caroline completed.

This method bore fruit after six months. By then they had been trying for several years. As Caroline said, 'It was not easy. We were both quite old, and it gets worse and worse, it's so painful – all your friends get pregnant and say, "I'm not sure I want to be pregnant," and you think, oh don't tell me this!'

The exigencies of the whole process – trying to get pregnant, being pregnant, and the demands of a baby – had gradually reduced their sex life to 'zilch'. At the beginning, though, the passion between them ran high. 'I can remember when we decided to live together,' said Kathleen, 'I said to a friend, "I don't think I can do this, sex every night, I'll be dead in three months!"'

Reversing previous patterns

For Kathleen, sex with Caroline was the best she'd ever had. She had certainly 'enjoyed' sex with her previous boyfriends, but it was never 'sincere'. Indeed, she said, 'for the first time in my life I loved someone, and that was a whole new experience. For the first time in my life I had actually given myself, which was something I'd never done before, not totally, not wholly, and I loved it.' She knew from the start, she said, 'that I was settled, this was it, I didn't want to go anywhere else'. She knew, because of a moment when she and Caroline had parted on a train and when Caroline climbed off, 'my whole world walked away from me'.

For Caroline, things were not so simple. While in her past relationships Kathleen had been the one to leave unwanted boyfriends, Caroline said, 'In every relationship they dumped me.' She had always been the pursuer, chasing 'cold, blond, thin upper-class men'. In her longest, seven-year relationship with a man called Richard, 'the harder I loved him, the less he loved me. He wouldn't say he loved me.' So when Kathleen settled on her, 'I was terrified. No one had ever loved me more than . . . I had always been the one who put my all into the relationship, and here was someone . . . it absolutely terrified me.'

Consequently, she began to demand 'space'.

KATHLEEN: I couldn't relate to that at all. No one ever asked me for space.

CAROLINE: I had never lived with anyone. I used to have aeons of time alone, writing and working on my bed, and relationships with men where I saw them once or twice a week. Now there was someone who wanted to run my baths for me and I couldn't stand it. She took care of people.

KATHLEEN: I always had done. I lived with my mother until she died when I was 29.

CAROLINE: And you look after people. She's the one who jumps up for the baby, makes the tea . . .

KATHLEEN: I do it by nature – I enjoy it. But it was the time we went to Paris – it was a wonderful time. My first time in France, I loved it, and I loved the idea of being with this woman I loved and adored. We were so together, weren't we—

CAROLINE: Mmm.

KATHLEEN: And then something happened. She was quiet, distant. On the train I asked her what was wrong. What did you come back with? It broke my heart.

CAROLINE: I thought it was when you were running me a bath and I said, don't run me a bath!

KATHLEEN: No, it started on the train – you said, 'I want to think', or something.

CAROLINE: All my life people have given me more space than I wanted.

KATHLEEN: I wanted to know and learn about every pore in this woman's body.

CAROLINE: I just wanted to be by myself. I'd seen you for a whole week and I felt, go away, let me sit in my room and open the window and look at the birds, I don't want to see your face.

KATHLEEN: That's what hurt me.

CAROLINE: I didn't say that.

KATHLEEN: No, but I knew.

CAROLINE: Yes, you cried. All through that year Kathleen loved me more. I remember saying one day, 'I guess you love me more than I love you at the moment,' and she said, 'That's all right.'

For Caroline and Kathleen, their relationship reversed all previous patterns. Kathleen, who had always held back before, now 'laid down her cap' without hesitation or doubt. Caroline, who had spent her adult life in pursuit of love from men who refused to give it, now found herself loved at last, but drew back and, like the boyfriends, began clamouring for space. Indeed, she said, 'I understood how those men, Richard, felt. Isn't that a terrible thing to say?'

But unlike those men, Caroline stayed in the relationship and gradually allowed herself to be loved. Kathleen learned how to give her some 'space'. What did this reversal of their past lives mean for them? What new thing were they forging together?

Kathleen's background

Kathleen came from a poor background in a small Irish town. Her geneogram looked quite chaotic: her mother had had eight children by several different men, one child had died, and there were miscarriages and stillbirths. Kathleen was her youngest.

When she was two, a stepfather entered her life. He was an alcoholic bookie, and although he earned good money, he gave Kathleen's mother almost none. Every Saturday night he came home and wrecked the house: the glass in the kitchen cupboard doors was always out, and Christmas decorations were pulled down on Christmas Eve. Kathleen remembered the ritual of Saturday evenings, when her mother bathed and dried the children in front of the fire, washed their hair and brushed it with a fine comb. Then she shunted them all into the back room and sat down to wait in terror for her husband's homecoming.

Kathleen spoke with triumph of the time, when she was 18, when she 'had him put out of the house'. There was an argument, 'He put his foot through the TV, so I got my cousin to come up the road and give him a few words, and he left. Mum and I slept in the same bed then. Unfortunately she brought him back. I think she pitied him.'

Until her mother died ten years ago, Kathleen always lived at home with her, and supported her financially. Although she said she had wanted to leave home since the age of 15, she couldn't because 'I couldn't leave her, there was no one else. She was a good woman, she looked after all of us.'

Kathleen had several relationships with men in her twenties – she even got engaged to her first boyfriend. But then, one evening, he got angry and pushed her up against a wall, and after that moment she withdrew, and soon ended the relationship. She said that after that she 'used men', that they were always after her, never she after them, and if a man wanted her company, he should be the one to pay. Mostly she was the one to end relationships.

Kathleen, in Caroline's words, was 'an uneducated, broad, bawdy Irish lass'. She was also a practising Catholic, and for their son's christening had managed to track down a priest liberal enough to make it a joyful celebration.

As for her work, with Caroline's support Kathleen had given up market research and moved into care work. She was a counsellor at a centre for young homeless people. 'I love the work,' she said. 'It's the first job I can honestly say I get satisfaction from.'

Caroline's background

Caroline was the oldest of three children in a solid middle-class, professional family. Her father was a solicitor, a moody and unpredictable man. Caroline said they were alike: 'self-centred, short-tempered, and hyper-sensitive, which he tries to push down'. She added, 'I understand Dad's badness. Everyone else in my family is like Mum: nice, sweet people. I'm not like that. They're all very dear people and I'm not.'

She likened her mother to Kathleen, 'loving and practical'. She was not especially close to her mother, however. 'When I shop for clothes with her, I might go into the shop and ask for a brown sweater and my mum will say "brown?? !" and I'll end up with the blue. My sister would say, "Bag it, Mum, I'm getting it," but I have to say, "I want the brown because this that and the other . . . I can't say no to her. I endlessly want her approval. I feel as if I'm always going, "Oh Mum, love me love me love me" – but it has the opposite effect.' Much like her ill-fated relationships with the cold blond upper-class men, in fact.

Caroline had grown up feeling 'all wrong' in her family. 'I wasn't pretty.' Her father told her cruelly that he would buy her a nose job for her eighteenth birthday, but he didn't tease any of the other children about their appearance. 'I was always the odd one out. When I left home a lodger took my place; she seemed to fit in much better, they were always laughing with her.'

The couple, the choice

Caroline had felt unable to win her parents' love. She had perpetuated her self-image as 'unlovable' throughout her twenties by seeking love from cold and unresponsive men. In her relationship with Kathleen, who was determined to love her, she had the opportunity to break the habit of a lifetime.

Learning to be loved

As she said, this was neither easy nor comfortable at first. Caroline was 'terrified' of being loved. How does one give up the familiar position of underdog and become a happy dog instead? For a while, Caroline even identified with her erstwhile prey, the cool blond men, and protected herself with demands for 'space'.

'And amazingly,' she said, 'Kathleen heard what I was saying.'

'And I accepted it,' said Kathleen. 'It was difficult for me, but I actually did understand what she was asking of me – to hold myself back.'

Gradually, Caroline began to relax. She never contemplated leaving the relationship, so she must have felt, despite the discomfort of the unfamiliar feeling of being loved, that something good was happening. Events glued them together as well: 'coming out' to their families, trying to have a baby. Now, seven years later, Caroline saw it like this: 'I've got stronger, because she loves me . . . she's not like "I love you I love you I love you", although she does say it a lot. But she loves my cooking, and she loves my work, and the way I look. She constantly says, what you do is so good, your cooking is so good, the way you look is so good. I hear other women talk about how their men don't say it, and they feel unconfident – I suppose I take it for granted now that someone should spend so much time loving and appreciating me. She has helped me to value myself, which is more precious than rubies.'

And did Caroline love back now? That Caroline still entertained doubts about her own capacity for loving was revealed in the final joint interview, in response to the question about how they had found their individual interviews. Kathleen had enjoyed hers, but Caroline said: 'I felt so unhappy after the last interview, on my own – Kathleen said her interview was so great . . . and because she is this great big loving character I felt like this critical . . . I can't describe it, as if I were coming across as this less effusive, joyful person than Kathleen. I was the one

wanting my space and Kathleen was this great big endlessly loving person, totally liberated by our relationship, you went in
with both feet and hands, and because it took me longer to
work out how it was going to work for me, I was this cautious
little person and you this bold brave person . . .' She wound up,
'I'm thinking that Kathleen came across much better than me.'

She seemed to be lamenting, and feeling guilty, that all
Kathleen's loving had not managed to fundamentally alter her
nature, to transform her into an equally 'warm and loving and
lovable' person. She seemed to be saying, 'Look, I've *still* got my
dad's badness inside me.' As long as Caroline had been the pur-
suant, super-loving one in her relationships, she could feel
virtuous, martyred perhaps, but her 'badness' was in check.
Once she became the loved one, her darker side took the opportunity to clamour to the fore, demanding to be allowed to exist
alongside the brighter aspects of her personality. This was her –
good and bad, loving and unloving, radiant and darkly moody.
Being loved by Kathleen had certainly helped her accept herself
more than before, as she said. But at other times she felt guilty
that all Kathleen's loving had not transformed her into one of
the 'nice, sweet ones – the dears' of the world.

Loving totally

If through her relationship with Kathleen Caroline had made
good some of her deficit of feeling loved, what, if anything, had
Kathleen repaired for herself? Was their relationship one of giver
and receiver, or did Kathleen receive too? It seemed that she did:
Caroline cooked her good food, Caroline had inspired her to
have a baby, Caroline had supported her in her move to the first
job she found truly satisfying. Above all, in Caroline Kathleen
had found someone with whom she could settle, as she could
not with the various men who courted her in her youth – with
Caroline, she had somewhere to lay her cap.

Perhaps one could say that with Caroline, Kathleen had
resurrected her mother, or rather the exclusive relationship that

she perhaps wished to have with her mother, undistorted by her stepfather. Said Caroline, 'When Kathleen takes someone on she wants them totally.'

When Caroline and Kathleen met, they longed for each other intensely and irresistibly. They sensed in each other the possibility of renewal, and the hope of making up for the past. To a great extent their hopes had been fulfilled: Kathleen had found someone to love and to care for 'totally and wholly'. Caroline had found someone who loved her, and with whom she dared to let herself be loved.

In these circumstances it was perhaps not surprising that their sex life had 'gone down the pan', as Caroline put it. Of course, their sex life had come under strain during the years they tried to conceive, and afterwards they suffered the exhaustion of all new parents. On top of that, the role of sexually charged lovers was probably the last on their mutual agenda. Top of the list was helping each other feel good about themselves, to make each other feel valued, loved and lovable. Whether one calls it good mothering or good therapy, their relationship was first and foremost about healing. If sex didn't fit into this framework, then perhaps it was a price they felt was not too high to pay for all the other things they gave each other.

CHAPTER SEVEN

The Interviews and the Interviewed

The Interview Sample

Of the sixteen couples[1] who were interviewed and whose stories make up the substance of this book, eight came by word of mouth and eight were selected from among those who replied to advertisements which I placed in *She* magazine[2] and *Voice* newspaper.[3]

This method of selection, and the small number involved, means that the sample is not 'scientific' or sociologically representative. But I was not attempting a 'scientific' study in this sense. I wanted to interview couples in sufficient depth to gain some understanding of their original choice of each other from a psychological point of view. To this end I interviewed each couple five times, representing 80 hours of interviews. I could have interviewed 80 couples for an hour each and gained a 'representative' sample, but I think I would have learned little to guide me in my quest to touch 'the unconscious choice'. I sought to build up complex, three-dimensional pictures of individual couples.

Despite its biases, I think my sample possesses a unique

value. I know of no other study of 'ordinary' couples in which the couples were interviewed in such depth both with regard to the topics of discussion and the period of time, that is, five interviews per couple. By 'ordinary' couples I here mean couples who were not the clients of marital therapists. Marital therapists may see couples for years, and go into great psychological depth with them. But the books they write are based on their clinical work, and must always be biased towards 'couples with problems' and, furthermore, couples who wanted to have help with their problems.

The writings of marital therapists make up the bulk of psychoanalytically orientated studies of couples. Studies by sociologists and social psychologists, when they use interviews, rarely use more than one. They collate observable data and base their interpretations and speculations on these, often by means of correlation. For example, they may observe that there is a positive correlation between couples who split up and get back together again during courtship, and divorce.[4] That is, if such couples marry they appear more likely than the average to end up divorced. Or they may try to define certain 'personality factors' that are often present in couples who divorce. One study lists mental disorder, excessive ambition, divorced parents, and bad health as the top 'personality factors' linked with divorce.[5]

To my mind, such observations and correlations may be useful as general pointers, but they don't explain much about why a specific couple gets together or separates. No attempt is made to discover motivations from the people themselves. Social scientists tend to believe that only observable, external data are reliable, and that what people say about themselves is of secondary use, perhaps to give padding and colour to a study. Psychoanalytically trained psychologists, by contrast, give great weight to what people say and show about themselves, and interpret these communications according to theories of the unconscious, but they rarely undertake large sample studies. It will have been seen in Chapter 1 that I draw mainly on psychoanalytic theory. So while this book can offer no social scientific conclusions, I believe that it offers a unique synthesis of the theory of couple dynamics and the real lives of individual couples (who were *not* in marital therapy); the focus being the personal, psychological motivation for their choice of partner.

The Interviews

Once a couple – or as it almost always was, the woman of the couple – showed an interest in the interviews, I sent them an information sheet. In it I outlined the subject of the book, gave details about how many interviews would be required, and emphasised that all interviews would be confidential. At the end of the last interview I often asked if the initial information had been adequate, and happily, no one complained of having been misled.

After a few days I followed up the information sheet with a phone call, and if the couple wanted to go ahead, as most did, a date for the first interview was set.

All interviews took place in the couple's home (except two individual interviews held in the deserted boardrooms of the subjects' workplaces). Each interview cycle comprised five one-hour sessions, usually spaced a week to ten days apart. Thus I met the couple over a period of at least five weeks, usually more, and so I often had the opportunity to watch the unfolding of something that was a particular issue in their lives at the time. This gave the interviews an extra dimension: I was privy not just to talk, but action too: responses to events in the family, for example, or the progress of a job application, or the waxing and waning of the couple's negotiations about an issue between them. Sometimes these have entered the narrative and the discussion of the choice and sometimes not, but they always contributed to a fuller picture of the couple.

For each interview I had a checklist of questions. These covered both objective information and subjective responses, so that comparative material could be elicited. However, I particularly encouraged free-ranging conversation, especially in the final interview.

The first interview

The first interview was a joint interview with both partners present. I asked each partner in turn to tell the story of how they met; what they had found attractive about each other; what their situation had been just before they met, and to describe the course of their relationship to the present. Throughout I tried to make sure that both partners had a chance to reply and that even if one partner was the more voluble, he or she was never allowed to take over completely.

The second interview

The second interview was also joint, and involved each partner drawing up a family tree, called a geneogram, and talking about their families and family relationships. (For an example of a geneogram, see page 266.) The geneogram shows three or four generations: the subject, his or her parents, grandparents, and children if there were any, as well as uncles, aunts, cousins, nieces and nephews (if they were very numerous just the most important ones could be singled out). It shows marriages, divorces and cohabitations; people's names, ages and occupations – in short, the family network in an easy-to-read format.

Additionally, I asked subjects to characterise their relationships with the most important family members by drawing connecting lines. For example, three lines connecting the subject to her mother meant 'very close'; a dotted line meant 'distant'; a zigzag line meant 'conflict', and so on. Conflict and closeness could coexist, of course, and sometimes people had to distinguish between their childhood and adulthood lines. Other notations could also be made; for example, in some families alcoholism was observed running through the generations, or short comments and descriptions could be written by the symbols, such as 'changed jobs every year' or 'loving but possessive', and so on.

The point of this exercise, which easily took up the second interview hour, was to learn as much as possible about family influences on the interviewees. Were their parents divorced or together? Were they the only child or part of a big family, and how close in age were the children? Was the family well off or poor? Did they spend their childhood living in one place or moving around? Had there been deaths and illnesses in the family? This and much more could be gleaned from the geneograms.

Often it was instructive to put the two partners' geneograms side by side. I might then see that an only child had got together with someone from a big family (as with Greg and Elaine, Chapter 2); or that someone from a well-ordered, middle-class family had chosen someone with a poverty-stricken and chaotic background (Caroline and Kathleen, Chapter 6); or that someone whose geneogram was marked by lots of lines denoting emotional intensity, both closeness and conflict, had married someone whose geneogram was altogether rather bare (Linda and James, Chapter 3). Naturally the interview couples often saw the same things as I did, and the geneograms could open the door to lively discussions. Many said that they enjoyed the geneogram exercise and found that the unfamiliar format prompted new insights. A few people were made sad or uneasy by what they drew, and one woman refused to draw one for fear of the pain it might cause her.

The third and fourth interviews

The third and fourth interviews were separate, one with each partner. Before them I explained that although the couple were welcome to compare notes and discuss them with each other, I would not reveal material from an individual interview in a joint one. Occasionally I was left guarding a secret; more often, I simply found that in individual conversation people would place a different emphasis on things. The individual interviews were a chance for me to hear 'one side of the story' without the necessity for people to tread as carefully as when their partner was present. Most couples want to show themselves in agreement, so in joint interviews would let alone an area of potential disagreement, or allow a contentious subject to drop.

One part of the individual interview was always set aside for discussion about previous relationships (if there were any), and another for further talk about the family, which there might not have been time for in the geneogram session. I also asked subjects to recall and describe what it felt like at the beginning of the relationship; and I asked them to describe themselves and then to describe their partner as they saw them now. Further, I asked about areas of conflict, disappointments, as well as pleasant surprises, and what changes, if any, there had been in the relationship. I usually also asked the question, 'Would you say that sex was an important part of your relationship?'

In addition to what people said, the individual interviews afforded me the opportunity to see how people were without their partners. Did they come across differently from when they were part of a couple? Were they more talkative and forthcoming, or less? Were they more lively or more subdued? Sometimes a man who in the joint interviews was somewhat reticent and allowed his female partner to take the lead, spoke with surprising ease and openness in his own interview. Conversely, in one instance a man who talked fluently and volubly in the joint interviews became almost tongue-tied on his own.

Most people seemed comfortable with the individual interviews. In one instance strong feelings were raised when one partner felt that the other had revealed something they should not have (which emerged when the two of them discussed their respective interviews afterwards). Often, to my surprise, partners said they had not discussed their separate interviews with each other. Their explanations for this ranged from saying lightly, 'I should think that whatever s/he said about me was true', to 'I trust him', to 'We have such similar thought patterns that we don't need to discuss them.'

The fifth interview

The fifth and final interview brought the two partners together again. It was the most loosely structured interview of the cycle. I asked how they had felt about the interviews, whether there was anything they regretted saying and, conversely, anything they felt had been left out, whether they had suggestions for how the interviews could have been done differently, and allowed the conversation to develop freely from there. Sometimes little new material emerged; sometimes the final interview added a whole new dimension to my perception of a couple – as with Linda and James (Chapter 3), who said that perhaps they had given me too rosy a picture of themselves and proceeded to have an argument, as if to make quite sure that I left with no false impressions. The most dramatic final interview was perhaps the one in which Louisa and Jason (Chapter 2), announced that they were going to have a trial separation.

Forms of expression

The stories in this book are closely founded on what I was told and what was said in the interviews. Quotations and dialogue come directly from the transcripts of the tape-recorded sessions. However, over five interviews there was time to observe other forms of expression as well. Differences between the way people were in the joint and individual interviews was one such form. It was also interesting to note which questions elicited a lively response and which led to a dead end. Another form of expression was 'body language': some people sat stiffly side by side on the sofa, others looked at each other and touched each other; some people talked to each other and some talked only to me. The interior of people's houses also contributed to the overall impression.

Where these forms of non-verbal expression were strong enough to influence the direction of my thoughts about a couple, I have clearly pointed it out in the story. But mostly I have avoided putting weighty interpretations on this kind of impression because of the distortions imposed by the interview situation. While most people seemed relatively relaxed, and increasingly so as the interviews progressed, there were some who obviously retained an element of 'best behaviour' throughout. People also had different conceptions of the interviews: while I believe most made a real effort to be as open and honest as they knew how, some clearly preferred to guard their privacy in certain areas.

Why Be Interviewed?

Having said that none of the couples were in therapy, but that they were 'ordinary' couples, dealing with their relationship without feeling the need to seek outside help, I nevertheless had to ask why they allowed a stranger to enter their lives during a period of five weeks or more. The commitment in terms of time and energy was significant (one woman commented that she always felt very tired after the interviews). There was no financial reward; all sixteen couples gave their time for free.

By 'ordinary' couples I naturally do not mean couples without problems. Indeed, as I argued in Chapter 1, the choice of partner is often 'problem-based'. That is, the hope is to have help, through one's choice of partner, to resolve or just to live with one's greatest emotional difficulties. So of course the couples I interviewed had their share of problems, on both the conscious and unconscious levels.

But as far as I could tell, their problems were contained within their relationship. These were 'ordinary' couples dealing with 'ordinary' problems as best they could: either trying to resolve them or living with them. If their relationships were imperfect, they were nevertheless real-life, working relationships. One bias of the sample is that all the couples considered themselves happy. They made clear in the interviews that they thought they had a 'good enough' relationship, and strong enough to risk exposure.

But did their problems bear any relation to their willingness to be interviewed? Could some of them have been hoping for a kind of lightweight counselling by allowing a neutral third party into their living-rooms to ask questions?

Curiosity and new insights

When I asked couples at the beginning why they wanted to take part in the interviews, most cited curiosity. They hoped to find out more about themselves and their partner. Many people said they were intrigued to hear what their partner would say. Many also seemed to hope for some fresh viewpoint or insight about their relationship.

At the end of the interviews I asked people whether their expectations had been fulfilled. 'It's been a deeper analysis than I've done before, or at least for some time,' said one man. Some people commented that doing the geneograms had prompted new thoughts about relationships within their families. Several people said it had been interesting to hear their partner's replies to questions. Others said that they had not thought about the beginning of their relationship for a long time and liked being reminded of it – the romance and the excitement of falling in love. One woman said in a card, 'Talking with you was a valuable experience for both of us and has given us much to talk about'; another said that the interviews had prompted her and her partner to talk more. If helping couples to talk and listen is something that counsellors do, then several couples may have put the interviews to use in this way in their relationships.

Negative comments included the expression of disappointment by one couple that they had *not* learned anything new about themselves. Two couples said they had an argument as a result of the interviews; one of them was angry about it and blamed the interviews while the other seemed to think it had been quite useful. One woman said she wished she had never started the whole thing. On the whole, however, the positive responses to the interviews far outweighed the negative – I hope through genuine feeling rather than politeness.

Hidden agendas: adjusting to change

Some of the eight couples who responded to my advertisements may, in different ways, have had something of a 'hidden agenda', a special reason for taking part in the interviews, in so far as they appeared to be either entering or in the midst of a process of change.

Linda and James, and Pippa and Timothy (Chapter 3) were both newly married: they were engaged in adjusting to the commitment, as well as shaping their new roles as 'husband' and 'wife'.

Jane and George, and Cheryl and Michael (see Chapter 4) certainly were at a turning point which may have prompted them to volunteer for interview. Elaine and Greg (Chapter 2) consciously acknowledged their position at a crossroads, and their dilemma about marriage and having children was a live subject in the interviews.

Perhaps then, for the 'couples at a crossroads', the interviews served as a means of talking about their current situation without pathologising it by 'seeking help'. The presence of a third party has several uses. For one thing, it forces one to sit down and to think and talk about oneself and one's relationship in a way that might seem strange and affected in the everyday run of life. Indeed, several people, not just the ones who made the first approach, said the interviews had made them 'take stock'.

Secondly, because the conversation is to some extent controlled by the interviewer, 'tricky' subjects can be negotiated without blowing up into hurtful exchanges or rows. And thirdly, as some people said, they had the opportunity to hear their partner say things in a way they had not heard before. The joint interviews were as even-handed as possible, with the same questions asked of both partners. Perhaps, then, some people were not only forced to communicate in an unusually direct and concentrated way – grunts to the accompaniment of the TV weren't good enough – but also forced to listen for longer than usual.

Finally, I think it was not just the newly weds who may have derived from the interviews an element of 'confirmation as a couple'. A period of change always brings uncertainty, which may tug at the foundations of even the most solid and secure relationship. To be interviewed *as a couple*, about one's marriage or relationship, could in itself be a kind of containment, a countermeasure against the strain of change.

Disguise and Distillation

All the people in this book have been thoroughly disguised. I have changed every detail about them – names, ages, occupations, where they lived, family constellations, etc. – which were not crucially part of the psychological narrative. Nevertheless, it is surprising how intricate the weave of meaning and circumstance, inner and outer reality, can be. For example, I could not have changed the age of Cheryl and Michael's youngest child, because at five he was starting school, and this event had profound repercussions on the couple's life and relationship. Similarly, I could not have disguised Elaine's position as the only child in her family, because it seemed an important factor in her and Greg's choice of each other. However, I trust that I have approached the task of disguise with sufficient care to make the couples unrecognisable to all but themselves.

No doubt many of the interview couples, if they read this

book, will be surprised at the way they have been represented. They may recognise what they said, as it appears in quotation marks and dialogue (taken verbatim from the transcripts of the tape recordings), but I alone bear responsibility for the interpretative context.

Naturally I did not make interpretations in the interviews. I asked some set questions, and plenty more that were prompted by the immediate discussion, and listened to what people told me without offering my own view. I only embarked on the writing after all the interviews were completed.

In Chapter 1 I established my theoretical framework for the psychology of choosing a partner, and it is within this that I have tried to understand and make sense of the interviews. When I have tried to show that an attraction was founded on 'complementarity', or 'shared defence', or the opportunity for 'repetition', this is not an interpretation that I and the interview couple would have discussed. Yet some couples clearly shared my 'psychological' way of looking at the world far more than others. Some were used to searching for unconscious motives in their lives, while for others events and facts counted for themselves and did not need to have psychological meanings ascribed to them. Such couples mostly explained their life choices in terms of external circumstances. Thus while all my interpretations are a kind of imposition, they are so much the greater in cases where we did not easily share a language and a way of seeing things. I believe that what I have written holds true in the theoretical framework of this book, but I accept that some couples might disagree.

Simplifying, and in a sense fictionalising, the couples' stories is an inevitable result of the need to synthesise rich and sometimes unwieldy material into a whole that makes sense. People's lives don't make sense in the way I show them in these narratives. I have concentrated on distilling the original, unconscious choice. In the process I have omitted plenty of detail that seemed unconnected, even if it was important to the couple in other ways.

The couples in this book are real, and yet their stories are coherent in a way that real lives are not. Or are they? I believe we all need to make sense of our lives, to find themes and recurrences that help us to understand why we do what we do, and why we feel the way we feel, and how the two interlace to form the lives we live. As will be clear from this book, I draw on the findings of psychoanalysis for inspiration in making meaning out of everyday lives. I hope that the readers of this book will find my suggestions and interpretations interesting and believable.

THE GENEOGRAM

Comment on Geneogram

This 'prototype' geneogram shows a family of three sisters, with Eleanor, the oldest, the interview subject. She is married and has a baby; her next sister Emma lives with her boyfriend, and her youngest sister Rose had a baby by a boyfriend from whom she subsequently split up, and is now a single mother. Eleanor describes herself as very close to her mother and close to Emma, but her relationship with Rose is characterised as conflictual, as is Rose's relationship with their mother. On the other hand, Rose and Emma are said to be very close. No one is very close to their father. In general it is noticeable that the relationship lines are concentrated on the maternal side.

Eleanor's mother Sarah, is also very close to her own mother, but she experienced conflict with her stepfather, the man her mother married after losing her first husband in the war. She had two more children by him, Sarah's step-brothers, with whom Sarah has only limited contact.

This sketched family tree provokes lots of questions; for example:

Where does father stand in this family of four women? Is he, as it looks, somewhat outside of things?

How did Rose's 'illegitimate' child affect the family? Did her conflict with their mother start before or after she became pregnant?

Why is the relationship between Eleanor and Rose conflictual?

If Emma and Rose are very close, were they always so, and did this mean Eleanor got left outside?

How is the relationship between mother and father?

etc.

Further Reading

Alibhai-Brown, Yasmin and Montague, Anne, *The Colour of Love: Mixed Race Relationships*, London, Virago Press, 1992.

Argyle, Michael and Henderson, Monika, *The Anatomy of Relationships*, Harmondsworth, Penguin Books, 1990.

Belsky, Jay and Kelly, John, *The Transition to Parenthood*, London, Vermilion, 1994.

Benjamin, Jessica, *The Bonds of Love: Psychoanalysis, Feminism, and the Problem of Domination*, London, Virago Press, 1992.

Bowlby, John, Attachment and Loss, volumes 1–3: *Attachment; Separation: Anxiety and Anger; Loss: Sadness and Depression*, Harmondsworth, Penguin Books, 1971–81.

Bowlby, John, *A Secure Base*, London, Routledge & Kegan Paul, 1988.

Bowlby, John, *The Making and Breaking of Affectional Bonds*, London and New York, Tavistock/Routledge, 1992.

Brown, Dennis and Pedder, Jonathan, *Introduction to Psychotherapy*, London and New York, Tavistock Publications, 1979.

Clulow, Christopher F., *To Have and To Hold: Marriage, the First Baby and Preparing Couples for Parenthood*, Aberdeen, Aberdeen University Press, 1982.

Clulow, Christopher F., *Marital Therapy: An Inside View*, Aberdeen, Aberdeen University Press, 1985.

Clulow, Christopher and Mattinson, Janet, *Marriage Inside Out: Understanding Problems of Intimacy*, Harmondsworth, Penguin Books, 1989.

Cole, M. and Dryden, Windy, *Sex Therapy in Britain*, Milton Keynes, Open University Press, 1988.

Coward, Rosalind, *Our Treacherous Hearts: Why Women Let Men Get Their Way*, London, Faber & Faber, 1992.

Diamond, Jared, *The Rise and Fall of the Third Chimpanzee*, London, Vintage, 1992.

Dicks, Henry, *Marital Tensions*, London and New York, Tavistock Publications, 1967.

Dryden, Windy, *Marital Therapy in Britain*, volumes I and II, London, Harper & Row, 1985.

Freeman, Dorothy, R., *Couples in Conflict*, Milton Keynes, Open University Press, 1990.

Hafner, Julian, *The End of Marriage*, London, Arrow Books, 1994.

Hawton, Keith, *Sex Therapy: a Practical Guide*, Oxford, Oxford University Press, 1985.

Jung, C.G., 'Marriage as a Psychological Relationship', in *Aspects of the Feminine*, London and New York, Routledge & Kegan Paul, 1986.

Klein, Josephine, *Our Need for Others and its Roots in Infancy*, London and New York, Tavistock Publications, 1987.

Litvinoff, Sarah, *The Relate Guide to Better Relationships*, London, Ebury Press, 1991.

Mansfield, Penny and Collard, Jean, *The Beginning of the Rest of Your Life? A Portrait of Newly-wed Marriage*, London, Macmillan, 1988.

Mattinson, Janet and Sinclair, Ian, *Mate and Stalemate*, London, Institute of Marital Studies, 1981.

Mooney, Bel (ed.), *The Penguin Book of Marriage*, Harmondsworth, Penguin Books, 1991.

Morley, Robert E., *Intimate Strangers*, London, Family Welfare Enterprises, 1984.

Norwood, Robin, *Women Who Love Too Much*, London, Arrow Books, 1986.

Pincus, Lily (ed.), *Marriage: Studies in Emotional Conflict and Growth*, London, Institute of Marital Studies, 1973.

Plato, *The Symposium*, translated by Walter Hamilton, Harmondsworth, Penguin Classics, 1951.

Reibstein, Janet and Richards, Martin, *Sexual Arrangements: Marriage and Affairs*, London, Heinemann, 1992.

Rose, Phyllis, *Parallel Lives: Five Victorian Marriages*, Harmondsworth, Penguin Books, 1985.

Rubinstein, Helge (ed.), *The Oxford Book of Marriage*, Oxford, Oxford University Press, 1990.

Skynner, Robin and Cleese, John, *Families and How to Survive Them*, London, Mandarin, 1989.

Solomon, Marion F., *Narcissism and Intimacy: Love and Marriage in an Age of Confusion*, New York and London, W.W. Norton, 1989.

Storr, Anthony, *Solitude*, London, Flamingo, 1989.

Tannen, Deborah, *You Just Don't Understand*, London, Virago, 1992.

Tannen, Deborah, *That's Not What I Meant!*, London, Virago, 1992.

Tysoe, Maryon, *Love Isn't Quite Enough: the Psychology of Male–Female Relationships*, London, Fontana, 1992.

Notes

Chapter 1: The Unconscious Choice

1   Dennis Brown and Jonathan Pedder, *Introduction to Psychotherapy*, London and New York, Tavistock Publications, 1979, pp. 15–16.
2   John A. Desteian, *Coming Together – Coming Apart: The Union of Opposites in Love Relationships*, Boston, Massachusetts, Sigo Press, 1989, pp. 73–4.
3   Frieda Fordham, *An Introduction to Jung's Psychology* (1953), Harmondsworth, Penguin Books, 1991, p. 77.
4   From John Donne's poem 'The Ecstasy'.
5   Plato, *The Symposium*, translated by Walter Hamilton, Harmondsworth, Penguin Books, 1951, p. 64.
6   Polly Young-Eisendrath, *Hags and Heroes: A Feminist Approach to Jungian Psychotherapy with Couples*, Toronto, Inner City Books, 1984, pp. 86–7 and elsewhere.
7   C.G. Jung, *Anima and Animus* in *Aspects of the Feminine*, London and New York, Routledge & Kegan Paul, 1986.
8   Plato, *Symposium*, pp. 59–61.
9   For an interesting and thorough review of theories about the development of perceptions of self and other, see Josephine Klein, *Our Need for Others and its Roots in Infancy*, London and New York, Tavistock Publications, 1987.

10   Referring to the nursery rhyme:
     Jack Sprat could eat no fat,
     His wife could eat no lean.
     And so betwixt them both, you see,
     They licked the platter clean.

11   The correct term is really 'projective identification' but because it
     seemed too unwieldy I have shortened it to 'projection'
     throughout.

12   Desteian, *Coming Together*, p. 8.

13   *Marriage – Studies in Emotional Conflict and Growth*, ed. Lily
     Pincus, London, Institute of Marital Studies, 1973, pp. 74–93.

14   Ibid., p. 219.

15   Janet Mattinson and Ian Sinclair, *Mate and Stalemate*, London,
     Institute of Marital Studies, 1981, p. 54.

16   Phyllis Rose, *Parallel Lives: Five Victorian Marriages*,
     Harmondsworth, Penguin Books, 1985. First published by Chatto
     and Windus, 1984.

17   Ibid., p. 242.

18   Ibid.

19   *New York Review of Books*, 4 March 1993, p. 59.

20   Christopher Clulow and Janet Mattinson, *Marriage Inside Out*,
     Harmondsworth, Penguin Books, 1989, p. 12.

21   C.S. Lewis, *A Grief Observed*, London: Faber & Faber, 1961.

22   G. Wilson and D. Nias, *Love Mysteries: The Psychology of
     Sexual Attraction*, London, Open Books, 1976, p. 128, cited in
     Michael Argyle and Monika Henderson, *The Anatomy of
     Relationships*, Harmondsworth, Penguin Books, 1990, p. 120.
     First published by William Heinemann Ltd, 1985.

23   John Bowlby, *The Making and Breaking of Affectional Bonds*,
     London, Tavistock/Routledge, 1992, p. 70.

24   H.F. Harlow and R.R. Zimmerman, 'Affectional Responses in
     the Infant Monkey,' *Science*, 130 (1959), pp. 421–32, cited in
     Bowlby, *Making and Breaking*, p.129.

25   Bowlby, *Making and Breaking*, p. 130.

26   Duncan J. Dormor, *The Relationship Revolution: Cohabitation,
     Marriage and Divorce in Contemporary Europe*, One Plus
     One Marriage and Partnership Research publication, 1992,
     p. 27.

27   D.W. Winnicott, *Through Paediatrics to Psycho-Analysis*,
     London, Hogarth Press, 1975, p. 99, cited in Brown and Pedder,
     Introduction to Psychotherapy, p. 111.

28 D.W. Winnicott, *Playing and Reality*, Harmondsworth, Penguin Books, 1974, p. 131. Copyright © 1971 by the Estate of D.W. Winnicott. Reproduced by permisssion of Mark Paterson on behalf of the Winnicott Trust.

29 Plato, *Symposium*, pp. 63–4.

30 Ibid., p. 62.

31 Clulow and Mattinson, *Marriage Inside Out*, p. 36.

32 Pincus (ed.), *Marriage*, p. 13.

33 Clulow and Mattinson, *Marriage Inside Out*, p. 52.

34 Ibid., pp. 54–7.

35 Cited in Jared Diamond, *The Rise and Fall of the Third Chimpanzee*, London, Radius, 1991, pp. 86–7.

36 Maryon Tysoe, *Love Isn't Quite Enough: The Psychology of Male–Female Relationships*, London, Fontana, 1992, p. 48.

37 Clulow and Mattinson, *Marriage Inside Out*, p. 57.

38 Ibid.

39 This couple were not part of my interview sample.

40 Marion F. Solomon, *Narcissism and Intimacy*, New York and London, W.W. Norton, 1989, pp. 140–7.

Chapter 2: To Commit or Not to Commit?

1 George Eliot, *Middlemarch*, (1871–2), Harmondsworth: Penguin Books, 1985, pp. 335–6.

2 R.M. Cate, T.L. Huston and J.R. Nesselroade, 'Premarital Relationships: toward the Identification of Alternative Pathways to Marriage,' *Journal of Social and Clinical Psychology*, 4 (1986), pp. 3–22, cited in Maryon Tysoe, *Love Isn't Quite Enough: The Psychology of Male–Female Relationships*, London, Fontana, 1992, p. 79.

3 Cited in Tysoe, *Love Isn't Quite Enough*, p. 20.

4 Statistics from Duncan J. Dormor, *The Relationship Revolution, Cohabitation, Marriage and Divorce in Contemporary Europe*, One Plus One Marriage and Partnership Research publication, 1992, p. 3. The statistics refer to England and Wales, 1990.

5 Jacqui Jackson is the co-author with Jill Bowler and Eileen

Loughridge of *Living Together: You, Your Partner and the Law*, London, Century, 1992, available from libraries.

6   Dormor, *Relationship Revolution*, p.13.
7   Ibid., p. 28.
8   Ibid.
9   A. Brown and K. Kiernan, 'Cohabitation in Great Britain: Evidence from the General Household Survey,' *Population Trends*, 25 (1981), pp. 4–10, cited in Michael Argyle and Monika Henderson, *The Anatomy of Relationships*, Harmondsworth: Penguin Books, 1990, p. 113. First published by William Heinemann Ltd, 1985.
10 Dormor, *Relationship Revolution*, p. 28.
11 Tysoe, *Love Isn't Quite Enough*, p. 68.
12 Couples Counsel, *She Magazine*, December 1991.
13 Quoted in Helge Rubinstein (ed.) *The Oxford Book of Marriage*, Oxford, Oxford University Press, 1990, p. 355.

Chapter 3: Setting Out

1   Anthony Storr, *Solitude*, London, Flamingo, 1989, p. ix. Storr's purpose in his book is to challenge this belief through examples of the lives of creative people who did not form conventional relationships.
2   Jung's characterisation of 'normal sex life' in *Marriage as a Psychological Relationship*, in *Aspects of the Feminine*, London and New York, Routledge & Kegan Paul, 1986, p. 44.
3   Penny Mansfield and Jean Collard, *The Beginning of the Rest of Your Life? A Portrait of Newly-wed Marriage*, London, Macmillan, 1988, pp. 37–8 and 162.
4   Entry for Friday 2 November 1917, in *The Diary of Virginia Woolf 1915–19*, ed. A.O. Bell, London, Chatto and Windus – The Hogarth Press, 1977. Reprinted by permission of the Estate of Virginia Woolf.
5   Storr, *Solitude*, p. 18.
6   Ibid., p. 20.
7   This is an edited transcript, mainly from the first interview, although the topics recurred in subsequent interviews. Sometimes statements made at different times on the same subject have been conflated.

8   Claire Tomalin, *Katherine Mansfield – A Secret Life*,
     Harmondsworth, Penguin Books, 1988, p. 224.
9   Ibid., p. 131.
10   Cited in Josephine Klein, *Our Need for Others and its Roots in
     Infancy*, London and New York, Tavistock Publications, 1987,
     pp. 104–7.

Chapter 4: Crossroads

1   Susie Orbach, *Fat is a Feminist Issue*, London: Hamlyn
     paperbacks edition, 1983, pp. 78–9 and elsewhere.
2   Christopher Clulow and Janet Mattinson, *Marriage Inside Out*,
     Harmondsworth, Penguin Books, 1989, p. 57.

Chapter 5: Conflict

1   Poula Jakobsen and Steen Visholm, *Parförhållanden–förälskelse,
     kris, terapi*, Alfabeta, 1933 (in Swedish translation from the
     Danish), p. 95 (author's translation into English).
2   Janet Mattinson and Ian Sinclair, *Mate and Stalemate*, London,
     Institute of Marital Studies, 1981, p. 54.
3   C.G. Jung, *Marriage as a Psychological Relationship*, in *Aspects
     of the Feminine*, London and New York, Routledge & Kegan
     Paul, 1986, p. 49.
4   C.G. Jung, *Anima and Animus*, ibid. pp. 56–7.
5   Polly Young-Eisendrath, *Hags and Heroes: A Feminist Approach
     to Jungian Psychotherapy with Couples*, Toronto, Inner City
     Books, 1984.

Chapter 6: Ways of Being

1   Christopher Clulow and Janet Mattinson, *Marriage Inside Out*,
     Harmondsworth, Penguin Books, 1989, p. 36.

Chapter 7: The Interviews and the Interviewed

1   Thirteen full accounts appear in the book; two more are used in Chapter 1 (Charles and Susannah, Katharine and Sally), and one was not used.

2   From 1990 to 1993 I and a marital counsellor wrote a monthly column in *She* magazine entitled 'Couples Counsel'. My research was written about in the editor's column, at my request, and interviewees advertised for as follows: 'What attracts people to one another, what makes them want to form a couple, and what persuades them to stay together or split are things which intrigue us all. Cathy Troupp, who works with our counsellor on Couples Counsel, is writing a book on the subject. She wants to interview couples of every kind: young, old and middle-aged, newly-weds and third time marrieds, gay and straight, black and white, mixed race and mixed culture. If both you and your partner (or even you and your ex-partner) are interested in being interviewed by Cathy – she'll want to talk to you together as well as separately – please write to her at . . .'

3   The advertisement read: 'Why were you attracted to your partner? I am a writer looking for interviewees for a book on the psychology of choosing a partner, to be published by Virago Press. Interviews are conducted with both partners of a couple, both jointly and individually. Interviews are confidential, names and details changed. Every kind of couple welcome as long as your relationship is at least 18 months old.'

4   B. Thornes and J. Collard, *Who Divorces?* London, Routledge & Kegan Paul, 1979, cited in Michael Argyle and Monika Henderson, *The Anatomy of Relationships*, Harmondsworth, Penguin Books, 1990, p. 168. First published by William Heinemann Ltd, 1985.

5   Ibid., p. 169.